Capabilities Equality

In what sense should persons be judged to be equal or unequal as a matter of justice? The capabilities approach to equality, developed by Amartya Sen and Martha Nussbaum, seeks to answer this important question.

While capabilities theory has avoided many of the conceptual difficulties that have undermined competing accounts of egalitarian justice, recent criticisms have raised questions regarding the focus, structure and justification of the theory. In this volume, leading scholars present new and original essays that address these controversies. The authors connect issues of egalitarian justice to practical political concerns, identify the strengths and weaknesses of the capabilities account of egalitarian justice and finally seek to realize real progress in the understanding of distributive justice.

This accessible volume will be essential reading for all scholars with an interest in distributive justice, and for students and researchers studying moral philosophy, social theory and political theory.

Alexander Kaufman is Assistant Professor of Political Theory at the School of Public and International Affairs at the University of Georgia.

Routledge innovations in political theory

1 **A Radical Green Political Theory**
Alan Carter

2 **Rational Woman**
A feminist critique of dualism
Raia Prokhovnik

3 **Rethinking State Theory**
Mark J. Smith

4 **Gramsci and Contemporary Politics**
Beyond pessimism of the intellect
Anne Showstack Sassoon

5 **Post-ecologist Politics**
Social theory and the abdication of the ecologist paradigm
Ingolfur Blühdorn

6 **Ecological Relations**
Susan Board

7 **The Political Theory of Global Citizenship**
April Carter

8 **Democracy and National Pluralism**
Edited by Ferran Requejo

9 **Civil Society and Democratic Theory**
Alternative voices
Gideon Baker

10 **Ethics and Politics in Contemporary Theory**
Between critical theory and post-Marxism
Mark Devenney

11 **Citizenship and Identity**
Towards a new republic
John Schwarzmantel

12 **Multiculturalism, Identity and Rights**
Edited by Bruce Haddock and Peter Sutch

13 **Political Theory of Global Justice**
A cosmopolitan case for the world state
Luis Cabrera

14 **Democracy, Nationalism and Multiculturalism**
Edited by Ramón Maiz and Ferrán Requejo

15 **Political Reconciliation**
Andrew Schaap

16 **National Cultural Autonomy and Its Contemporary Critics**
Edited by Ephraim Nimni

17 **Power and Politics in Poststructuralist Thought**
New theories of the political
Saul Newman

18 **Capabilities Equality**
Basic issues and problems
Edited by Alexander Kaufman

Capabilities Equality

Basic issues and problems

Edited by Alexander Kaufman

Routledge
Taylor & Francis Group
NEW YORK AND LONDON

First published 2006
by Routledge
270 Madison Ave, New York, NY 10016

Simultaneously published in the UK
by Routledge
2 Park Square, Milton Park, Abingdon, Oxon OX14 4RN

Routledge is an imprint of the Taylor & Francis Group

Typeset in Times New Roman by Wearset Ltd, Boldon, Tyne and Wear
Printed and bound in Great Britain by MPG Books Ltd, Bodmin

Library of Congress Cataloging in Publication Data
A catalog record for this book has been requested

British Library Cataloguing in Publication Data
A catalogue record for this book is available from the British Library

ISBN 0–415–36055–2

Contents

Contributors

Sabina Alkire is a research associate at the Global Equity Initiative at Harvard University's Asia Center. A student of Amartya Sen's, she has served as a development economist at the World Bank and a senior research associate at the Von Hugel Institute, University of Cambridge. Her book *Valuing Freedom: Sen's Capability Approach and Poverty Reduction* (New York: Oxford University Press, 2002) is generally recognized as a major contribution to the capabilities theory literature.

Richard Arneson is Professor of Philosophy, the University of California, San Diego. He was department chair from 1992 to 1996. He has written numerous articles on distributive justice, several of which are recognized as classics in the field.

David A. Crocker is Senior Research Professor, Center for Philosophy and Public Policy, University of Maryland (College Park). He has written numerous articles on political and moral philosophy, with a particular emphasis on issues of distributive justice.

Timothy Hinton is Associate Professor of Philosophy, North Carolina State University. His research focuses on the nature of justice, equality and the challenges of pluralism.

Victoria Kamsler is Visiting Professor of Political Philosophy, Princeton Institute for Advanced Study. Her work focuses on deliberative democracy and German Idealism.

Alexander Kaufman is Assistant Professor of Political Theory, School of Public and International Affairs, University of Georgia. His book *Welfare in the Kantian State* (Oxford: Clarendon Press, 1999) examines the basis in Kant's political and moral theory for institutions designed to secure social conditions of equality. He has published articles on German Idealism, issues of distributive justice, and philosophy of law.

Martha C. Nussbaum is Ernst Freund Distinguished Professor of Law and Ethics at the University of Chicago, appointed in the Philosophy Department, the Law School, the Divinity School, and the College. Her most recent books include *Women and Human Development* (Cambridge: Cambridge University Press, 2000) and *Upheavals of Thought: Intelligence and the Emotions* (Cambridge: Cambridge University Press, 2001).

Peter Vallentyne is Professor of Philosophy, University of Missouri–Columbia. His primary research interests are in the areas of distributive justice, ethics and philosophy of law. His recent work in political philosophy includes *Contractarianism and Rational Choice* (edited; Cambridge: Cambridge University Press, 1991), *The Origins of Left-Libertarianism* (co-edited; Basingstoke, UK: Palgrave, 2000), *Left-Libertarianism and Its Critics* (co-edited; Basingstoke, UK: Palgrave, 2000), and *Equality and Justice*, five volumes (edited; New York: Routledge, 2003).

David Wasserman is Research Scholar at the Center for Philosophy and Public Policy, University of Maryland (College Park). Among his research interests are biotechnology and disability policy, the preservation of human environments and cultures, and ethical issues in probability, statistical inference, and legal proof. He is co-editor, with Robert Wachbroit, of *Genetics and Criminal Behavior: Methods, Meanings, and Morals* (Cambridge: Cambridge University Press, 1998).

Introduction

Alexander Kaufman

In what sense should persons be judged to be equal or unequal as a matter of justice? Persons inherit differing endowments of goods and abilities; are born into differing social positions; and exercise differing degrees of power and influence. As a result, they enjoy differing degrees of opportunity to realize their abilities and experience different degrees of affluence or poverty. Accounts of egalitarian justice measure and characterize these differences. In order to perform these tasks, an egalitarian theory must, as G. A. Cohen notes, address two distinct questions (1994: 117). First, in what respect should persons be counted equal or unequal – what "currency of egalitarian justice" should be employed to measure the individual's well-being? Second, how should the degree of existing inequality be measured; that is, how should we calculate the *degree* of inequality that exists in a given distribution of social goods?

The capabilities approach originated as a response to the first question. In "What Is Equality?", Amartya Sen (1980) criticized two leading contemporary accounts of the currency of egalitarian justice. The first account, *equality of welfare*, argues that egalitarians are concerned most fundamentally with the welfare that a given distribution of goods produces, and not with the literal distribution of goods; while the second account, *equality of resources*, argues that egalitarians are most fundamentally concerned to assure that all members of society receive equal shares of resources.

Neither of these theories, Sen argued, provides a satisfactory account of fundamental egalitarian concerns. Egalitarians are not simply concerned with the distribution of *resources*, since persons vary in their efficiency in transforming resources into well-being. A person with a large body mass is not, for example, treated equally if he or she is provided with precisely the same share of food as a person with a much smaller body mass. Egalitarians are not, in fact, primarily concerned with the literal allocation of goods; rather, egalitarians are concerned with what goods do for persons. But this concern is not, Sen argued, well described by equality of *welfare*. What goods do for persons goes beyond the satisfaction of preferences or the generation of happiness. Tiny Tim may be happier and more satisfied with his share of goods than Scrooge is with his share, but this fact should not lead an egalitarian to redistribute goods from Tiny Tim to Scrooge.

As an alternative to welfare or resources, Sen argues for *capabilities* as the currency of egalitarian justice. Capabilities are the person's freedoms to *be* or *do* certain fundamentally important things. A person's quality of life, Sen argues, is a function of what the person is able to be (e.g. well or poorly nourished) and do (e.g. perform more or less meaningful work). Sen refers to the various states of being and doing relevant to the assessment of a person's well-being as *functionings* (Sen 1985: 10). The combination of functionings that a person achieves constitutes the form of life that the person leads.

Capabilities are defined as the various combinations of functionings that the person can achieve (Sen 1993: 40). A person's capability set represents the alternative combinations of simultaneously attainable functionings that are available to the person. Sen argues that a capability set therefore reflects "the person's freedom to lead one type of life or another" (1992: 40).

Recent scholarship has extended the capabilities approach beyond an account of the currency of equality. Martha Nussbaum, in particular, argues for a political approach based on ideas of capability and functioning. Working from an account of the minimal conditions necessary for truly human functioning, Nussbaum argues for minimum capabilities guarantees that a just society should extend to its members (see Nussbaum 1988, 1990, 1995, 2000).

The capabilities approach thus can claim to expand the descriptive and analytic resources of egalitarian discourse. In fact, it has been the apparent success of this approach in addressing central egalitarian concerns that has helped to establish it as an important strand in contemporary egalitarian thought. Nevertheless, the approach faces important challenges. In particular, critics (i) object to the priority that the capabilities approach assigns to securing thresholds levels of basic capabilities; and (ii) argue that the view fails to present an account of egalitarian concerns that is clearly differentiated from competing accounts. In this introduction, I will describe (i) achievements of the capabilities approach in addressing egalitarian concerns; and (ii) the challenges to that approach raised and addressed by chapters in this volume.

Achievements: capabilities and responsibility

The recent egalitarian literature has focused on two fundamental concerns. The first reflects the intuition that the individual's share of social goods should not be determined by factors that are distributed according to a "natural lottery," and whose distribution is therefore "arbitrary from a moral point of view" (Rawls [1971] 1999: 72, 74). Such factors include endowments of wealth, social position and talent. Both equality of welfare and equality of resources aim to neutralize or correct for the role of morally arbitrary factors in determining the distribution of goods. The second concern reflects the intuition that egalitarian justice should only correct for inequalities of condition for which it is inappropriate to hold the person responsible. Ronald Dworkin, for example, argues that persons should be compensated for welfare deficits deriving from their circumstances, but not from their choices; others adopting a similar view include Richard Arneson, G. A. Cohen, Matt Matravers, and John Roemer (see Arneson 1989, 2000; Cohen 1989, 1993; Matravers 2002; Roemer 1985, 1986). Elizabeth Anderson, Timothy Hinton, Alexander Kaufman, and Samuel Scheffler, among others, have disputed this view, arguing that such a focus on responsibility reflects an unattractive ideal of egalitarian justice (see Anderson 1999; Hinton 2001; Kaufman 2004; Scheffler 2003). Disagreement regarding the role that intuitions regarding responsibility for disadvantage should play in constraining the aspirations of egalitarian theory has thus complicated the task of designing an acceptable account of the currency of egalitarian justice.

Two questions regarding responsibility have proved especially problematic for contemporary egalitarians. First, to what extent is it reasonable to hold a person responsible for his or her tastes and preferences? Second, to what extent is it reasonable to hold a person responsible for his or her level of ambition? The failure of equality of welfare and equality of resources to provide persuasive responses to these questions has left both theories vulnerable to important objections. Moreover, neither of the two leading attempts to address this failing – equality of access to advantage and equality of opportunity for welfare – resolves these concerns in a satisfactory manner.

Responsibility for tastes and preferences

If a person requires the satisfaction of exorbitantly expensive tastes in order to avoid a welfare deficit, must the egalitarian satisfy these tastes or compensate for the deficit? Must the egalitarian, as Kenneth Arrow suggested, satisfy the epicure's taste for prephylloxera claret and plover's eggs in order to secure a just distribution of goods (1973: 254)? This question has constituted a serious problem for equality of welfare. While equality of welfare's commitment to equalizing levels of subjective preference satisfaction is apparently well designed to eliminate the influence of morally arbitrary factors (e.g. class rank, wealth, talent) on the distribution of social goods, such an approach seems to require that egalitarians compensate Arrow's claret-lover even if his expensive tastes were formed willfully.[1]

Symmetrically, equality of welfare appears to require no special compensation for persons whose preferences have been deformed by morally arbitrary cultural or contextual influences. If a "tamed housewife" is no worse off than others in terms of preference satisfaction, despite living under conditions of inequality and domination, equality of welfare's concerns are satisfied.

In each case, equality of welfare fails to take proper account of the degree to which it is appropriate to hold the individual responsible for the content of his or her preference set. While it would seem reasonable to hold the person responsible for voluntary expensive tastes, welfare equality fails to do so and simply compensates for deficits in the satisfaction of such tastes. In the case of involuntary cheap tastes, where it would seem unreasonable to assign responsibility for preferences to the person, welfare equality refuses to compensate for welfare deficits, implicitly holding the person responsible for his or her distorted preference set.

Responsibility for ambition

Like equality of welfare, equality of resources aspires to neutralize the influence of morally arbitrary factors on the distribution of social goods. In order to avoid over-resourcing persons with expensive tastes, equality of resources argues that egalitarian theory must be ambition sensitive. That is, egalitarians should not compensate for inequalities deriving from choices to consume rather than invest, or to consume more expensively rather than less, or to work in less rather than more profitable ways.[2] Egalitarians should, however, compensate for inequalities deriving from the effects of morally arbitrary endowments of wealth, position, and talent. Thus, Ronald Dworkin argues, egalitarian justice should pair ambition-sensitivity with endowment-insensitivity. Equality of resources would therefore compensate individuals impoverished through a lack of talent, but not those impoverished through an expensive taste for leisure.

Equality of resources may, however, introduce the notion of responsibility into the egalitarian analysis too aggressively. Dworkin's discussion of the role of insurance in transforming differences in fortune from brute luck to option luck provides a representative example of resource equality's employment of the notion of responsibility. Assume, Dworkin suggests, that two victims of an accident had an equal chance of going blind and an equal opportunity to insure against going blind, but only one chose to insure. The uninsured victim could expect no compensation from the insured victim, even if the uninsured person were the only one blinded. The failure to insure would convert the difference in circumstances between the insured and uninsured victims from bad brute luck to option luck. By analogy, Dworkin argues, if everyone had the same risk of suffering such a catastrophe, knew the odds, and had adequate opportunity to insure, no victim could assert a legitimate claim to compensation against other members of society (2000: 77).

Uninsured victims could assert no legitimate claims for compensation, under such circumstances, because the choice not to insure transforms the element of misfortune that distinguishes the victim's condition from that of his or her fellows into the product of his or her own choice. Equality of resources respects this choice and assigns responsibility for a person's condition to that person, Dworkin tells us, because the choice reflects the victim's preference for a certain form of life – a life that "contains, as an element, the factor of risk" (Dworkin 2000: 74). To redistribute resources to the victim would therefore deprive the victim of the form of life that he or she prefers (ibid.: 75).

But this claim appears to trade on an ambiguity in the notion of risk employed. Most persons, it seems reasonable to assume, are willing to assume a significant *economic* risk of downward mobility in order to preserve the possibility of upward mobility. The risk of seriously disabling injury, however, is of quite a different order; and Dworkin's claim that persons should be held responsible for the preference for risk in such a case highlights the degree to which equality of resources applies the idea of responsibility overly aggressively. In *Sovereign Virtue*, Dworkin argues that equality of resources appropriately assigns full responsibility to the individual, even while conceding that preferences are in many cases not voluntarily chosen, because tastes and preferences are constitutive of the individual's conception of the good life (2000: 289; see also Dworkin 1995: 293). It is incoherent, Dworkin suggests, to argue that a preference could be simultaneously constitutive of a conception of the good life and a limitation on the realization of that conception (2000: 293; see also Dworkin 1995: 295).

Even if Dworkin argued persuasively that the choice not to insure reflected the uninsured victim's preference for a life that contains risk, however, he could not consistently assign a central role to such a preference in determining the nature of a just distribution. Dworkin defines brute luck as "a matter of how risks fall out that are not . . . deliberate gambles" (2000: 73). The inheritance of risk-seeking preferences therefore constitutes an instance of brute luck. In order to vindicate his constitutive commitment to neutralizing the influence of morally arbitrary factors, and in particular the influence of brute luck, on life chances, then, Dworkin must concede that the uninsured victim *can* assert a legitimate claim to compensation against other members of society.

Defining an acceptable standard of responsibility for preferences

Both *equality of opportunity for welfare* and *equality of access to advantage* attempt to resolve concerns regarding responsibility for preferences by attempting to identify a category of preferences that are free from morally arbitrary influences. G. A. Cohen's theory of *equality of access to advantage* offers a carefully circumscribed account of responsibility: individuals are to be held responsible for the consequences of preferences that they have not chosen freely only if the preferences "are so *intrinsically connected* with [the individual's] commitments that their bearer would not choose to be without them" (Cohen 1989: 937).[3] Even if such preferences are, in fact, affected by the contingent influence of context or genetic endowment, the intrinsic connection of these preferences to the individual's constitutive commitments can be understood to transform such choices from merely contingent to genuinely autonomous.

Yet this approach is no more successful than equality of resources in addressing the problem of involuntary cheap tastes. Indeed, as John Roemer notes, such an approach "would direct society *not* to redress the situation of the tamed housewife" (1996: 275; my emphasis). In fact, the tamed housewife appears to fit precisely G. A. Cohen's description of a person suffering a welfare deficit resulting from preferences intrinsically connected to the person's fundamental commitments. It is precisely because involuntary cheap preferences are intrinsically connected to the individual's commitments that such preferences are so problematic: the individual has, apparently, freely chosen to incorporate the preferences imposed upon her into her conception of the good life. The notion of an intrinsic connection between certain involuntarily formed preferences and the individual's constitutive commitments does not provide the basis for an adequate litmus test for identifying those preferences that are truly "genuine."

Richard Arneson's *equality of opportunity for welfare* rejects responsibility for preferences as an appropriate basis for the distribution of social goods.[4] Instead, like welfare equality, equality of opportunity for welfare argues for equalizing preference satisfaction; but, like resource equality, opportunity equality also argues against disproportionate compensation for expensive tastes. In order to avoid such over-resourcing, opportunity equality limits compensation to the satisfaction of the individual's "ideally considered preferences," defined as "those [preferences] I would have if I were to engage in thorough-going deliberation about my preferences with full pertinent information, in a calm mood ... making no reasoning errors" (Arneson 1989: 82–83).

Yet it is not clear that opportunity egalitarianism avoids over-resourcing expensive tastes. While "ideally considered preferences" are the product of thoroughgoing deliberation, it is not clear whether such deliberation would persuade Arrow's claret-lover to modify her taste for luxury goods. It seems quite possible, in fact, that such deliberation would confirm and reinforce preferences for expensive but high-quality goods over goods that are inexpensive but prosaic.

While this failure to deal decisively with the problem of voluntary expensive tastes is problematic, equality of opportunity for welfare seems even less well equipped to address the effects of involuntary cheap tastes. The problem is perhaps best illustrated by examining Arneson's attempt to operationalize the notion of ideal deliberation over preferences (1990: 163–164). In Arneson's example, individual X prefers beer to champagne, but considers the possibility that his rational preference *should* be for champagne. Should X, after ideal deliberation, abandon or reaffirm his preference for beer? Arneson argues that X should reach his judgment by comparing, after ideal deliberation: (i) the pleasure he now derives from drinking beer; and (ii) the maximum pleasure he might be able to derive from champagne. If, after ideal deliberation, X concludes that he will derive the greatest pleasure from "drinking beer with unenlightened gusto," then beer will remain the better option for him. Thus, X's judgment should be determined by X's "enlightened judgment of [his] perhaps unenlightened preferences" (ibid.: 164).

It is far from certain, however, that such ideal deliberation could adequately address the influence of involuntary cheap tastes on the tamed housewife or the discouraged worker. Suppose, for example, that a tamed housewife is considering a strategy designed to redefine her social role and status. Suppose, in addition, that redefining her role would cause a great deal of pain. Her relations with her husband, children, parents and extended family will be strained, perhaps to the breaking point. She has little confidence in her academic skills; yet she will need to return to school to acquire certain skills. Finally, her social conditioning has made her submissive, and she is terrified of provoking disapproval. Even when deliberating from a fully enlightened standpoint, she does not believe she can bear the stress, disruption, and disapproval necessary to redefine her role. Her enlightened judgment of her unenlightened preferences requires that she remain as she is.

Yet it is possible that she would weigh the costs and benefits of self-assertion differently when viewing them retrospectively, after, say, she has successfully completed medical training and is in practice. In retrospect, she may believe that the costs incurred are significantly outweighed by the benefits. Thus, her retrospective enlightened preferences may favor her choice to assert her independence.

Arneson does not ignore the possibility that ideally considered preferences may change over time. In order to incorporate the possibility of changes in ideally considered preferences in his account, Arneson "tentatively" suggests comparing the weighted sums of the sets of ideally considered preferences generated over a complete lifetime ("lifetime preference satisfaction"; 1990: 166). Each weighted sum would aggregate values assigned to sets of ideally considered preferences generated "moment by moment" over the full course of a person's life. The weight to be assigned to each of the sets of preferences to be summed would be determined according to the importance the set of preferences would have for the (hypothetically rational) agent at the moment in which it was generated. The highest total sum would identify the agent's ideally considered lifetime set of ideally considered preferences.

Yet Arneson's procedure does not solve the problem. Suppose that, during her medical training, the woman in my example experienced all of the evils she had anticipated. Her husband divorced her; she became estranged from her children and family; and the disapproval of her friends and family caused her constant discomfort. As a result, her sets of ideally considered preferences during the period of her training were colored by the (unrealizable) desire to undo her choice and restore her previous condition. The weight and intensity of these preferences far outweighed the weight and intensity of her later preference to endorse her choice to pursue medical training. Thus, the weighted sum of the lifetime set of ideally considered preferences that included her early preference to pursue medical training would not produce the highest possible sum, and would therefore be rejected under Arneson's procedure. Yet the woman's considered retrospective judgment endorsed her choice.

Retrospective endorsement of this choice does not, of course, demonstrate that the choice was objectively correct for the individual. It could plausibly be argued that present preferences to avoid pain should be privileged over anticipated future preferences that do not require such painavoidance. Equality of opportunity for welfare, however, would lead us to endorse the woman's prospective preferences without considering whether her retrospective preferences might provide a compelling countervailing consideration. Thus, the view contains a status-quo bias that would reinforce the influence of adaptive preferences, and thus arbitrary contingency, on the distribution of social goods.

Arneson, in his most recent work, modifies his argument, asserting that egalitarians should give priority to assisting those who are badly off and, in particular, those who "are not substantially responsible for their condition" (2000: 340). The basic character of his theory, however, remains the same. The apparently novel element in his recent work is provided by the priority to be assigned to the needs of those who are badly off and "not substantially responsible" for their disadvantage. Yet this element was characteristic of Arneson's earlier theory as well. In that work, Arneson divided the world into (i) those who *were not* responsible for disadvantage experienced (that is, who had not been provided with equal opportunity to realize their ideally considered preferences); and (ii) those who *were* responsible for disadvantage (those who had been provided with such equal opportunity); and he assigned priority to the claims of the persons who were not responsible their for their disadvantage (Arneson 1989). Arneson's recent work does not provide a new standard of responsibility to guide egalitarian judgment in determining when a person should be viewed as "substantially responsible" for his or her condition.

Thus, equal opportunity for welfare, like equal access to advantage, fails to incorporate intuitions regarding responsibility for disadvantage successfully into an acceptable account of egalitarian concerns. Both theories attempt, ultimately unsuccessfully, to identify a set of ideally considered – or genuine – preferences that have escaped the influence of arbitrariness.

The capabilities approach

The capabilities approach does not attempt to identify a set of preferences that are free from the influence of arbitrary factors; as a result, the approach avoids many of the problems that entangle opportunity and access equality. Rather, the capabilities approach argues for a distinctly practical object of egalitarian fundamental concern: egalitarian policy is to assess the ability of individuals to *be* and *do* certain things. The approach is distinct from equality of resources in arguing that egalitarian theory should focus on the *effects* of distributions of resources rather than on the distribution of resources *per se*; and from equality of welfare in arguing for a focus on the ability to function rather than end-states measured in terms of well-being. Most significantly, the theory argues for a positive account of the interests and needs essential to purposive agency.

The capabilities approach appears to address successfully the problems concerning responsibility for preferences and choices that undermined welfare, resource, access, and opportunity egalitarianism. This approach avoids allowing the distribution of social resources to be determined by preferences that are determined or affected by the contingent effects of genetics or context, since the distribution of social goods is to be grounded in a positive account of interests and needs. In addition, the capabilities approach does not impose an excessively strict standard of responsibility, since the approach is committed to assuring the capability to act effectively, regardless of the choices made by the individual.

Finally, as Elizabeth Anderson argues, the capabilities approach "conceives of equality as a relation among people rather than merely as a pattern in the distribution of divisible goods," and therefore "offers a superior way to understand the expressive demands of justice – the demand to act only on principles that express respect for everyone" (1999: 336–337). Samuel Scheffler suggests that "questions about egalitarian distributive norms must be controlled by some broader understanding of equality" (2003: 23), and the capabilities approach offers an attractive broader understanding to perform such a role.

Controversies

Recent criticism in the philosophical and theoretical literature has raised fundamental questions regarding the character and justification of the capabilities approach. One set of objections focuses on what critics describe as the sufficientarian nature of the approach. Critics who offer such objections argue that a capabilities approach would: (i) overcompensate persons whose disadvantage is the product of voluntary choice; and (ii) undercompensate anyone else requiring assistance by aiming to ensure too modest a threshold level of functioning to too large a class of persons (see Arneson 2000; Dworkin 2000). A second objection suggests that the view fails to present a clearly differentiated account of egalitarian concerns; capabilities equality, it is suggested, collapses into either equality of resources or equality of welfare, because the theory in fact reflects a fundamental concern either with resources or with the welfare derived from resources (Dworkin 2000: 106–143).

The chapters of this book address these concerns. Chapters in Part I examine the objection that the capabilities approach is sufficientarian; chapters in Part II examine the objection that the capabilities approach is not a clearly differentiated view; and chapters in Part III address various issues and problems arising in the context of efforts to implement the capabilities approach.

Part I: "A sufficientarian approach?"

Richard Arneson's chapter (Chapter 1) extends and develops his ongoing critique of the capabilities approach. Arneson focuses on the approach's commitment to securing threshold levels of basic capabilities. The centrality of this commitment, he argues, establishes that the theory is sufficientarian – that is, the theory aims to assure that everyone has access to a *good enough* level of functioning. What happens beyond this "good enough" level, Arneson asserts, is a "don't care" from the standpoint of the capabilities account of justice. The problem with such an approach is that a sufficiency doctrine goes wrong in suggesting that one can nonarbitrarily pick out some level of capability whose achievement should take strict priority over the achievement of further gains for those above that level. No sufficiency threshold, he notes, could justify absolute priority over other questions of distributive justice. Moreover, sufficiency accounts of social justice become increasingly plausible as they are progressively modified *to weaken or eliminate their sufficientarian character*. The most reasonable approach, Arneson concludes, is to abandon sufficientarianism.

Martha Nussbaum's chapter (Chapter 2) offers a defense of the capabilities approach's focus on defining and protecting a definite set of basic capabilities. In order to fulfill its potential as a basis of a normative account of social justice with critical potential for gender issues, Nussbaum argues, the capabilities approach requires an account, for political purposes, of what the central capabilities are. Such an approach, she asserts, is both justified, on the basis of politically liberal arguments grounded in shared ideals of humanity; and essential for the identification and analysis of unjust conditions.

Alexander Kaufman's note (Chapter 3) disputes the view that the character of the capabilities approach is unqualifiedly sufficientarian. In fact, Kaufman suggests, the approach neither limits its attention to securing threshold levels of capabilities nor assigns absolute priority to the goal of securing such thresholds.

Part II: "A clearly differentiated approach?"

Vallentyne, in Chapter 4, argues that the capabilities approach does not define an account of egalitarian concerns that is distinct from the view – favored by Arneson, Cohen, and Roemer – that justice is concerned with something like the distribution of opportunities for well-being. Rather, Vallentyne argues, although some versions of the capability view are incompatible with some versions of the opportunity for well-being view, the most plausible version of the capability view is identical to a slight generalization of the opportunity for well-being view.

Timothy Hinton's chapter (Chapter 5) develops the basis for a response to Vallentyne's argument in the context of an exploration of the capabilities approach's treatment of gender. Hinton critiques and proposes an extension of Nussbaum's analysis of gender inequality: in focusing so carefully on inequalities in the treatment of women, Hinton suggests, Nussbaum overlooks the inequalities in social power that generate this unequal treatment. Hinton begins to develop a response to Vallentyne by distinguishing the *social* ideal animating the capabilities approach from the *distributive* ideal that motivates opportunity accounts of equality. The capabilities approach aspires to sustain a society of free political equals, Hinton notes, while opportunity conceptions of equality aim to guarantee people (access to) equally worthwhile lives.

Alexander Kaufman in Chapter 6 examines a second feature that distinguishes the capabilities approach from opportunity accounts of equality in the context of responding to G. A. Cohen's argument that the capabilities approach suffers from confusing duality in its account of fundamental egalitarian concerns. Sen's pluralistic view of those fundamental concerns, Kaufman argues, undermines neither the coherence nor the practical value of the capabilities approach. In adopting such a pluralistic view, as opposed to the monistic views (identifying the distribution of welfare or midfare as the sole fundamental concern of distributive justice) favored by opportunity accounts of equality, Kaufman argues that the capabilities approach in fact expands the descriptive and analytic range of egalitarian thought.

Part III: "Issues in Implementation"

The chapters by Sabina Alkire, David Crocker, Victoria Kamsler, and David Wasserman address questions relating to the implementation in policy of the commitments of the capabilities approach.

Alkire, in Chapter 7, argues that implementation of the policies required to ensure adequate opportunity to realize fundamental capabilities in the context of a democratic political culture characterized by reasonable pluralism requires sustained and substantive participation by members of society in ongoing deliberations regarding the commitments of distributive justice within a democratic society. Her chapter explores the potential that "forms" of participatory discussion have for enabling communities to identify common value judgments and priorities.

Crocker argues in Chapter 8 that recent work in the deliberative theory of democracy appropriately supplements Sen's capabilities approach to international development and enriches Alkire's efforts to apply Sen's theory with a value-oriented conception of participation to micro-projects. His chapter first sketches four different levels of governmental and non-governmental fora in which public deliberation and deliberative democracy might reasonably play a role. Second, Crocker examines Sen's capabilities approach to international development and argues that this approach requires democracy and would benefit from explicit adoption of a version of deliberative democracy. Third, as resources to strengthen the social choice dimension of the capabilities approach, Crocker discusses the theory and practice of deliberative democracy and draws on several useful theoretical versions and institutional experiments. Finally, Crocker argues that a version of deliberative democracy also enriches Sabina Alkire's effort to "operationalize" the capabilities approach for use in improving the theory and practice of participation in small-scale, grassroots development initiatives.

Kamsler's chapter (Chapter 9) considers the way that capability lists enable the inclusion of environmental issues in a theory that is anthropocentric in its standard formulation. Do we add environmental issues to the list of human capabilities, or revise the basic understanding of capability to make it inclusive of other forms of flourishing? Recently, Martha Nussbaum has sought to extend the account of capabilities to the flourishing of individual non-human animals. Kamsler considers the significance and limitations of this approach.

Wasserman's contribution (Chapter 10) examines the implications of the capabilities approach for policies to address the needs of people with major sensory, motor, and cognitive impairments. Nussbaum, Wasserman notes, has modified her initial account of core capabilities in two important ways: (i) broadening the individuation of the core capabilities to accommodate a significantly wider range of ways they can be acquired and exercised; and (ii) holding that justice requires the acquisition not of equal, but only of minimum levels of each capability, achievable by almost all human beings, while continuing to reject trade-offs among capabilities in assessing justice and well-being. These features allow Nussbaum to recognize the possibilities of flourishing for people with severe impairments, while maintaining that justice demands the resources and environmental modifications necessary for them to achieve minimum levels.

Wasserman's chapter endorses the first modification but questions the second. It argues that achieving minimum levels of each capability is more difficult than Nussbaum assumes and that justice may require trade-offs among individuals and capabilities that leave some people below the mimima for some capabilities – even if they could achieve them with sufficient resources and accommodation. This argument for the moral necessity of trade-offs converges in several respects with Arneson's critique of the priority Nussbaum accords to the acquisition of minimum levels of each capability, an approach he characterizes as "sufficientarian."

Notes

1 The problem of expensive tastes, in fact, constitutes merely one dimension of a deeper issue. In order to equalize preference satisfaction, the welfarist will need to tie distributive decisions to a variety of given tastes and preferences. For example, a literal reading of the welfarist approach would seem to require the fine-tuning of emergency energy subsidies to the propensity for discomfort of the recipient. As G. A. Cohen notes, "[p]eople vary in the amount of discomfort which given low temperatures cause them" (1989: 920). But a propensity to discomfort, like a preference for rare burgundy, is affected, if not determined, by morally arbitrary natural endowments and cultural influences. Thus, welfare egalitarians wish to equalize the satisfaction of subjective preferences that are themselves, in significant part, arbitrarily distributed.

2 This paraphrases Dworkin's claim that egalitarians should not be concerned with inequalities deriving from different attitudes to the questions of whether "to invest rather than consume, or to consume less expensively rather than more, or to work in more rather than less profitable ways" (1981: 311).

3 Equality of opportunity for welfare operationalizes this commitment by providing access to sufficient information, varied perspectives, and counselling to allow individuals to revise their choices, so that individuals may reasonably be deemed to identify with the choices they make.

4 "[I]t is far from clear why … affirming [one's preferences and values] and identifying them as essential to one's self precludes demanding or accepting compensation for these preferences in the name of distributive equality" (Arneson 1989: 81).

References

Anderson, E. (1999) "What is the Point of Equality?" *Ethics* 109 (2): 287–337.

Arneson, R. (1989) "Equality and Equal Opportunity for Welfare," *Philosophical Studies* 56: 77–93.

Arneson, R. (1990) "Liberalism, Distributive Subjectivism, and Equal Opportunity for Welfare," *Philosophy and Public Affairs* 19: 158–194.

Arneson, R. (2000) "Luck Egalitarianism and Prioritarianism," *Ethics* 110: 339–349.

Arrow, K. J. (1973) "Some Ordinalist-Utilitarian Notes on Rawls's Theory of Justice," *Journal of Philosophy* 70: 245–263.

Cohen, G. A. (1989) "On the Currency of Egalitarian Justice," *Ethics* 99: 906–944.

Cohen, G. A. (1993) "Equality of What?", in M. C. Nussbaum and A. Sen (eds) *The Quality of Life*, Cambridge: Cambridge University Press, pp. 9–29.

Cohen, G. A. (1994) "Review: Amartya Sen's Unequal World," *New Left Review* (January): 117–129.

Dworkin, R. (1981) "What Is Equality? Part 2: Equality of Resources," *Philosophy and Public Affairs* 10: 283–345.

Dworkin, R. (1995) "Foundations of Liberal Equality," in S. Darwall (ed.) *Equal Freedom*, Ann Arbor: University of Michigan Press.

Dworkin, R. (2000) *Sovereign Virtue*, Cambridge, MA: Harvard University Press.

Hinton, T. (2001) "Must Egalitarianism Choose between Fairness and Respect?" *Philosophy and Public Affairs* 30 (1): 72–87.

Kaufman, A. (2004) "Choice, Responsibility and Equality," *Political Studies* 52: 819–836.

Matravers, M. (2002) "Responsibility, Luck and the 'Equality of What' Debate," *Political Studies* 50: 558–572.

Nussbaum, M. C. (1988) "Nature, Function and Capability: Aristotle on Political Distribution," *Oxford Studies in Ancient Philosophy*, suppl. vol.: 145–184.

Nussbaum, M. C. (1990) "Aristotelian Social Democracy," in R. B. Douglass, G. R. Mara, and H. S. Richardson (eds) *Liberalism and the Good*, New York: Routledge.

Nussbaum, M. C. (1995) "Human Capabilities, Female Human Beings," in M. C. Nussbaum and J. Glover (eds) *Women, Culture and Development*, Oxford: Clarendon Press.

Nussbaum, M. C. (2000) *Women and Human Development: The Capabilities Approach*, Cambridge: Cambridge University Press.

Rawls, J. ([1971] 1999) *A Theory of Justice*, Cambridge, MA: Harvard University Press.

Roemer, J. (1985) "Equality of Talent," *Economics and Philosophy* 1: 151–187.

Roemer, J. (1986) "Equality of Resources Implies Equality of Welfare," *Quarterly Journal of Economics* 101: 751–784.

Roemer, J. (1996) *Theories of Distributive Justice*, Cambridge, MA: Harvard University Press, 1996.

Scheffler, S. (2003) "What Is Egalitarianism?" *Philosophy and Public Affairs* 31 (1): pp. 5–39.

Sen, A. (1980) "Equality of What?" in S. M. McMurrin (ed.) *The Tanner Lectures on Human Values*, Salt Lake City: University of Utah Press.

Sen, A. (1985) *Commodities and Capabilities*, Amsterdam: North-Holland.

Sen, A. (1992) *Inequality Reexamined*, Cambridge, MA: Harvard University Press.

Sen, A. (1993) "Capability and Well-Being," in M. C. Nussbaum and A. Sen (eds) *The Quality of Life*, Oxford: Clarendon Press.

Part 1

A sufficientarian approach?

1 Distributive justice and basic capability equality

"Good enough" is not good enough

Richard Arneson

Amartya Sen has developed important conceptual clarifications and criticisms for the theory of justice. He has so far been reluctant to affirm a theory of justice (or a component of such a theory) in his own voice. This chapter urges that the criticisms Sen has made against utilitarian and Rawlsian measures of people's condition are inconclusive, pending the elaboration and defense of an objective account of human well-being. Such an account would enable us to select among the myriad capabilities to function in various ways that people always have and identify some capabilities as the ones that matter for purposes of the theory of justice. In several essays, Martha Nussbaum has worked to elaborate such an account. The Nussbaum and Sen approach to social justice theorizing merits close scrutiny.

The Nussbaum and Sen approach can usefully be interpreted as sufficientarian. On this view, justice above all requires that each and every person be sustained at a threshold adequate level of capability to function in all of the ways that are important for human well-being. This chapter examines capability sufficiency doctrine and finds it wanting. The nub of the difficulty with sufficiency is that it overstates the moral importance of sustaining each and every person at the "good enough" level, come what may. In this respect the doctrine that has become known as prioritarianism is to be preferred.

The Nussbaum and Sen approach to social justice significantly maintains that justice requires fair provision of real freedom or capability to function in important ways to all persons, rather than assurance that individuals reach any particular life outcomes assessed in terms of functioning levels. At least, Nussbaum if not Sen himself is committed to the idea that capability, not functioning, is the proper measure of people's condition for use by the theory of justice. For example, justice involves assurance of freedom of religion to all, not assurance that people achieve any particular sort of religious functioning. For another example, the just society is concerned to provide all people the capability to engage in satisfying sexual relations but does not regard any part of its proper business to be bringing it about that people actually function sexually to any degree. The issue of capability versus functioning as the proper measure of people's condition for a theory of justice goes to the heart of liberalism, regarded as a philosophy of individual freedom for modern times. Giving priority to capability is appealing for many reasons. Nonetheless, this chapter argues against giving priority to capability at the level of fundamental moral theory. What ultimately matters, and should matter for the theory of justice, is the actual quality of life that people attain, not the capabilities, freedoms, and opportunities they enjoy.

Amartya Sen is a renowned economist who has also made important contributions to philosophical thinking about distributive justice. These contributions tend to take the form of criticism of inadequate positions and insistence on making distinctions that will promote clear thinking about the topic. Sen is not shy about making substantive normative claims, but thus far he has avoided commitment to a theory of justice, in the sense of a set of principles that specifies what facts are relevant for policy choice and determines, given a full characterization of any situation in terms of these relevant facts, what ought to be done in that situation. Moreover, Sen has expressed skepticism about the existence of a fully adequate theory in this sense. According to Sen, there is a plurality of moral considerations that bear on choice of action and policy, and no particular reason to think that weights can be attached nonarbitrarily to each consideration to yield a theory (see Sen 1982, 1985a, b, 1987, 1992).

"Sen's proposal is that distributive justice entails equalizing midfare levels across persons," writes John Roemer (1996: 189). "Other things being equal," one has to add by way of correction to Roemer's formulation. Sen holds that we should be concerned with the extent of people's capability or freedom to attain midfare as well as the midfare level actually reached. Sen holds that distributive values including equality must be balanced against, and should sometimes be sacrificed to, aggregative values. We should care about how much of the good things of life people get as well as how evenly they are distributed. Also, what Roemer is calling "midfare" is, according to Sen, not one thing but itself a plurality: the many functionings (doings and beings) that people have reason to value so far as they are seeking their own well-being. Sen does not affirm that there is a single canonical measure of these functionings, so the ideal of equality of midfare is in an important sense indeterminate. Besides well-being as midfare functionings and freedom to get well-being, the just society also properly promotes and distributes agency achievement, the attainment of goals one has reason to value, and freedom to attain agency goals.

In short, Sen's message to any would-be theorist of justice is that things are more complicated than you think. Current theories on offer ride roughshod over distinctions that are consequential for right policy choice and ignore considerations that are morally important. The paradigm foil in this enterprise as Sen pursues it is utilitarianism, which achieves elegant simplicity by failure to register the actual complexity of the reasons that bear on evaluation. Sen has developed an approach to the understanding of social justice rather than a theory of justice.

In this chapter I argue that Sen's official position is unstable. To vindicate his criticisms of subjectivist versions of utilitarianism, one must have good reason to affirm an objective account of human well-being – objective in the sense that items are identified as intrinsically enhancing the well-being of a person independently of the person's own opinions and attitudes toward these items.[1] Otherwise, the criticisms he lodges against desire satisfaction accounts of distributive justice can be turned against his own proposals. In several essays, Martha Nussbaum (1988, 1990, 1991, 1992, 1999, 2000a), registering appreciation of this point, proposes a set of capabilities to function as definitive of a good human life, and proposes that social justice requires that every person should have the capability to achieve a decent or good enough level of functioning for each and every one of the types of functioning that together constitute a good human life. This proposal dovetails with suggestions that recur in Sen's own writings to the effect that the core of social justice is basic capability equality, a state of affairs in which each person equally has the capability to attain all of the designated important basic types of functionings, and so is able if he or she chooses to function at a good enough threshold level with respect to each and every one of the types of functionings deemed basic or essential (see, for example, Sen 1982). The Sen and Nussbaum approach to social justice decisively affirms claims that Sen only suggests, and to which he himself is not then committed. But the approach is valuable for working through some of Sen's hints and suggestions, so one can see what they might amount to. The idea that social justice is basic capability equality is attractive in its own right, and is worthy of careful examination. Moreover, versions of the idea have elicited assent on the part of other moral philosophers and theorists of justice (see Anderson 1999; Scheffler 1981; Crisp 2003).

In this chapter I criticize the ideal of basic capability equality, in large part by touting the merits of an alternative theory of justice. To the extent that these criticisms are plausible, some cold water is incidentally thrown on Sen's skepticism regarding the prospects for a genuine theory of justice. In the welter of normative complexity, the great tangles of which Sen has helped us appreciate, some simplicity may also be discerned. Or so I shall claim.[2]

From utility and primary goods to basic capability equality

Sen's view emerges by way of criticisms of other theorists' answers to the question, what is distributive justice concerned to distribute? In other words, insofar as justice requires fair shares for individuals, we need some measure of a person's condition that is relevant for determining whether the allocation of goods and alterable aspects of circumstances to the person is fair. For example, if justice requires equality, we need some measure of people's condition so that we can determine whether their conditions are equal or unequal.

Sen supports an emphasis on the measures of functionings and functioning capabilities by pointing to inadequacies in the Rawlsian and the standard utilitarian interpersonal comparison measures. John Rawls (1999) has proposed primary social goods as the measure.[3] These are goods it is rational for every person to want, whatever else he or she wants. The Rawlsian primary social goods are general-purpose means that will be useful for furthering a wide variety of rational plans of life. The standard utilitarian view is that the proper standard of interpersonal comparison for social morality is utility, construed as pleasure and the absence of pain or as desire satisfaction.

The objection to primary social goods as the basis of interpersonal comparison is that individuals differ in their personal traits and in particular in their abilities to transform resources into fulfillment of their aims or achievement of values. Suppose two individuals espouse the same life aims but differ in their personal traits, and have identical resources and means. They may be able to fulfill any reasonable aims to markedly different extents. Sen suggests that we should be concerned directly with what people are enabled to be and do with their resources, given their traits and circumstances. Focusing on means rather than on the extent of freedom is fetishistic. Suppose that what people seek from life is running and jumping and two individuals are given equal means: a pair of well-fitting athletic shoes and access to paths and roads. But one has healthy legs and the other is lame. A theory of justice that measures people's condition by the means and resources they possess must judge the two individuals to be equal in resources, but this assessment is overshadowed by the very unequal extent to which the two persons are enabled by their resources to achieve aims they affirm and have reason to pursue.

Sen objects to the utilitarian measures of interpersonal comparisons on the ground that people's mental states tend to adjust to their condition, whatever it is. Living in hell, one ceases to desire cool-weather activities; such desires are unsatisfiable and thus pointless. In hell there is nothing to do but suffer heat, but people may become inured to the unpleasantness of the situation, and experience little pain. Hellish conditions might also distort the formation of desire – cause me to desire odd things the getting of which would bring me no satisfaction and serve no sensible purpose. Living on earth in a normal lifestyle may be more valuable for an individual than living in hell in many ways that do not register in utilitarian assessment but that should matter to us all the same.

Sen is not denying that it may be perfectly reasonable and prudent if one can to try to adjust one's desires to one's circumstances, actively to desire only what is likely to be obtainable, and to steel oneself so one feels less pain and gets more pleasure from small bits of good fortune. These reasonable tactics will lessen or perhaps entirely eliminate the gap in utility between those placed in disadvantageous circumstances and lucky people fortunately placed. Sen's point is that desire satisfaction and degree of pleasure are inadequate measures of how good a life a person is having. There are other things that matter besides desire satisfaction and pleasure. Moreover, oppressive conditions can have the effect of truncating people's desires, but then a high degree of satisfaction of these reduced desires should not persuade us that the person is really well off, as utilitarian measures must insist.

Sen's position is that the right basis of interpersonal comparison for a theory of justice is neither the resources made available to the individual nor the quality of the mental states of the individual induced by what he or she does and becomes by utilizing those resources. Instead we should focus directly on the doings and beings of the individual, which Sen calls "functionings," and on his or her real freedom to choose among different possible combinations of these doings and beings. We can single out those doings and beings that pertain to the individual's well-being, how well the individual's life is going for him or her. A person's achievement of these doings and beings at a time or summed over time is a vector of functionings. A person's capability to function is the set of vectors of functionings, any one of which an individual can choose.[4] Each vector is a combination of the different functionings that are possible together for that individual. (We can contrast well-being functionings and the capability to function with the wider idea of the person's freedom to achieve goals he or she has reason to value, the person's own well-being among them.)

The problem with functionings is that there are too many of them. My functionings at any particular time include some important ones and countless trivial ones such as twitching my nose or finger or hand, and so on, one way or another or another. This is a problem, because unless some regimentation is imposed, some ranking of functionings as more or less important and valuable, different persons' capabilities will almost always be noncomparable. Each person will have available to him or her many unique types of functionings that others lack.

Suppose we say in a democratic spirit that each individual's valuation of the capabilities he or she has and might come to have is the relevant standard for assessing that person's condition. Straightaway, the problems of adaptation to bad conditions and distortion of preference and value formation that the introduction of the capability standard was supposed to avoid will have come back to haunt us. The docile housewife, cowed, may value only capabilities to function in trivial homemaker ways, while others value more ambitious capabilities. Suppose we instead say, as Sen suggests, that we use the intersection of everyone's ranking of capabilities to guide policy choice. Social prejudice and distorted evaluation may once again be calibrating the standard that is to measure the degree to which people are fairly treated. If some people think it is inappropriate for women to pursue a career of scientific research or administrative leadership, the capabilities to achieve these functionings will not be valued when the person whose condition we are assessing is a woman.

Sen has painted himself into a corner from which I see only one viable exit.[5] Sen's criticisms of resource-based and utility-based measures of interpersonal comparison implicitly appeal to our sense that we can rank people's functionings and capabilities overall and nonarbitrarily affirm that one person's options or chosen life path is better or worse, objectively speaking, than another's. If this conviction cannot be vindicated, Sen's criticisms of alternative measures lose their force. His position, which coyly refuses assertion of an objective standard of value, is unstable.

Sen asserts that desire satisfaction or life-aim fulfillment is an inadequate basis of interpersonal comparison for a theory of justice, because desires and aims can be distorted and truncated. The oppressed peasant may come to have only small desires, and might be reasonable to shave his or her desires in this way. Our sense that the peasant's satisfaction of these truncated desires does not constitute a good human life depends on our background convictions as to what are the major components of a genuinely good life. Either these background convictions, thought through rigorously, will yield a defensible objective conception of human well-being or they will not. In the latter case, our basis for disparaging the quality of life of the contented peasant with satisfied small desires collapses. To press Sen's criticisms of subjectivist conceptions of human well-being successfully, it is necessary to develop and defend a nonsubjectivist alternative.

In this dialectical situation, Martha Nussbaum's extension of Sen's capability approach is of paramount importance. She decisively grasps the nettle that Sen's writings gingerly touch.[6]

Besides unequivocally insisting that the capability approach must be yoked to an objective account of human good, Nussbaum commits herself to two further claims about social justice that appear in Sen's writings but without receiving the stamp of his endorsement. One claim is that the just society provides *capability to function* in certain valuable ways at adequate threshold levels to all persons, not actual *functioning* in these ways at these levels to all. Justice requires real freedom for all, not actual attainment by all. Nussbaum ties the insistence on capability, not functioning, to liberal values in the theory of justice.

The second further claim is that the fundamental social justice principle is sufficientarian. What matters morally above all else from the standpoint of social justice is that each person has the capability to gain a sufficient or good enough level of attainment with respect to each and every one of the functionings that are singled out as crucial elements in a good human life. In terms that Sen has used, justice requires basic capability equality: policies and actions should be set so that each person equally has freedom to attain an adequate level of basic capabilities.

The idea that all persons should have basic capability equality is an interesting and attractive ideal, one that Sen's writings do much to clarify and advance. The view admits of many versions and variations, and part of my aim in this chapter is to identify the most plausible versions. This Sen and Nussbaum approach to social justice is well worth study and evaluation in its own right, quite aside from the complex exegetical issues that arise in attributing one or another component of the view to one or both of these authors. My primary aim in this chapter is to arrive at a reasoned verdict on the position as I shall characterize it. The extent to which either Sen or Nussbaum holds the position is a hard and tricky issue, and one that is not at the focus of my attention. For the reasons stated in the first paragraphs of this chapter, attributing any definite theory to Sen involves misrepresenting his contributions, which tend not to take the form of theory espousal.

Sufficiency

The idea that social justice is basic capability equality includes two controversial notions. One is that the principles of justice should promote capability or freedom to attain well-being rather than well-being itself. The other controversial aspect of the proposal is sufficientarianism.

The doctrine of sufficiency states that justice requires above all that everyone should have a sufficient amount, or enough. Enough for what? I shall suppose, in agreement with Nussbaum, that the sufficient level is a good enough level of well-being, a decent threshold of quality of life. In coming to grips with the doctrine, the next phrase that requires interpretation is "requires above all." Some sort of priority is imputed to the moral goal of getting everyone to the good enough level. The strictest form of the doctrine of sufficiency holds that the sufficiency goal has strict lexical priority over any other justice values there might be. This means that gaining the slightest increase or averting any loss, no matter how small in terms of the sufficiency value, should be chosen in preference to achieving any gains of any size, or averting any losses, however huge, in any or all other values. Sufficiency rules the roost.

Prominent sufficientarian theorists such as Nussbaum and Elizabeth Anderson shy away from strict lexical priority. Nonetheless, my discussion concentrates on this version. For one thing, I believe that the implausibility of the lexical priority version of the doctrine also attaches to versions that relax lexical priority, though to a reduced degree, depending on the strength of the priority that remains. Also, beyond asserting that sufficiency is a very important value, no one who backs away from the strictest version of the doctrine to my knowledge proposes any specific alternative view.[7]

Another needed clarification answers the question, "When must sufficiency obtain?" One possibility is that justice requires that each person be brought to the good enough capability level and must be maintained at that level throughout the life course (unless disability or disease makes this literally impossible). Another possibility is that justice requires that each person be enabled to gain a sufficient level of well-being achievements over the course of his or her life. This might require access to school and roller-coaster rides in youth, good jobs, vacation travel, and family responsibilities during the middle years, and respected social status and comfortable surroundings in old age. On this view, different components of sufficiency might be supplied at different ages, maybe at different times of life to different sorts of people, such that by the end of life each person will have had access to all of the components of full sufficiency at the good enough level. (This view abstracts from the problem of premature death.) A third possibility introduces the idea of a canonical moment, perhaps the onset of adulthood. The sufficiency requirement is that at the canonical moment each person should be able to choose and pursue a reasonable plan of life that will gain for him or her a sufficient level of well-being throughout the person's life. If the person does not choose that reasonable sufficiency-ensuring life plan, to some extent his or her life may deviate downward from the sufficient level consistent with the requirements of sufficientarian justice. On this view, if entirely unforeseeable events occur as random shocks that threaten to lower people's access to well-being below what they can reasonably anticipate on their chosen plan of life, justice requires that the shortfall due to the unexpected shocks should be restored. On this third view, the sufficiency doctrine incorporates some of the features of opportunity for welfare conceptions of justice.[8]

Nussbaum opts for the first possibility of the three delineated just above. In the just society, social life is arranged so that, as far as is possible, each person has access to the sufficient level of functioning throughout his or her life. My critical discussion then concentrates on the first possibility. Sorting out the comparative merits of possibility 3 versus the rest would require exploring the question of how the sufficient doctrine might be yoked to a plausible view concerning personal responsibility. Nussbaum and Sen tend not to say much about this issue, and, so far as I can see, it would remain wide open even if we were to accept the components of the sufficiency doctrine that they espouse and defend. I simply record my opinion that the second possible answer to "When sufficiency?" described above is more plausible than the first answer, the answer that the doctrine's proponents actually tend to embrace.

Another range of variation in sufficiency doctrines comes into view if we ask who is to be included in the "everyone" who should be assured capability to function at the good enough level. To their credit, Nussbaum and Sen tend to interpret "everyone" in the widest possible way, so that the sufficiency entitlement extends to all persons at all times and locations. For practical purposes this means everyone on earth now and in the future. Let's call this the *global sufficiency doctrine*. The scope of the principle could be limited in a variety of ways: to presently living persons only, or to persons living in a particular nation-state for whom a theory of justice is being formulated, to name two obvious limits. But "everyone" could be limited to all members of a tribe or race or clan or ethnic or religious group, or to all men or women or to all heterosexuals or gays, and so on. This discussion ignores these scope limits and takes the doctrine under review to be global sufficiency.

Another large interpretive issue is how to understand access to the good enough well-being level construed as capability to function in specified ways. Nussbaum explicitly identifies a number of functionings taken to be essential to a decent human life and insists that each person should be sustained at capability to attain each and every one of the designated functionings at the good enough level. She does not say much by way of defense of this insistence. Her idea appears to be that if we identify functionings that are necessary to a decent human life, no shortfall in any of the dimensions can be allowed to afflict a person without dropping that person below the good enough level.

Peter Vallentyne (personal communication) disagrees, and I entirely concur. If we are going to adopt a sufficiency view, we should allow trade-offs among the various functionings, just so long as the total well-being from all functionings to which one has access exceeds the threshold level. In making this point I assume that well-being scores can be assigned to all functionings to which one has access, the scores indicating the gain one would get from any given level of achievement of the functioning and thus the comparative importance of the different functionings. This way of interpreting the sufficiency justice requirement is especially compelling if one is considering situations in which individuals by their voluntary choices of life plans alter their access to various functionings over time. Suppose I give up some level of good health security in order to pursue other goals that matter more to me. I continue doing scientific research, for example, even though by eschewing stressful work I could reduce the probability of suffering a devastating heart attack to a reasonable level. Or I continue to pursue a dangerous sport even though with increasing age and steady participation in the sport the dangers of suffering serious debilitating injury increase beyond acceptable levels, so that I come to lack access to secure good health functioning. Or I insist on fulfilling a lifelong dream of completing a pilgrimage to Mecca or paying for my child's wedding even though undertaking either of these expenses precludes payment for extra cancer therapy in ways that would prolong my life by at least two years. In all of these cases, dropping below a threshold acceptable capability to function in one specific way that is essential according to Nussbaum is not morally problematic if accompanied by a more than compensating gain in access to other capabilities.[9] One might allow a narrower or broader range of trade-offs so long as an overall good enough capability level is sustained. On the narrower option, it would be acceptable to sufficiency if one falls below one or more of the sufficient capability levels for some of the functionings singled out as essential so long as one's overall capability level stays high enough. One's overall capability level is computed by adding up the well-being value of the remaining essential functioning capabilities. On the broader option, no restriction is placed on the types of functionings whose value contributes to the overall capability level that sufficiency requires must be sustained at the good enough level. Even trivial capabilities that are only slightly valuable – capability to eat cotton candy and similar nonessential freedoms – are counted in the computation of the individual's overall capability level. The idea here is simply that gains of varying size in less important capabilities can add up to an overall capability gain that can offset a drop below the designated good enough level of any of the capabilities accorded essential status.

Another way to put the point is to challenge the idea that one can identify a sufficient level for each of a set of functionings such that attainment of the sufficient level for each is necessary for a good enough life, and attainment of the sufficient level of all of these designated functionings is sufficient for a good human life. Call this the set of *essential functionings*. Depending on the context, including how much of other functionings one has, one can reasonably judge that very little or none of any particular functioning is necessary for a good human life. Sexual and romantic pleasures are good, but one can attain a good human life even if one endures lifelong enforced celibacy. The same holds for friendship. Yet great friendship attainment can be a significant element of a life that is very good for the one who lives it, so it would be utterly implausible to ignore this functioning in an assessment of the quality of any person's life. Yet it will not qualify as an essential functioning, so the conception of capability for a good life that takes it to be a function only of capability for each of the essential functionings must ignore it.

Against sufficiency

One route to the sufficiency doctrine begins by noticing an oddity in some intuitive arguments to the conclusion that it is unjust that people gain unequal quality of life.[10] The intuitive arguments point to the grim quality of the lives of the poor and contrast this with the luxuries and great advantages enjoyed by those who are very fortunate in their circumstances and inherited personal traits. The contrast is supposed to make it plausible that the condition of the advantaged and the disadvantaged be rendered more equal, and the suggested principle that delivers this verdict is some version of equality of condition. The oddity is that one might agree that in these circumstances a transfer from rich to poor might be required by justice without attaching any intrinsic moral value to equalizing people's conditions. After all, the gap between rich and poor could also appear in a contrast between rich and super-rich, but the moral imperative of transfer of resources to aid the rich seems far from compelling, or even nonexistent. If the moral reason to seek improvement in the condition of the disadvantaged in the initial example is the bad quality of the lives they must lead and the fact that this can be alleviated, then comparison between the situation of worse off and better off is perhaps doing no work. The principle that delivers this result is that everyone should have enough.

Doubts about the sufficiency doctrine should ensue once the question is posed, "How much is enough?" No answer is plausible. A human life can be better or worse for the one who lives it. Well-being varies by degree. But it is not so clear that there is a natural way to identify a good enough level, a threshold such that it is of paramount moral importance to get people to the threshold but a matter of relative indifference what happens to them above the threshold. This difficulty takes on a more distinct shape as an objection to sufficiency once we notice that we do not have to choose between some version of equality and some version of sufficiency to support the generic idea that justice can require transfers of goods and resources from better off to worse off people. Without accepting sufficiency, we can take on board the idea that it does not intrinsically matter morally how well off one person is compared to how well or badly off other persons are. The moral value of your eating a hamburger is not affected by whether others are better off, eating steak, or worse off, reduced to eating beans. Agreeing with this point does not commit us to sufficiency.[11]

According to the priority family of moral principles, one ought always to maximize a function of human well-being that gives weight to two factors: the greater the well-being gain for a person that one can achieve, the greater the moral value of the gain; and the lower the person's lifetime well-being level would be in the absence of this gain, the greater the moral value of the gain. Institutions and actions should be set to maximize moral value so understood. This formulation characterizes a family of views. To arrive at a specific moral principle within this family it is necessary to set weights on the comparative value of increasing aggregate well-being and obtaining well-being gains for the badly off. Even as roughly characterized, priority provides an explanation of how there can be moral reason to transfer resources from better-off to worse-off persons – moral value is thereby increased. According to priority, it is morally more urgent (gains more moral value) to obtain a one-unit well-being gain for a person, the lower the person's lifetime well-being otherwise would be.

Consider this version of sufficiency: As many as possible of those who shall ever live should be brought to the good enough threshold level of lifetime well-being. This principle is understood to have strict lexical priority over other justice values, including gains to those above and below the good enough threshold that do not alter the numbers of people who are sustained at sufficiency. Call this principle *the strict sufficiency doctrine*.

From a prioritarian standpoint the essential objection to sufficiency so construed is that there is no way to set the sufficiency threshold in such a way that this level of well-being can have the moral importance that sufficiency assigns to it. The objection is not exactly that there is no nonarbitrary way to set the threshold. Surely it is nonarbitrary that the "good enough" level of well-being must be above the zero level of well-being – that is, the level of well-being such that the slightest decrease in the lifetime goods or increase in the lifetime bads the person gets makes his or her life on the whole intrinsically bad for that person (so it would be better for the person never to have lived at all). We might then appeal to intuition and reflective equilibrium methods to establish a rough range in which the sufficiency level must lie. My point is that reflective equilibrium methods will not indicate that there is any threshold level of well-being or threshold range of well-being levels that can play the role that sufficiency assigns to it.

The strict sufficiency doctrine assigns trumping moral weight to getting individuals just to the sufficiency threshold. This view is extremely implausible when we consider cases in which we can achieve great gains in well-being for people, perhaps great numbers of people, who fall into either or both of two categories. Category 1 consists of people who are leading unavoidably below-threshold lives, hellish lives let us say, that can in no way be brought to sufficiency. Category 2 consists of people who are unavoidably above the threshold. Whatever policy is chosen, their above-threshold status will not change. Both categories become invisible and are required to be ignored under the rule of strict sufficiency. Suppose we can choose either (i) a policy that brings one person from just barely below to just across the sufficiency threshold; or (ii) a policy that brings about great improvements in the well-being of many people who are unavoidably below threshold (billions are moved from hell to tolerable limbo existence); or (iii) a policy that brings about great improvements in the lives of a great many people who are already above threshold (billions and billions are moved from a modest existence to perfectionist bliss). Whatever the numbers of people who would gain and the amounts of gain they would get if (ii) or (iii) is chosen, strict sufficiency must always demand that we ought morally to choose policy (i). There is no way that the sufficiency level, wherever we place it on the smooth continuum that marks improvements in a person's well-being, can be reasonably viewed as of such transcendent moral urgency as strict sufficiency implies.[12]

This criticism suggests a weaker and more plausible form of the sufficiency doctrine. Call this *moderate sufficiency*, which consists of three claims: (a) there is a good enough level of well-being, such that moral priority should be given to achieving well-being gains for those who are below the threshold; (b) the further an individual is below the threshold, the greater the moral value of securing a well-being gain of a given size for that individual; and (c) above the threshold, well-being gains and losses count for something in determining what to do, but achieving any gain or avoidance of loss for any person below threshold has strict lexical priority over achieving instead any gain or avoidance of loss of any size for any number of individuals who are and will always be above the threshold.

Compared to *strict sufficiency*, *moderate sufficiency* makes large concessions to the priority view. In all cases where our choice of action or policy affects only individuals who are below the threshold, moderate sufficiency just is priority. (Like priority, moderate sufficiency characterizes a family of principles rather than a specific principle. To obtain a specific principle in either case, one would have to assign weights to the value of obtaining a small increment of well-being for a person at each well-being level.) To my mind, the fact that bending a sufficiency doctrine toward the shape of priority renders it more plausible suggests that we might well do better to go the whole hog for priority and abandon sufficiency altogether.

To test this surmise, consider scenarios in which moderate sufficiency and priority will yield conflicting moral judgments concerning right policy choice. Imagine that we have to choose between (i) bringing a single individual from just barely below the sufficiency line to just across it, giving that person a tiny well-being boost; and (ii) bringing about a very large gain in well-being for a very large number of persons all of whom will certainly be above the sufficiency threshold whatever we do. Whatever the size of the well-being gain and the numbers of people affected in (ii), the moderate sufficiency view tells us we must choose (i). But why discount gains to the well-being of the better off so ruthlessly? To make this radical discounting credible, we would need to be told a story that explains and justifies the claim that the sufficiency threshold is of paramount moral importance. But how can inching one's way up a bit along a measure of overall lifetime well-being have that sort of significance? Perhaps it would be rash to insist that no such story could be told; but no sufficiency advocate has begun to tell even the barest outline of such a story.[13] Pending the offering of some justification of the moral significance of the sufficiency threshold, I submit that acceptance of sufficiency even in moderate form is unreasonable.

The same point holds if we relax condition (c), so that the priority assigned to below-threshold well-being gains over above-threshold well-being gains is less than lexical. The residual difficulty that will not go away is that we still need some plausible justification of why the sufficiency line is drawn in one place rather than somewhere else and why this particular line is morally significant. But notice also that nothing in the priority view as characterized here rules out the possibility that priority gradually tapers off as well-being levels increase and eventually becomes vanishingly small. Consistently with priority, one might maintain that very little priority attaches to gaining a small benefit for Rich (a person with extremely high lifetime well-being) as opposed to achieving a same-sized benefit for Very Rich (a person with a higher yet lifetime well-being). So once we relax condition (c) as indicated, there need be no difference in the practical implications of relaxed sufficiency and priority, as they might embrace the same function relating the degree of priority attached to a small well-being gain to the potential recipient's lifetime well-being level absent this gain.

The prioritarian insists on continuity – roughly, the idea that a small shift in the values of the factors that morally matter should not generate a large shift in what we morally ought to do.[14]

But continuity is itself deeply controversial. The moderate sufficientarian can defend the lexical priority he or she upholds by pressing on our attention examples in which the bland toleration of aggregation of benefits in the determination of what to do, embraced by priority, looks problematic. If only finite extra weight is given to gaining benefits for people, the worse off in absolute terms they are, there are bound to be cases of this sort: Either we can get a tiny, tiny benefit, such as a single bite of chocolate, to many, many people who are already leading lives that are wonderful, far above the sufficiency threshold; or we can instead get a huge (lifesaving, say) benefit to a tiny number of extremely badly off persons. We must choose one or the other action; we cannot do both. Which to choose? The prioritarian will say it depends on the numbers. But it is guaranteed by the prioritarian's position that if the number of beneficiaries is large enough on the side of the chocolate-bite eaters and small enough on the side of those severely disadvantaged persons who stand to gain an incredible windfall benefit, the prioritarian must say that the right answer is to stuff the extremely well off with extra chocolate. In contrast, the moderate sufficientarian, who attaches strict lexical priority to achieving gains for those below the sufficiency threshold, can insist that the numbers do not matter; morality demands that we help the below-threshold worse off.

In reply: the tyranny of aggregation should be accepted, not resisted.[15] (Of course, if you accept it, it will seem like legitimate government, not tyranny at all.) This same issue recurs throughout morality, and cuts across consequentialism versus deontology conflicts. The consequentialist might accept or reject lexical priority rankings, and the deontologist might accept or reject the idea that any individual right, however sacred, must give way if it is opposed by sufficiently bad consequences that will ensue unless the right is infringed, and furthermore, sufficiently bad consequences can always take the form either of a few big bads or a large enough number of very small individual bads.

The point is arithmetic: any huge finite number, however large, can be eclipsed by an even larger number that is formed by taking a very small but not infinitesimal number and adding that same number to itself a sufficient number of times. Bites of chocolate, if sufficiently numerous, can morally have more weight than a single premature death.

Notice that the lexical priority versus aggregation issue is independent of the issue of whether or not a justification can be given for singling out a single well-being level (or a broad band of levels) and according great moral importance to getting a person to that level. Even if further moral investigation does reveal a nonarbitrary sufficient level and establishes its importance, so long as the moral weight attached to attainment of sufficiency or the moral weight attached to degrees of distance from sufficiency is finite, a version of the bites of chocolate case can be posed for the advocate of sufficiency. For example, suppose we have to choose between either obtaining a huge well-being boost for a single individual or the utterly trivial well-being boost of a tiny bite of chocolate to a great many individuals – all of the persons in the example being below the sufficiency threshold. I say the moderate sufficiency advocate should accept with equanimity the implication of conditions (a) and (b), together with the further proviso that the priorities they assign are finite in strength. The implication is that if the number of potential chocolate bite recipients is large enough, the sufficiency advocate should abort the lifesaving rescue mission and channel the resources to the chocolate dispenser.

My tentative view is that no version of the sufficiency doctrine is plausible when one considers the prioritarian alternative. Hence, although at the level of practical policy, trying to achieve basic capability for all may be laudable, at the level of fundamental moral principle, basic capability equality is not morally acceptable.

Capability or functioning?

The core of the capability approach to social justice is that what we owe each other morally is capability, not functioning.[16] In the just world, each person has the capability (for example) to be adequately nourished, but does not necessarily actually attain the functioning of being adequately nourished. Between the capabilities of the agent and the functionings of the agent the agent's own voluntary choices intervene. The individual with the capability to be adequately nourished might choose to fast, perhaps to join a political protest, even to his or her own death. This dramatic shortfall in functioning does not signal any sort of injustice inflicted on the fasting person, according to the capability approach. Sen links the insistence on capability, not functioning, with a liberal respect for individual freedom and also with an appropriate accommodation of an ideal of individual responsibility. He writes, "In dealing with responsible adults, it is more appropriate to see the claims of individual on the society in terms of *freedom to achieve* rather than *actual achievements*." (1992: 148).

The issue joined here is complex and tricky. More needs to be said about Sen's understanding of the ideas of freedom and capability in order to assess his position. My discussion approaches Sen's actual view in stages.

At the outset it may be useful to state my own position in a nutshell. The fundamental requirement of justice and social morality is to bring it about that fair shares of well-being (the attainment of the items on the objective list, properly weighted) accrue to persons. The just society maximizes a function of human well-being that properly balances aggregative and distributive concerns (more well-being is better, and well-being more fairly distributed is better). In Sen's terms, the just society is concerned to promote functioning, not capability. Freedom enters this account in four different ways. Wide freedom of action and traditional civil liberties are important means to bringing about fulfillment of the just social welfare function. Freedoms of particular sorts are constituents of some important goods that are items on the objective list. Third, provision of wide freedom to follow valuable pursuits fosters experimentation and evaluation of options, and helps individuals to form sensible and reasoned aims and values. Finally, an ideal of personal freedom and autonomy itself constitutes one item on the objective list, a good having which intrinsically makes one's life go better in a way that contributes to one's well-being. But the basic justice value, the stuff to which people are entitled according to the fundamental moral principles, is well-being (in Sen's terms, well-being functionings), not freedom to attain well-being.

Let's begin by identifying capability to function with real freedom to function. If I have the real freedom to go to Paris, then if I choose to go to Paris (and undertake some course of action that is open to me and that I can choose), I go to Paris. Real freedom contrasts with merely formal freedom. I am formally free to go to Paris if the laws do not prohibit my going and nobody would interfere with me (in certain familiar ways) if I chose to go. As just defined, having real freedom to *X* is compatible with lacking the real freedom *not to X*. I have the real freedom to go to Paris but not the real freedom not to go to Paris if I go to Paris, whether I choose to do so or not. So perhaps we had better identify capability with *real option freedom*. I have real option freedom to go to Paris only (i) if I choose to go to Paris (and undertake some course of action that is open to me and that I can choose), I go to Paris; and (ii) if I choose not to go to Paris (and undertake some course of action that is open to me and that I can choose), I do not go to Paris.[17]

The objection to taking provision of capability to function in certain valuable ways that constitute well-being as the fundamental justice aim is simply stated. At least, the objection is simple if capability is understood as real option freedom. Consider a case in which provision of the capability to an individual is expensive and the capability, if provided, will certainly yield nothing valuable. It will be ignored or wasted or mishandled by the individual to whom it is provided. If this fact is certainly known, then surely any justice obligation to provide the capability vanishes. But this judgment presupposes that we are thinking of capabilities as means, valuable not for their own sake but for their contribution to some further goal. If capability provision were the ultimate end of justice, then it would make no difference that in the case we are imagining, provision of capability would be pointless. Provision would be morally valuable just the same. I submit that the implausibility of this implication flows back to render dubious the conception of justice as concerned fundamentally to provide capabilities to persons.

Expansion of real option capability can sometimes predictably bring about a decrease in well-being functioning. With some money, I go to the opera and play football and have a good life. With more money, and cocaine legally available, I indulge too often, and lead a worthless life. In such a case, denying me access to extra cash or prohibiting cocaine use can lower my capability to function in ways that constitute well-being but raise my functioning levels in ways that constitute well-being. In such a case, justice principles should look beyond capability to the functioning levels justice generates.

Another way to put the point acknowledges, as briefly stated above, that real freedom is crucial for human well-being, so any theory of justice that takes the basis of interpersonal comparison to be the individual's well-being over the life course will be registering the value of real freedom as means to well-being and as a constituent of well-being. But all of this falls short of holding that the basis of interpersonal comparison should be the real freedom of the individual to attain well-being. The basis of interpersonal comparison in the theory of justice identifies who is better off and who worse off and tells us what we should aim to promote if we wish to improve the condition of the worse off. To get a handle on this disagreement we need to consider cases in which the principles of justice that tell us to seek fair shares of capability for all yield recommendations for policy that conflict with principles of justice that tell us to seek fair shares of well-being (in Sen's terms, well-being functioning) for all.

Sometimes more freedom will be a matter of indifference to individuals, or even disavowed. Suppose the individual has five options. We can either sweeten the already best option, the one the individual is going to choose come what may, or we could instead add to the individual's choice set some significantly different and attractive options, good but less good than the five already on offer. Surely in some cases of this sort the theory of justice that tells us to promote capability will tell us it is better to add extra options than to sweeten the option that is anyway best and the one the individual will choose. The theory that tells us to promote well-being for individuals might sometimes endorse this verdict. Perhaps providing more, and more significantly diverse, options sharpens people's appreciation of all options, including the ones they actually choose, so more freedom means better choice and more value from what is chosen. But in some other cases, the aims of obtaining more capability for freedom well distributed and obtaining more well-being functioning for people better distributed will diverge. In such a case, why prefer more freedom over more well-being? If we value freedom just as a means to well-being or as part of well-being, one will never rationally prefer more freedom when that yields less well-being overall. Putting this case in a sufficientarian framework does not change the reasonable verdict on the case. Suppose the person with five options is below the sufficient capability level. No matter, I say.

This critique of justice as capability provision presupposes the real option freedom account of capability. The critique misfires as it stands, for two distinct reasons.[18] One is that Sen has a different understanding of capability than the one I have been employing. The second is that we need to take account of the relationships among agency achievement, agency freedom, well-being achievement, and well-being freedom (which Sen calls capability). Let's address the second point first.

Agency achievements are achievements of goals one has reason to value. These might be goals that have nothing to do with one's own well-being. One might have the agency goal of helping other people, or of saving the whales from extinction, and so on. Corresponding to a person's actual agency achievements we can note the person's agency freedom, his or her real freedom to achieve agency goals. One agency goal one might well have is one's own well-being (what makes one's life go better for oneself), and corresponding to a person's actual well-being achievement we may note his or her well-being freedom. Sen holds that the theory of justice must pay attention to all four concerns – well-being achievement and agency achievement and well-being freedom and agency freedom – and not narrow the concern to just some of the four. Sometimes an expansion of freedom for an individual will lead to less well-being for that individual, because that person reasonably chooses to pursue some agency goal other than his or her own well-being. There is no puzzle here and there need be nothing problematic or untoward about holding that justice requires expansions of a person's freedom in such cases, even though the person's well-being predictably suffers (Sen 1992: ch. 4).

My response is that none of this proliferation of helpful distinctions does anything to mitigate the objection against taking well-being freedom (capability) to be of rock-bottom importance for a theory of justice. In the case discussed three paragraphs back, let it be stipulated that agency achievement and agency freedom (other than the well-being component of each) are not involved. Postulating that well-being freedom is of intrinsic moral importance and should sometimes be sought even at the expense of well-being is fetishistic, in much the same way that concentrating on means to freedom as though it were valuable in itself is thought by Sen to be fetishistic.

Should agency freedom and agency achievement be accorded a place in the formulation of fundamental principles of social morality? This is a large issue. My response here must be quick. Let us distinguish my desire that some goal, not involving my own well-being and thought to be impersonally valuable, be fulfilled, from my desire that such a goal be fulfilled through my own significant agency. The former we can call agency goals proper. I say that the fact that I embrace such a goal does not mean that the just society owes me help to achieve the goal. It is not for my sake that the goal should be fulfilled, but rather it should be fulfilled on the ground that it is morally important in its own right. Maybe society ought to save the whales, but, if so, this is not because I myself happen to embrace the goal, and my entitlements under a sound theory of justice do not include the satisfaction of such aims.

Now consider my desire that the whales be saved through my significant agency. This is a mixed goal, part impartial and altruistic, part self-concerned. The impersonal part was dealt with in the previous paragraph. Consider the residue, what remains of my desire that the whales be saved through my agency when one subtracts my desire that the whales be saved, period. This is a self-interested desire. When such a desire is reasonable, its satisfaction, on many sensible views of well-being, improves the agent's well-being. Catering to such desires can be important for social justice: consider a parent's desire not just that her children come to have good lives, but that they come to have good lives, in part, through her exercise of responsible parenting. So my response to Sen's distinction between agency goals and well-being goals is that it is morally appropriate that the theory of justice should be concerned only to promote the well-being of persons (and other sentient beings; for simplicity we leave this important addition aside). Agency achievements register in fundamental morality in terms of their final results, their benefits to persons. The self-interested component of people's aim to achieve agency goals through the exercise of their own agency does register in a well-being measure and so does properly affect the determination of what the individual is owed under fundamental principles of social morality, principles of justice.

Turn now to the second reason that my initial critique of making capability the distribuendum of justice misfired and needed to be loaded and shot again.

Sen proposes that where some might be tempted to see a conflict between increasing a person's freedom and doing what is, all things considered, advantageous for that person (contributes to the person's agency achievement), we would do better to see the conflict as between different notions or ideals of freedom. Let's set aside cases in which an increase in agency freedom decreases well-being freedom and well-being achievement. Sen wants simply to accept that more agency freedom can bring about lessening of freedom and achievement on the well-being dimension. What he finds confusing is talk of agency freedom increases that result in lesser agency achievement, and well-being freedom increases that result in lesser well-being achievement. Here clarification of the notion of freedom (and capability) can promote clear thinking.

His account begins with the thought that the freedom of a person in a recognizable and significant sense can obtain with respect to some feature of his or her condition even though he or she herself does not control whether or not the feature will exist. To illustrate the point, Sen uses the example of the freedom to have one's book printed as one would like. A proofreader corrects the printed text and does so, let us suppose, more efficiently than one would have done if one had done the proofreading oneself. One does not have the option of correcting or declining to correct this or that error in the text. The proofreader controls this choice. But if "the levers of control are systematically exercised in line with *what I would choose* and *for that exact reason*" (Sen 1992: 64), then one has freedom even if not control with respect to this matter.

The idea proposed here is that one is free with respect to some aspect of one's condition X provided that: (i) I get X; (ii) if I had a choice, I would choose to get X; and (iii) the fact that (ii) is true is the reason that (i) is true. In other words, (iii) says that the agents who bring it about that (i) is true do so for the reason that (ii) is true. Notice that (i) through (iii) can all be true in a situation in which I actually have no choice whether or not to get X.

If we plug this account of being free into the norm of basic capability equality, the scope for conflict between attainment of desirable basic functionings and attainment of basic capability might appear to diminish. Consider components of basic good health such as being adequately nourished. Assume a scenario in which if we provide real option freedom to be adequately nourished, people will fail to be adequately nourished, because of weakness of will that drives them toward junk food diets. If we provide only healthy food diet options, people get adequately nourished, and the counterfactual test for being free in this respect is satisfied. That is to say, (i) people get adequately nourished; (ii) if they had a choice, people would choose to be adequately nourished; and (iii) the fact that (ii) is true is the reason that (i) is true. In this setting, people's capability includes being adequately nourished, because whatever combination of accessible functionings anyone chooses, it will include being adequately nourished.

For another example, suppose that we have to construct university facilities years in advance if people at a given future time are to have the freedom to attend university. The social planner correctly estimates the number of people who would choose to go to college at that time if they had the open option at that time, and builds accordingly. When the time comes, there are places at university for only 10 percent of people, but it is the case that whatever people get by way of university provision (a place or no place), it is true that what they get, they would choose if they had the choice, and this fact is what brings it about that they do or do not now have access to university. People are then free in the counterfactual sense with respect to their university access.

I do not deny that the counterfactual sense of freedom is coherent and can be yoked to the account of capability. But something that had been billed as important to the capability account is perhaps lost thereby.

The first thing to notice is that we really do have two quite different and opposed ideals of capability – what I have labeled *real option freedom* and *counterfactual freedom*. Which to choose? Alternatively, how are they to be integrated? So far as I can see, advocates of the capability approach have not yet clarified what answers they would give to these questions. (To say this is not of course to deny that the questions are answerable.)

My objection to capability as real option freedom from the standpoint of a view that fundamentally values people's achieved functionings or well-being outcomes is that taking provision of real option freedom to be the goal exaggerates the moral value of freedom *per se*. In many contexts, adding extra valuable options and thus increasing a person's real option freedom would come at a cost of lesser achieved well-being, and in these contexts we should favor achieving more functioning. Beyond some point, expansion of real option freedom is wasteful of resources that are better spent targeted at boosting functioning.

My objection to capability as counterfactual freedom is different. This view exaggerates the moral significance of people's getting what they want. According to counterfactual freedom, a person enjoys more capability the more it is the case that the world is so arranged that the person gets or achieves what he or she would choose given the opportunity to choose. But sometimes the person's choices would not do well at achieving his or her well-being and might even directly oppose it. This could be so whether we are using what the person actually would choose as the measure or what the person would choose if he or she were fully informed. The objection here is essentially the same as the objection to desire satisfaction or ideally informed desire satisfaction as the measure of human good.

Consider an anorexic whose desires and hypothetical choices are ideally informed. This person values above all conformity to an extreme ideal of beauty as maintenance of a thin body, and wants above all to fulfill this ideal even if this means she cannot ingest enough calories to sustain life and will swiftly die. As I imagine the case, the person is not suffering from mental disease, but is merely making a gross normative error about what is worthwhile and how best to live her life. According to the counterfactual freedom account as described, the person enjoys capability freedom to the extent the world is arranged so that she achieves and gets what she would choose if she had the opportunity to choose – which in this case is reduced caloric intake and consequent maintenance of a thin body ideal.

In contrast, consider the application of Martha Nussbaum's ideal of justice as capability (2000a) to this scenario. She holds that justice requires that for each and every person, we must provide that the person throughout the course of his or her life maintains the capability to function at a decent threshold level in each of the valuable ways that are core components of a good life. She is insistent that her view requires provision of capability, not functioning. In a recent discussion she associates her capability approach with a Rawlsian affirmation that "each person possesses an inviolability founded on justice that even the welfare of society as a whole cannot override" (John Rawls quoted in Nussbaum 2004: 328). Rights to capability rest on the dignity of each person and the fundamental moral equality of all persons, which mere claims to more functioning cannot override.

Her view would then hold that we must continue to provide full capability to function in all of the ways that matter as the anorexic person goes about fulfilling her thin body ideal. Whether the person achieves any good functionings for herself is her responsibility, not the proper business of society. I suppose this view of justice might well demand what I have called wasteful opportunity provision: allocating resources to a person that we know for certain he will not use and does not want and which will in that case go to waste. It is not entirely clear to me what Nussbaum would say about cases in which the person's self-regarding choices now have the effect of reducing unavoidably the degree to which she enjoys capabilities to function throughout her life subsequently. At some point, my pursuit of a thin body ideal will mean that whatever society provides or does not provide, I will lack the energy and bodily and mental capacities to function at the decent threshold level in the ways Nussbaum's theory singles out as crucially important. In some cases these self-induced capability deficits will be irreversible. Perhaps Nussbaum would say that society has an absolute obligation to sustain each person at threshold capability in all the ways that matter to the good life except insofar as the person's voluntary self-regarding actions preclude maintenance of some capabilities at the threshold levels.

In contrast, the bottom line for my functioning-oriented approach to social justice is the level of well-being the person reaches (and brings about for others, of course). Capabilities are valued as means (and in the other ways described earlier in this chapter), not as intrinsically morally valuable. So in the case of the ideally informed anorexic, in principle my approach would countenance paternalistic restriction of liberty for the person's own good, although such recommendation would be inhibited by all of the many instrumental reasons that J. S. Mill offers in *On Liberty* ([1859] 1977) (to the considerable extent that these reasons withstand critical scrutiny, a big topic I cannot pursue here). In practice, there may be nothing sensible that concerned individuals acting on their own or social policy can do to prevent the anorexic from starving herself and dying prematurely, although this will be regarded as a tragic loss. But just suppose there is some sensible liberty-restricting intervention that would be successful in prioritarian terms. Temporary forced hospitalization and treatment would alert the person to her normative error and initiate a process whereby she comes to shed the thin body ideal and develops sounder priorities, let us say. Or perhaps, let us say; a law backed by social norms can be of service in preventing such scenarios from arising – perhaps a law that requires prospective parents to take a battery of psychological tests and take classes in sound parenting methods if the tests reveal they have proclivities that are likely to lead to conflict with their children of a sort that induces the aspiration to autonomy to assume perverse forms. On my view, justice demands that we adopt sensible policies if such there be that efficiently promote good lives for people, not merely opportunities for good lives.

This is a toy example, but it should serve to illustrate the fundamental division between a functioning-oriented approach to social justice and the capability approach, whether capabilities are interpreted as real option freedom or as counterfactual freedom.

My criticisms of the two different interpretations to the capability approach stick only if the capability theorist is really proposing that capability provision be regarded as intrinsically morally desirable, the basic justice value that should be upheld rather than functioning. Nussbaum does fit that description. She holds that the basic justice rights are rights to capability. It is not clear to me that Sen means to commit himself on this issue as I have formulated it.

My criticism leaves open the possibility that the two interpretations of capability might be combined in some single set of principles that is not vulnerable to my objections. My hunch is that such a combined view would inherit the flaws of each of the two capability approaches in a mixed measure, depending on the exact combination proposed. But judgment on this issue would be premature pending the elaboration of such a hybrid view.

My own view is that an approach to social justice that takes capability provision to be morally of fundamental rock-bottom importance will be plausible only to the degree that it succeeds in mimicking a functioning-oriented approach. But this is just an opinion, not a claim I can say I have supported by definitive argument in this chapter. I do hope that I have succeeded in showing that the issue of capability versus functioning (like the prior issue of whether or not capability needs to be given content via an objective list account of human good, and like the independent issue of sufficiency versus priority) is consequential for the theory of justice. Moreover, the functioning approach has a lot going for it.

Notes

Thanks to Steven Wall for his sharp criticism provided at the September, 2004 meeting of the American Political Science Association. My understanding of Sen on capability has been altered by my reading of Alexander Kaufman's excellent essay "Capabilities and Freedom" (*Journal of Political Philosophy*, forthcoming).

1 The text here is referring to the Objective List conception of well-being, according to which there are correct answers to the question, What is good for someone? I shall usually assume that well-being admits of cardinal interpersonal comparability, so that there are correct answers to the question of whether Smith has more well-being than Jones and how much more the one who has more has. On the Objective List conception, see Parfit (1984). On objective list accounts of well-being and social justice, see Arneson (1999a, 2000).

2 See Richard Arneson (1999c). For the locus classicus on the priority view, see Parfit (2000). See also Weirich (1983) and Scheffler (1994).

3 See also Rawls (1982). Rawls's idea of primary goods has shifted over time. In the original edition of *A Theory of Justice* (1971), primary social goods are defined as goods distributable by society that a rational person will prefer to have more rather than fewer of, whatever else he or she wants. In his later writings, primary social goods are defined as those goods distributable by society that a rational person who gives priority to his or her Kantian interests in developing and exercising his or her capacities for a sense of justice and a conception of the good will want more rather than fewer of, whatever else that person wants.

4 In this chapter I often use the term "capability" loosely to mean "freedom," and speak of a person's capability to achieve some particular functioning. This marks a departure, I hope an innocent departure, from Sen's usage.

5 The statement in the text needs more argument than I provide. For all that I say, Sen could avoid embracing an objective list account of human good and instead adopt an informed desire satisfaction account that would be used to rank the importance of different capabilities. The ones that matter would be the ones that would enable informed desire satisfaction. I doubt this gambit would work, because I agree with familiar criticisms of ideally informed desire accounts of human good. But this issue would need to be explored in order to nail down the claim I make in the text. Thanks to Steven Wall for this point.

6 A qualification should be added to the statement in the text. In her writings from about 1988 to 1992, Nussbaum yokes Sen's capability approach to broadly Aristotelian claims about human well-being. A reasoned commitment to claims about what is objectively valuable in human life is supposed to inform the theory of justice. In later writings, especially *Women and Human Development: The Capabilities Approach* (2000a), Nussbaum backtracks from these claims, and sees her project in Rawlsian "political liberalism" terms. She takes herself to be developing a political conception of justice in Rawls's sense, one that avoids commitment to any controversial comprehensive conception of the good or the right. Instead, what is proposed is to be a thin conception of good on which partisans of all reasonable conflicting comprehensive doctrines can agree as an appropriate charter for common life. For example, she states that the threshold level of the basic capabilities that is essential to a good enough human life should be settled by the political process of constitutional democracies, so might vary from country to country depending on the outcome of such a process. For this last suggestion, see her contribution to a symposium on Martha Nussbaum's political philosophy (Nussbaum 2000b).

7 In fairness, I should note that the prioritarian view I embrace is also not a specific doctrine, but rather a broad family of alternative principles. Living then in a glass house, the prioritarian should not throw stones at other theorists' windows.

8 See Arneson (1989) and Cohen (1989). For criticism of equal opportunity for welfare, see Christiano (1991), Fleurbaey (1995), and Lippert-Rasmussen (1999); also Arneson (1999b).

9 Nussbaum's list of basic capabilities excludes higher achievements and includes only goods that any normal person in reasonably favorable circumstances should be able to attain. But the issue raised in the text remains pertinent. I see no reason not to allow the good enough level (whether of capability or functioning) to which everyone is to be entitled to reflect an "all things considered" assessment of the person's condition, so subpar scores on some basic dimensions of capability such as health can be offset by superior scores on other dimensions and by excellent scores on exquisite nonbasic dimensions.

10 Harry Frankfurt (1987) asserts this line of thought.
11 Straight aggregative act-utilitarianism can of course recommend transfers of resources from better-off to worse-off persons without assuming that how well or badly off one person is compared to others has any intrinsic moral weight. Utilitarianism recommends transfers when that is utility maximizing. I regard as egalitarian a moral view that proposes equalizing transfers sometimes even when they are not utility maximizing. Any view that gives some weight to equality of condition *per se* will count as egalitarian. So will leximin and maximin, which say (roughly) that one should do whatever would produce the greatest benefit to the worst off. In contrast, priority (also known as weighted utilitarianism), another egalitarian view, holds that one ought to maximize moral value, given that moral value (a) consists of well-being gains and avoidance of well-being losses, and (b) is greater, the larger the well-being gain (loss avoidance) a person would get from a benefit, and (c) is greater, the lower in absolute terms the person's lifetime well-being worse would be absent that benefit. In addition, I impose a further condition on the views I call "priority" in the text: a lexical priority relation does not obtain in either direction between the moral value gained through well-being increase (clause (b) just above) and the moral value gained through channeling benefits to the worse off (clause (c)). I myself want to identify priority with a "middling" balancing of the moral value of aggregation of well-being and distribution of well-being but I do not have any proposal about how to formulate a specific proposal that captures this vague idea.
12 This criticism of strict sufficiency appears in Arneson (2002).
13 But for a contrary view, see Crisp (2003).
14 This is guaranteed by the characterization of prioritarianism in note 11 of this chapter.
15 Aggregation is the claim that for any loss or evil, however great its magnitude, that befalls one person, there is a greater loss or evil constituted by the sum of much smaller losses or evils suffered by a large number of persons.
16 Sen himself is rather noncommittal on capability versus functioning. Nussbaum does insist that justice requires sustaining all persons at the good enough capability level, not the good enough functioning level. According to her, in the just society an individual will have sexual functioning capability but may choose to be celibate, will have adequate nutrition capability but may choose to fast, and so on.
17 Real option freedom as characterized in the text leaves it open what happens if I do not make a choice either to go or not to go to Paris.
18 For useful discussion, see Pettit (2001).

References

Anderson, E. (1999) "What Is the Point of Equality?", *Ethics* 109: 287–337.

Arneson, R. (1989) "Equality and Equal Opportunity for Welfare," *Philosophical Studies* 56: 77–93.

Arneson, R. (1999a) "Human Flourishing versus Desire Satisfaction," *Social Philosophy and Policy* 16: 113–142.

Arneson, R. (1999b) "Equal Opportunity for Welfare Defended and Recanted," *Journal of Political Philosophy* 7: 488–497.

Arneson, R. (1999c) "Egalitarianism and Responsibility," *Journal of Ethics* 3: 225–247.

Arneson, R. (2000) "Perfectionism and Politics," *Ethics* 111: 37–63.

Arneson, R. (2002) "Why Justice Requires Transfers to Offset Inequalities of Income and Wealth," *Social Philosophy and Policy* 19, 172–200.

Christiano, T. (1991) "Difficulties with the Principle of Equal Opportunity for Welfare," *Philosophical Studies* 62: 179–185.

Crisp, R. (2003) "Equality, Priority, and Compassion," *Ethics* 13: 745–763.

Cohen, G. A. (1989) "On the Currency of Egalitarian Justice," *Ethics* 99: 906–944.

Fleurbaey, M. (1995) "Equal Opportunity or Equal Social Outcome?" *Economics and Philosophy* 11: 35–55.

Frankfurt, H. (1987) "Equality as a Moral Ideal," *Ethics* 98: 21–43.

Lippert-Rasmussen, K. (1999) "Arneson on Equality of Opportunity for Welfare," *Journal of Political Philosophy* 7: 478–487.

Mill, J. S. ([1859] 1977) *On Liberty*, reprinted in Mill, *Collected Works*, ed. J. Robson, vol. 18, Toronto: University of Toronto Press, pp. 212–310.

Nussbaum, M. (1988) "Nature, Function, and Capability: Aristotle on Political Distribution," *Oxford Studies in Ancient Political Thought*, supp. vol. 1, 145–84.

Nussbaum, M. (1990) "Aristotelian Social Democracy," in R. Douglas, G., Mara, and H. Richardson (eds) *Liberalism and the Good*, New York: Routledge, pp. 203–252.

Nussbaum. M. (1991) "Aristotle on Human Nature and the Foundations of Ethics," in J. Altham and R. Harrison (eds) *World, Mind, and Ethics: Essays on the Ethical Philosophy of Bernard Williams*, Cambridge: Cambridge University Press, pp. 86–131.

Nussbaum, M. (1992) "Human Functioning and Social Justice: In Defense of Aristotelian Essentialism," *Political Theory* 20: 202–246.

Nussbaum, M. (1999) "Women and Cultural Universals," in *Sex and Social Justice*, Oxford: Oxford University Press, pp. 29–54.

Nussbaum, M. (2000a) *Women and Human Development: The Capabilities Approach*, Cambridge: Cambridge University Press.

Nussbaum, M. (2000b), "Aristotle, Politics, and Human Capabilities: A Response to Antony, Arneson, Charlesworth, and Mulgan," *Ethics* 111: 102–140.

Nussbaum, M. (2004) *Hiding from Humanity: Disgust, Shame, and the Law*, Princeton, NJ: Princeton University Press.

Parfit, D. (1984) *Reasons and Persons*, Oxford: Oxford University Press.

Parfit, D. (2000) "Equality or Priority?" in M. Clayton and A. Williams (eds) *The Ideal of Equality*, New York: St. Martin's Press.

Pettit, P. (2001) "Capability and Freedom: A Defence of Sen," *Economics and Philosophy* 17: 1–20.

Rawls, J. (1971) *A Theory of Justice*, Cambridge, MA: Harvard University Press.

Rawls, J. (1982) "Social Unity and Primary Goods," in A. Sen and B. Williams (eds) *Utilitarianism and Beyond*, Cambridge: Cambridge University Press, 159–186.

Rawls, J. (1999) *A Theory of Justice*, rev. edn, Cambridge, MA: Harvard University Press.

Roemer, J. (1996) *Theories of Distributive Justice*, Cambridge, MA: Harvard University Press.

Scheffler, S. (1981) "Natural Rights, Equality, and the Minimal State," in J. Paul (ed.) *Reading Nozick: Essays on "Anarchy, State, and Utopia,"* Totowa, NJ: Rowman & Littlefield: 148–168.

Scheffler, S. (1994) *The Rejection of Consequentialism*, 2nd edn., Oxford: Oxford University Press.

Sen, A. (1982) "Equality of What?", in *Choice, Welfare and Measurement*, Cambridge, MA: MIT Press.

Sen, A. (1985a) "Well-Being, Agency and Freedom," *Journal of Philosophy* 82: 169–203.

Sen, A. (1985b) *Commodities and Capabilities*, Amsterdam: North-Holland.

Sen, A. (1987) *The Standard of Living*, Cambridge: Cambridge University Press.

Sen, A. (1992) *Inequality Reexamined*, Cambridge, MA: Harvard University Press.

Weirich, P. (1983) "Utility Tempered with Equality," *Nous* 17: 423–439.

2 Capabilities as fundamental entitlements

Sen and social justice

Martha C. Nussbaum

Amartya Sen has made a major contribution to the theory of social justice, and of gender justice, by arguing that capabilities are the relevant space of comparison when justice-related issues are considered. This chapter supports Sen's idea, arguing that capabilities supply guidance superior to that of utility and resources (the view's familiar opponents), but also to that of the social contract tradition, and at least some accounts of human rights. But I argue that capabilities can help us to construct a normative conception of social justice, with critical potential for gender issues, only if we specify a definite set of capabilities as the most important ones to protect. Sen's "perspective of freedom" is too vague. Some freedoms limit others; some freedoms are important, some trivial; some good, and some positively bad. Before the approach can offer a valuable normative gender perspective, we must make commitments about substance.

The capabilities approach and social justice[1]

Throughout his career, Amartya Sen has been preoccupied with questions of social justice. Inequalities between women and men have been especially important in his thinking, and the achievement of gender justice in society has been among the most central goals of his theoretical enterprise. Against the dominant emphasis on economic growth as an indicator of a nation's quality of life, Sen (1980, 1982, 1985, 1992, 1999) has insisted on the importance of *capabilities*, what people are actually able to do and to be. Frequently his arguments in favor of this shift in thinking deal with issues of gender (see, for example, Sen 1990, 1995, 1999). Growth is a bad indicator of life quality because it fails to tell us how deprived people are doing; women figure in the argument as people who are often unable to enjoy the fruits of a nation's general prosperity. If we ask what people are actually able to do and to be, we come much closer to understanding the barriers societies have erected against full justice for women. Similarly, Sen (1990, 1995) criticizes approaches that measure well-being in terms of utility by pointing to the fact that women frequently exhibit "adaptive preferences," preferences that have adjusted to their second-class status. Thus, the utilitarian framework, which asks people what they currently prefer and how satisfied they are, proves inadequate to confront the most pressing issues of gender justice. We can only have an adequate theory of gender justice, and of social justice more generally, if we are willing to make claims about fundamental entitlements that are to some extent independent of the preferences that people happen to have, preferences shaped, often, by unjust background conditions.

This critique of dominant paradigms in terms of ideas of gender justice is a pervasive feature in Sen's work, and it is obvious that one central motivation for his elaboration of the "capabilities approach" is its superior potential for developing a theory of gender justice. But the reader who looks for a fully formulated account of social justice generally, and gender justice in particular, in Sen's work will not find one; he or she will need to extrapolate one from the suggestive materials Sen provides. *Development as Freedom* develops one pertinent line of thought, arguing that capabilities provide the best basis for thinking about the goals of development (Sen 1999). Both when nations are compared by international measures of welfare and when each nation strives internally to achieve a higher level of development for its people, capabilities provide us with an attractive way of understanding the normative content of the idea of development. Thinking of development's goal as increase in GNP per capita occluded distributional inequalities, which are particularly central when we are thinking about sex equality. It also failed to disaggregate and separately consider important aspects of development, such as health and education, that are demonstrably not very well correlated with GNP, even when we take distribution into account. Thinking of development's goal in terms of utility at least has the merit of looking at what processes do for people. But utility, Sen argues, is inadequate to capture the heterogeneity and noncommensurability of the diverse aspects of development. Because it fails to take account of the fact of adaptive preferences, it also biases the development process in favor of the status quo, when used as a normative benchmark. Finally, it suggests that the goal of development is a state or condition of persons (e.g. a state of satisfaction), and thus understates the importance of agency and freedom in the development process.

All these failings, he stresses, loom large when we confront the theory with inequalities based on sex: for women's lives reflect a striving after many different elements of well-being, including health, education, mobility, political participation, and others. Women's current preferences often show distortions that are the result of unjust background conditions. And agency and freedom are particularly important goals for women, who have so often been treated as passive dependents. This line of argument has close links with the feminist critique of utilitarianism and dominant economic paradigms (e.g. Anderson 1993; Agarwal 1997). It also connects fruitfully with writings by activist-scholars who stress the importance of women's agency and participation (e.g. Chen 1983; Agarwal 1994).

Not surprisingly, I endorse these arguments. But I think that they do not take us very far in thinking about social justice. They give us a general sense of what societies ought to be striving to achieve, but because of Sen's reluctance to make commitments about substance (which capabilities a society ought most centrally to pursue), even that guidance remains but an outline. And they give us no sense of what a minimum level of capability for a just society might be. The use of capabilities in development is typically comparative merely, as in the *Human Development Reports* of the UNDP. Thus, nations are compared in areas such as health and educational attainment. But concerning what level of health service, or what level of educational provision, a just society would deliver as a fundamental entitlement of all its citizens, the view is suggestive, but basically silent.

A different line of argument pursued by Sen in works from "Equality of What?" (1980) to *Inequality Reexamined* (1992) seems more closely related to concerns of social justice. This argument begins from the idea of equality as a central political value (Sen 1992). Most states consider equality important, Sen argues, and yet they often do not ask perspicuously enough what the right space is within which to make the relevant comparisons. With arguments closely related to his arguments about the goals of development, Sen argues that the space of capabilities provides the most fruitful and ethically satisfactory way of looking at equality as a political goal. Equality of utility or welfare falls short for the reasons I have already summarized. Equality of resources falls short because it fails to take account of the fact that individuals need differing levels of resources if they are to come up to the same level of capability to function. They also have differing abilities to convert resources into actual functioning.

Some of these differences are straightforwardly physical: a child needs more protein than an adult to achieve a similar level of healthy functioning, and a pregnant woman more nutrients than a nonpregnant woman. But the differences that most interest Sen are social, and connected with entrenched discrimination of various types. Thus, in a nation where women are traditionally discouraged from pursuing an education it will usually take more resources to produce female literacy than male literacy. Or, to cite Sen's famous example (1980), a person in a wheelchair will require more resources connected with mobility than will the person with "normal" mobility, if the two are to attain a similar level of ability to get around.[2]

Sen's arguments about equality seem to have the following bearing on issues of social justice and public policy: to the extent that a society values the equality of persons and pursues that among its social goals, equality of capabilities looks like the most relevant sort of equality to aim at. And it is clear that equality is a central goal for women who pursue social justice; once again, then, the arguments have particular force and relevance in the context of feminism. But Sen never says to what extent equality of capability *ought* to be a social goal,[3] or how it ought to be combined with other political values in the pursuit of social justice. Thus, the connection of his equality arguments with a theory of justice remains as yet unclear.

In this chapter I shall suggest that the capabilities approach is indeed a valuable way to approach the question of fundamental entitlements, one that is especially pertinent to issues of sex equality.[4] I shall argue that it is superior to other approaches to social justice in the Western tradition when we confront it with problems of sex equality. It is closely allied to, but in some ways superior to, the familiar human rights paradigm, in ways that emerge most vividly in the area of sex difference. And it is superior to approaches deriving from the Western notion of the social contract because of the way in which it can handle issues of care, issues that are fundamental to achieving sex equality, as recent feminist work has demonstrated.[5]

I shall argue, however, that the capabilities approach will supply definite and useful guidance, and prove an ally in the pursuit of sex equality, only if we formulate a definite list of the most central capabilities, even one that is tentative and revisable, using capabilities so defined to elaborate a partial account of social justice, a set of basic entitlements without which no society can lay claim to justice.

Capabilities and rights

The capabilities that Sen mentions in illustrating his approach, and those that are part of my more explicit list, include many of the entitlements that are also stressed in the human rights movement: political liberties, freedom of association, the free choice of occupation, and a variety of economic and social rights. And capabilities, like human rights, supply a moral and humanly rich set of goals for development, in place of "the wealth and poverty of the economists," as Marx (1844) so nicely put it. Thus, capabilities have a very close relationship to human rights, as understood in contemporary international discussions. In effect, they cover the terrain covered by both the so-called "first-generation rights" (political and civil liberties) and the so-called "second-generation rights" (economic and social rights). And they play a similar role, providing both a basis for cross-cultural comparison and the philosophical underpinning for basic constitutional principles.

Both Sen and I connect the capabilities approach closely to the idea of human rights, and in Nussbaum (2001a: ch. 1) I have described the relationship between the two ideas at some length (see also Nussbaum 1997). The human rights approach has frequently been criticized by feminists for being male-centered, and for not including as fundamental entitlements some abilities and opportunities that are fundamental to women in their struggle for sex equality. They have proposed adding to international rights documents such rights as the right to bodily integrity and the right to be free from violence in the home, and from sexual harassment in the workplace. My list of capabilities explicitly incorporates that proposal, and Sen's would appear to do so implicitly.[6] But the theoretical reasons for supplementing the language of rights with the language of capabilities still require comment.

Capabilities, I would argue, are very closely linked to rights, but the language of capabilities gives important precision and supplementation to the language of rights. The idea of human rights is by no means a crystal-clear idea. Rights have been understood in many different ways, and difficult theoretical questions are frequently obscured by the use of rights language, which can give the illusion of agreement where there is deep philosophical disagreement. People differ about what the *basis* of a rights claim is: rationality, sentience, and mere life have all had their defenders. They differ, too, about whether rights are prepolitical or artifacts of laws and institutions. They differ about whether rights belong only to individual persons, or also to groups. They differ about whether rights are to be regarded as side-constraints on goal-promoting action, or rather as one part of the social goal that is being promoted. They differ, again, about the relationship between rights and duties: if A has a right to S, then does this mean that there is always someone who has a duty to provide S, and how shall we decide who that someone is? They differ, finally, about what rights are to be understood as rights *to*. Are human rights primarily rights to be treated in certain ways? Rights to a certain level of achieved well-being? Rights to resources with which one may pursue one's life plan? Rights to certain opportunities and capacities with which one may make choices about one's life plan?

The capabilities approach has the advantage of taking clear positions on these disputed issues, while stating clearly what the motivating concerns are and what the goal is. The relationship between the two notions, however, needs further scrutiny, given the dominance of rights language in international feminism.

Regarding fundamental rights, I would argue that the best way of thinking about what it is to secure them to people is to think in terms of capabilities. The right to political participation, the right to religious free exercise, the right of free speech – these and others are all best thought of as secured to people only when the relevant capabilities to function are present. In other words, to secure a right to citizens in these areas is to put them in a position of capability to function in that area. To the extent that rights are used in defining social justice, we should not grant that the society is just unless the capabilities have been effectively achieved. Of course, people may have a prepolitical right to good treatment in this area that has not yet been recognized or implemented; or it may be recognized formally and yet not implemented. But by defining the securing of rights in terms of capabilities, we make it clear that a people in country C do not really have an effective right to political participation – for example, a right in the sense that matters for judging that the society is a just one –

simply because this language exists on paper: they have really been given a right only if there are effective measures to make people truly capable of political exercise. Women in many nations have a nominal right of political participation without having this right in the sense of capability: for example, they may be threatened with violence should they leave the home. In short, thinking in terms of capability gives us a benchmark as we think about what it is really to secure a right to someone. It makes clear that this involves affirmative material and institutional support, not simply a failure to impede.

We see here a major advantage of the capabilities approach over understandings of rights – very influential and widespread – that derive from the tradition within liberalism that is now called "neoliberal," for which the key idea is that of "negative liberty." Often, fundamental entitlements have been understood as prohibitions against interfering state action, and if the state keeps its hands off, those rights are taken to have been secured; the state has no further affirmative task. Indeed, the US Constitution suggests this conception directly: for negative phrasing concerning state action predominates, as in the First Amendment:

> Congress shall make no law respecting an establishment of religion, or prohibiting the free exercise thereof; or abridging the freedom of speech, or of the press; or the right of the people peaceably to assemble, and petition the Government for a redress of grievances.

Similarly, the Fourteenth Amendment's all-important guarantees are also stated in terms of what the state may not do:

> No State shall make or enforce any law which shall abridge the privileges or immunities of citizens of the United States; nor shall any State deprive any person of life, liberty, or property, without due process of law; nor deny to any person within its jurisdiction the equal protection of the laws.

This phraseology, deriving from the Enlightenment tradition of negative liberty, leaves things notoriously indeterminate as to whether impediments supplied by the market or by private actors are to be considered violations of fundamental rights of citizens (Nussbaum forthcoming a).

The Indian Constitution, by contrast, typically specifies rights affirmatively.[7] Thus, for example: "All citizens shall have the right to freedom of speech and expression; to assemble peaceably and without arms; to form associations or unions; …" (Art. 19). These locutions have usually been understood to imply that impediments supplied by nonstate actors may also be deemed to be violative of constitutional rights. Moreover, the Indian Constitution is quite explicit that affirmative action programs to aid the lower castes and women are not only not incompatible with constitutional guarantees, but are actually in their spirit. Such an approach seems very important for gender justice: the state needs to take action if traditionally marginalized groups are to achieve full equality. Whether a nation has a written constitution or not, it should understand fundamental entitlements in this way.

The capabilities approach, we may now say, sides with the Indian Constitution, and against the neoliberal interpretation of the US Constitution.[8] It makes it clear that securing a right to someone requires more than the absence of negative state action. Measures such as the recent constitutional amendments in India that guarantee women one-third representation in the local *panchayats*, or village councils, are strongly suggested by the capabilities approach, which directs government to think from the start about what obstacles there are to full and effective empowerment for all citizens, and to devise measures that address these obstacles.

A further advantage of the capabilities approach is that, by focusing from the start on what people are actually able to do and to be, it is well placed to foreground and address inequalities that women suffer inside the family: inequalities in resources and opportunities, educational deprivations, the failure of work to be recognized as work, insults to bodily integrity. Traditional rights talk has neglected these issues, and this is no accident, I would argue: for rights language is strongly linked with the traditional distinction between a public sphere, which the state regulates, and a private sphere, which it must leave alone.

The language of capabilities has one further advantage over the language of rights: it is not strongly linked to one particular cultural and historical tradition, as the language of rights is believed to be. This belief is not very accurate, as Sen has effectively argued: although the term "rights" is associated with the European Enlightenment, its component ideas have deep roots in many traditions (Sen 1997; Nussbaum 2000a). Nonetheless, the language of capabilities enables us to bypass this troublesome debate. When we speak simply of what people are actually able to do and to be, we do not even give the appearance of privileging a Western idea. Ideas of activity and ability are everywhere, and there is no culture in which people do not ask themselves what they are able to do and what opportunities they have for functioning.

If we have the language of capabilities, do we also need the language of rights? The language of rights still plays, I believe, four important roles in public discourse, despite its unsatisfactory features. First, when used as in the sentence "A has a right to have the basic political liberties secured to her by her government," it reminds us that people have justified and urgent claims to certain types of urgent treatment, no matter what the world around them has done about that. It imports the idea of an urgent claim based upon justice. This is important particularly for women, who may lack political rights. However, the capabilities approach can make this idea of a fundamental entitlement clear in other ways, particularly, as I shall be arguing, by operating with a list of capabilities which are held to be fundamental entitlements of all citizens based upon justice.

Rights language also has value because of the emphasis it places on people's choice and autonomy. The language of capabilities, as both Sen and I employ it, is designed to leave room for choice, and to communicate the idea that there is a big difference between pushing people into functioning in ways you consider valuable and leaving the choice up to them. Sen makes this point very effectively in *Development as Freedom* (1999). But we make this emphasis clear if we combine the capabilities analysis with the language of rights, as my list of capabilities does at several points, and as the Indian Constitution typically does.[9]

Endorsing a list

One obvious difference between Sen's writings and my own is that for some time I have endorsed a specific list of the Central Human Capabilities as a focus both for comparative quality-of-life measurement and for the formulation of basic political principles of the sort that can play a role in fundamental constitutional guarantees.

The basic idea of my version of the capabilities approach, in *Women and Human Development* (2000a), is that we begin with a conception of the dignity of the human being, and of a life that is worthy of that dignity – a life that has available in it "truly human functioning," in the sense described by Marx in his 1844 *Economic and Philosophical Manuscripts*. With this basic idea as a starting point, I then attempt to justify a list of ten capabilities as central requirements of a life with dignity. These ten capabilities are supposed to be general goals that can be further specified by the society in question, as it works on the account of fundamental entitlements it wishes to endorse (Nussbaum 2000a: ch. 1). But in some form all are part of a minimum account of social justice: a society that does not guarantee these to all its citizens, at some appropriate threshold level, falls short of being a fully just society, whatever its level of opulence. Moreover, the capabilities are held to be important for each and every person: each person is treated as an end, and none as a mere adjunct or means to the ends of others. And although in practical terms priorities may have to be set temporarily, the capabilities are understood as both mutually supportive and all of central relevance to social justice. Thus a society that neglects one of them to promote the others has shortchanged its citizens, and there is a failure of justice in the shortchanging (Nussbaum 2001b). (Of course someone may feel that one or more of the capabilities on my list should not enjoy this central status, but then he or she will be differing with me about what ought to be on the list, not about the more general project of using a list to define a minimal conception of social justice.)

The list itself is open-ended and has undergone modification over time;

no doubt it will undergo further modification in the light of criticism. But here is the current version.

The Central Human Capabilities

1 *Life*. Being able to live to the end of a human life of normal length; not dying prematurely, or before one's life is so reduced as to be not worth living.
2 *Bodily health*. Being able to have good health, including reproductive health; to be adequately nourished; to have adequate shelter.
3 *Bodily integrity*. Being able to move freely from place to place; to be secure against violent assault, including sexual assault and domestic violence; having opportunities for sexual satisfaction and for choice in matters of reproduction.
4 *Senses, imagination, and thought*. Being able to use the senses, to imagine, think, and reason – and to do these things in a "truly human" way, a way informed and cultivated by an adequate education, including, but by no means limited to, literacy and basic mathematical and scientific training. Being able to use imagination and thought in connection with experiencing and producing works and events of one's own choice: religious, literary, musical, and so forth. Being able to use one's mind in ways protected by guarantees of freedom of expression with respect to both political and artistic speech, and freedom of religious exercise. Being able to have pleasurable experiences and to avoid nonbeneficial pain.
5 *Emotions*. Being able to have attachments to things and people outside ourselves; to love those who love and care for us, to grieve at their absence; in general, to love, to grieve, to experience longing, gratitude, and justified anger. Not having one's emotional development blighted by fear and anxiety. (Supporting this capability means supporting forms of human association that can be shown to be crucial in their development.)
6 *Practical reason*. Being able to form a conception of the good and to engage in critical reflection about the planning of one's life. (This entails protection for the liberty of conscience and religious observance.)
7 *Affiliation*:

- Being able to live with and toward others, to recognize and show concern for other human beings, to engage in various forms of social interaction; to be able to imagine the situation of another. (Protecting this capability means protecting institutions that constitute and nourish such forms of affiliation, and also protecting the freedom of assembly and political speech.)
- Having the social bases of self-respect and nonhumiliation; being able to be treated as a dignified being whose worth is equal to that

of others. This entails provisions of nondiscrimination on the basis of race, sex, sexual orientation, ethnicity, caste, religion, national origin.

8 *Other species*. Being able to live with concern for and in relation to animals, plants, and the world of nature.
9 *Play*. Being able to laugh, to play, to enjoy recreational activities.
10 *Control over one's environment*:

- Political. Being able to participate effectively in political choices that govern one's life; having the right of political participation, protections of free speech and association.
- Material. Being able to hold property (both land and movable goods), and having property rights on an equal basis with others; having the right to seek employment on an equal basis with others; having the freedom from unwarranted search and seizure. In work, being able to work as a human being, exercising practical reason and entering into meaningful relationships of mutual recognition with other workers.

Because considerations of pluralism have been on my mind since the beginning, I have worked a sensitivity to cultural difference into my understanding of the list in several ways.

First, I consider the list as open-ended and subject to ongoing revision and rethinking, in the way that any society's account of its most fundamental entitlements is always subject to supplementation (or deletion).

I also insist, second, that the items on the list ought to be specified in a somewhat abstract and general way, precisely in order to leave room for the activities of specifying and deliberating by citizens and their legislatures and courts that all democratic nations contain. Within certain parameters, it is perfectly appropriate that different nations should do this somewhat differently, taking their histories and special circumstances into account. Thus, for example, a free speech right that suits Germany well might be too restrictive in the different climate of the United States.

Third, I consider the list to be a free-standing "partial moral conception," to use John Rawls's phrase – that is, it is explicitly introduced for political purposes only, and without any grounding in metaphysical ideas of the sort that divide people along lines of culture and religion.[10] As Rawls says, we can view this list as a "module" that can be endorsed by people who otherwise have very different conceptions of the ultimate meaning and purpose of life; they will connect it to their religious or secular comprehensive doctrines in many ways.

Fourth, if we insist that the appropriate political target is capability and not functioning, we protect pluralism here again.[11] Many people who are willing to support a given capability as a fundamental entitlement would feel violated were the associated functioning made basic. Thus, the right to vote can be endorsed by believing citizens who would feel deeply violated by mandatory voting because it goes against their religious conception. (The American Amish are in this category: they believe that it is wrong to participate in political life, but they endorse the right of citizens to vote.) The free expression of religion can be endorsed by people who would totally object to any establishment of religion that would involve dragooning all citizens into some type of religious functioning.

Fifth, the major liberties that protect pluralism are central items on the list: the freedom of speech, the freedom of association, the freedom of conscience.[12] By placing them on the list we give them a central and nonnegotiable place.

Sixth and finally, I insist on a rather strong separation between issues of justification and issues of implementation. I believe that we can justify this list as a good basis for political principles all round the world. But this does not mean that we thereby license intervention with the affairs of a state that does not recognize them. It is a basis for persuasion, but I hold that military and economic sanctions are justified only in certain very grave circumstances involving traditionally recognized crimes against humanity (Nussbaum 2002). So, it seems less objectionable to recommend something to everyone, once we point out that it is part of the view that state sovereignty, grounded in the consent of the people, is a very important part of the whole package.

Where does Sen stand on these questions? I find a puzzling tension in his writings at this point. On the one hand, he speaks as if certain specific capabilities are absolutely central and nonnegotiable. One cannot read his discussions of health, education, political and civil liberties, and the free choice of occupation without feeling that he agrees totally with my view that these human capabilities should enjoy a strong priority and should be made central by states the world over, as fundamental entitlements of each and every citizen (although he says little about how a threshold level of each capability would be constructed). In the case of liberty, he actually endorses giving liberty a considerable priority, though without giving an exhaustive enumeration of the liberties that would fall under this principle. His role in the formulation of the measures that go into the *Human Development Reports*, moreover, clearly shows him endorsing a group of health- and education-related capabilities as the appropriate way to measure quality of life across nations.

On the other hand, Sen has conspicuously refused to endorse any account of the central capabilities. Thus, the examples mentioned above remain in limbo: clearly, they are examples of some things he thinks very important, but it is not clear to what extent he is prepared to recommend them as important goals for all the world's people, goals connected with the idea of social justice itself. And it is equally unclear whether there are other capabilities not mentioned so frequently that might be equally important, and, if so, what those capabilities might be. The reason for this appears to be his respect for democratic deliberation.[13] He feels that people should be allowed to settle these matters for themselves. Of course, as I have said above, I do too, in the sense of implementation. But Sen goes further, suggesting that democracy is inhibited by the endorsement of a set of central entitlements in international political debate, as when feminists insist on certain requirements of gender justice in international documents and deliberations.

In *Development as Freedom* (Sen 1999), things become, I believe, even more problematic. For Sen speaks throughout the work of "the perspective of freedom" and uses language, again and again, suggesting that freedom is a general all-purpose social good, and that capabilities are to be seen as instances of this more general good of human freedom. Such a view is not incompatible with ranking some freedoms ahead of others for political purposes, of course. But it does seem to go in a problematic direction.

First of all, it is unclear whether the idea of promoting freedom is even a coherent political project. Some freedoms limit others. The freedom of rich people to make large donations to political campaigns limits the equal worth of the right to vote. The freedom of businesses to pollute the environment limits the freedom of citizens to enjoy an unpolluted environment. The freedom of landowners to keep their land limits projects of land reform that might be argued to be central to many freedoms for the poor. And so on. Obviously these freedoms are not among those that Sen considers, but he says nothing to limit the account of freedom or to rule out conflicts of this type. Indeed, we can go further: any particular freedom involves the idea of constraint, for person P is only free to perform action A if other people are constrained from interfering with A.[14]

Furthermore, even if there were a coherent project that viewed all freedoms as desirable social goals, it is not at all clear that this is the sort of project someone with Sen's political and ethical views ought to endorse. The examples I have just given show us that any political project that is going to protect the equal worth of certain basic liberties for the poor, and to improve their living conditions, needs to say forthrightly that some freedoms are central for political purposes, and some are distinctly not. Some freedoms involve basic social entitlements, and others do not. Some lie at the heart of a view of political justice, and others do not. Among the ones that do not lie at the core, some are simply less important, but others may be positively bad.

For example, the freedom of rich people to make large campaign contributions, though defended by many Americans in the name of the general good of freedom, seems to me not to be among those freedoms that lie at the heart of a set of basic entitlements to which a just society should commit itself. In many circumstances it is actually a bad thing, and constraint on it a very good thing. Similarly, the freedom of industry to pollute the environment, though cherished by many Americans in the name of the general good of freedom, seems to me not to be among those freedoms that should enjoy protection; beyond a certain point, the freedom to pollute is bad, and should be constrained by law. And while property rights are certainly a good thing up to a point and in some ways, the freedom of large landowners in India to hold property under gender-discriminatory ceiling laws – laws that some early Supreme Court decisions have held to enjoy constitutional protection – is not part of the account of property rights as central human entitlements that a just society would want to endorse. To define property capabilities so broadly is actually a bad thing, because giving women equal access to land rights is essential to social justice (see generally Agarwal 1994).

To speak more generally, gender justice cannot be successfully pursued without limiting male freedom. For example, the "right" to have intercourse with one's wife whether she consents or not has been understood as a time-honored male prerogative in most societies, and men have greatly resented the curtailment of liberty that followed from laws against marital rape – one reason why about half of the states in the United States still do not treat nonconsensual intercourse within marriage as genuine rape, and why many societies the world over still lack laws against it. The freedom to harass women in the workplace is a tenaciously guarded prerogative of males the world over: the minute sexual harassment regulations are introduced, one always hears protests invoking the idea of liberty. Terms like "femi-nazis" are used to suggest that feminists are against freedom for supporting these policies. And of course in one sense feminists are indeed insisting on a restriction of liberty, on the grounds that certain liberties are inimical both to equalities and to women's liberties and opportunities.

In short, no society that pursues equality or even an ample social minimum can avoid curtailing freedom in very many ways, and what it ought to say is: those freedoms are not good, they are not part of a core group of entitlements required by the notion of social justice, and in many ways, indeed, they subvert those core entitlements. Of other freedoms, for example the freedom of motorcyclists to drive without helmets, a society can say, these freedoms are not very important; they are neither very bad nor very good. They are not implicit in our conception of social justice, but they do not subvert it either.

In other words, all societies that pursue a reasonably just political conception have to evaluate human freedoms, saying that some are central and some trivial, some good and some actively bad. This evaluation also affects the way we will assess an abridgment of a freedom. Certain freedoms are taken to be entitlements of citizens based upon justice. When any one of these is abridged, that is an especially grave failure of the political system. In such cases, people feel that the abridgment is not just a cost to be borne; it is a cost of a distinctive kind, involving a violation of basic justice. When some freedom outside the core is abridged, that may be a small cost or a large cost to some actor or actors, but it is not a cost of exactly that same kind, one that in justice no citizen should be asked to bear. This qualitative difference is independent of the cost, at least in terms of standard subjective willingness-to-pay models. Thus, motorcyclists may mind greatly a law that tells them to wear a helmet. In terms of standard willingness-to-pay models, they might be willing to pay quite a lot for the right to drive without a helmet. On the other hand, many citizens probably would not think that not being able to vote was a big cost. In terms of standard willingness-to-pay models, at least, they would not pay much for the right to vote, and some might have to be paid for voting. And yet I would want to say that the right to vote is a fundamental entitlement based upon justice, whereas the right to drive without a helmet is not (Nussbaum 2001b).

Sen's response to these questions, in public discussion (Bielefeld, July 2001), has been to say that freedom *per se* is always good, although it can be badly used. Freedom, he said, is like male strength: male strength is *per se* a good thing, although it can be used to beat up women. I am not satisfied by this reply – for so much depends on how one specifies the freedoms in question. Some freedoms include injustice in their very definition. Thus, the freedom to rape one's wife without penalty, the freedom to hang out a sign saying "No Blacks here," the freedom of an employer to discriminate on grounds of race or sex or religion – those are freedoms all right, and some people zealously defend them. But it seems absurd to say that they are good *per se*, and bad only in use. Any society that allows people these freedoms has allowed a fundamental injustice involving the subordination of a vulnerable group. Of other freedoms – for example, the freedom of the motorcycle rider to ride without a helmet – we should not say, "good in itself, bad only in use," we should say, "neutral and trivial in itself, probably bad in use." Once again, attention to the all-important issue of content is vital.

Thus, Sen cannot avoid committing himself to a core list of fundamental capabilities, once he faces such questions. If capabilities are to be used in advancing a conception of social justice, they will obviously have to be specified, if only in the open-ended and humble way I have outlined. Either a society has a conception of basic justice or it does not. If it has one, we have to know what its content is, and what opportunities and liberties it takes to be fundamental entitlements of all citizens. One cannot have a conception of social justice that says, simply, "All citizens are entitled to freedom understood as capability." Besides being wrong and misleading in the ways I have already argued, such a blanket endorsement of freedom/capability as goal would be hopelessly vague. It would be impossible to say whether the society in question was just or unjust.

Someone may now say, sure, there has to be a definite list in the case of each nation that is striving for justice, but why not leave the list-making to them, and to their processes of public discussion? Of course, as I have already said, in the sense of *implementation,* and also in the sense of *more precise* specification, I do so. So, to be a real objection to my proposal, the question must be, why should we hold out to all nations a set of norms that we believe justified by a good philosophical argument, as when feminists work out norms of sex equality in documents such as CEDAW, rather than letting each one justify its own set of norms? The answer to this question, however, is given in all of Sen's work: some human matters are too important to be left to whim and caprice, or even to the dictates of a cultural tradition. To say that education for women, or adequate healthcare, is not justified just in case some nation believes that it is not justified seems like a capitulation to subjective preferences of the sort that Sen has opposed throughout his career. As he has repeatedly stated: capabilities have intrinsic importance. But if we believe that, we also believe that it is right to say to nations that do not sufficiently recognize one of them: you know, you too should endorse equal education for girls, and understand it as a fundamental constitutional entitlement. You too should provide a certain level of healthcare to all citizens, and view this as among their fundamental constitutional entitlements. Just because the United States does not choose to recognize a fundamental right to healthcare, that does not make the United States right, morally justified. A very important part of public discussion is radical moral statement and the arguments supporting those statements. Such statements may be justified long before they are widely accepted. Such was true of the statements of Gandhi, of Martin Luther King, Jr., of early feminists. Where feminist demands are not yet widely accepted, it is true of those demands today: although public debate has not yet accepted them, they are a part of that debate right now, and a part that has already presented adequate moral justification for basic human entitlements.

In short: it makes sense to take the issue of social justice seriously, and to use a norm of justice to assess the various nations of the world and their practices. But if the issue of social justice is important, then the content of a conception of justice is important. Social justice has always been a profoundly normative concept, and its role is typically critical: we work out an account of what is just, and we then use it to find reality deficient in various ways. Sen's whole career has been devoted to developing norms of justice in exactly this way, and holding them up against reality to produce valuable criticisms. It seems to me that his commitment to normative thinking about justice requires the endorsement of some definite content. One cannot say, "I'm for justice, but any conception of justice anyone comes up with is all right with me." Moreover, Sen, of course, does not say that. He is a radical thinker who has taken a definite stand on many matters, including matters of sex equality. He has never been afraid to be definite when misogyny is afoot, or to supply a quite definite account of why many societies are defective. So, it is somewhat mysterious to me why he has recently moved in the direction of endorsing freedom as a general good. Certainly there is no such retreat in his practical policies regarding women. In recent writing such as "The Many Faces of Misogyny" he is extremely definite about what is just and unjust in laws and institutions, and one can infer a rich account of fundamental human entitlements from his critique (Sen 2001). But then it would appear that he cannot actually believe that the content of an account of fundamental entitlements should be left up for grabs.

Such leaving-up-for-grabs is all the more dangerous when we are confronting women's issues. For obviously enough, many traditional conceptions of social justice and fundamental entitlements have made women second-class citizens, if citizens at all. Women's liberties, opportunities, property rights, and political rights have been construed as unequal to men's, and this has been taken to be a just state of affairs. Nor have traditional accounts of justice attended at all to issues that are particularly urgent for women, such as issues of bodily integrity, sexual harassment, and, as my next section will describe, the issue of public support for care to children, disabled people, and elderly people.

Some supporters of a capabilities approach might be reluctant to endorse a list because of concerns about pluralism.[15] But here we may make two points that pertain specifically to the norm of respect for pluralism. First, the value of respect for pluralism itself requires a commitment to some cross-cultural principles as fundamental entitlements. Real respect for pluralism means strong and unwavering protection for religious freedom, for the freedom of association, for the freedom of speech. If we say that we are for pluralism and yet refuse to commit ourselves to the nonnegotiability of these items as fundamental building blocks of a just political order, we show that we are really half-hearted about pluralism.

I am sure that Sen would agree with this. I am sure, too, that he would say the same about other items on my list, such as health and education: if a nation says that it is for human capabilities, but refuses to give these special protection for all citizens, citing reasons of cultural or religious pluralism, Sen will surely say that that nation is not making a good argument, or giving genuine protection to pluralism. Instead, such nations are, very often, denying people (often, women in particular) the chance to figure out what culture and form of life they actually want. So, they are actually curtailing the most meaningful kind of pluralism, which requires having a life of one's own and some choices regarding it. And that goal surely requires a certain level of basic health and education. But then we are both, in effect, making a list of such entitlements, and the only question then must be: what shall go on the list, and how long will it be?

The second argument is one that derives from the Rawlsian idea of political liberalism, and I am not certain that Sen would endorse it. The argument says that classical liberalism erred by endorsing freedom or autonomy as a general good in human life. Both earlier liberals such as John Stuart Mill and modern comprehensive liberals such as Joseph Raz hold that autonomy and freedom of choice are essential ingredients in valuable human lives, and that society is entitled to promote freedom across the board. Rawls, and I with him, hold that this general endorsement of freedom shows deficient respect for citizens whose comprehensive conceptions of the good human life do not make freedom and autonomy central human values. People who belong to an authoritarian religion cannot agree with Raz or Mill that autonomy is a generally good thing. Mill responds, in chapter 3 of *On Liberty* ([1859] 1977), by denigrating such people (he understands Calvinists to be such people). Presumably the Millean state would denigrate them too, and would design education and other institutions to disfavor them, although their civil liberties would not be restricted. Rawls and I agree that this strategy shows deficient respect for a reasonable pluralism of different comprehensive conceptions of the good life. We should respect people who prefer a life within an authoritarian religion (or personal relationship), so long as certain basic opportunities and exit options are firmly guaranteed.

I hold that this respect for pluralism is fostered both by making capability and not functioning the appropriate political goal, and by also endorsing a relatively small list of core capabilities for political purposes. Thus, we say two things to religious citizens. We say, first, that endorsing the capabilities list does not require them to endorse the associated functioning as a good in their own lives, a point I have stressed earlier in this section. And we say, second, that the very fact that it is a short list shows that we are leaving them lots of room to value other things in mapping out their plan of life. We do not ask them to endorse freedom as a general good – as we might seem to do if we talked a lot about freedom but failed to make a list. Instead, we just ask them to endorse this short list of freedoms (as capabilities) for political purposes and as applicable to all citizens. They may then get on with the lives they prefer.

The expectation is that a Roman Catholic citizen, say, can endorse this short list of fundamental liberties for political purposes without feeling that his or her view of Church authority and its decisive role in his or her life is thereby being denigrated. Even an Amish citizen, who believes that all participation in public life is simply wrong, can still feel that it is all right to endorse the capabilities list for political purposes, because no general endorsement of autonomy as an end tells him or her that his or her life is less worthwhile than other lives. And, as I argued in Nussbaum (2000a: chs. 1 and 3), even a woman who believes that the seclusion of women is right may endorse this small menu of liberties and opportunities for all women, though she herself will use few of them – and she will feel that the conception is one that respects her, because it does not announce that only autonomous lives are worthwhile.

I am not certain whether Sen is in this sense a comprehensive liberal like Raz, or a political liberal like Rawls and me. But to the extent that he finds Rawls's arguments on this score persuasive, he has yet a further reason to endorse a definite and relatively circumscribed list of capabilities as political goals, rather than to praise freedom as a general social good.

The question of how to frame such a list, and what to put on it, is surely a difficult one, in many ways. But I have argued that there is no way to take the capabilities approach forward, making it really productive for political thought about basic social justice, without facing this question and giving it the best answer one can.

Capabilities and the social contract tradition[16]

One further issue, fundamental to concerns about gender justice, will help us to see both why the capabilities approach is superior to other approaches to social justice within the liberal tradition, and why a definite list of entitlements is required if the approach is to deliver an adequate conception of justice. This is the all-important issue of care for people who are physically and/or mentally dependent on others: children, disabled people, elderly people. This is a central issue for gender justice, because most of the caregiving for such dependents is done by women, often without any public recognition that it is work. The time spent on this caregiving disables women from many other functions of life, even when a society has in other respects opened those functions to them. For this reason, a large body of feminist writing pursuing this issue has developed; and the 1999 *Human Development Report* devoted special attention to it as an issue of gender justice. To appreciate why this problem has not been adequately addressed, and why the capabilities approach does better, we must now contrast it with approaches familiar within the social contract tradition.

Insofar as the capabilities approach has been used to articulate a theory of social justice, or part of such a theory, it has been in dialogue from the start with the ideas of John Rawls and the Western liberal social contract tradition (Rawls 1971, 1996). In "Equality of What?" Sen (1980) already argued for the capabilities approach by contrasting it with Rawls's approach, which defines justice in terms of the distribution of "primary goods," prominently including wealth and income. My account of capabilities in *Women and Human Development* takes the argument further, comparing capabilities to Rawlsian primary goods at several points and endorsing the idea of an overlapping consensus (Nussbaum 2000a: ch. 1). Sen and I both argue that Rawls's theory would be better able to give an account of the relevant social equalities and inequalities if the list of primary goods were formulated as a list of capabilities rather than as a list of things.[17]

But there is another problem that ought to trouble us, as we ponder the social contract tradition as a source of basic principles of justice, particularly with women's lives in view. All well-known theories in the social contract tradition imagine society as a contract for mutual advantage. They therefore imagine the contracting parties as rough equals, none able to dominate the others and none asymmetrically dependent upon the others.

Whatever differences there are among the different founders of that tradition, all accept the basic Lockean conception of a contract among parties who, in the state of nature, are "free, equal, and independent" (Locke [1698] 1960). Thus, for Kant, persons are characterized by both freedom and equality, and the social contract is defined as an agreement among persons so characterized. Contemporary contractarians explicitly adopt this hypothesis. For David Gauthier, people of unusual need are "not party to the moral relationships grounded by a contractarian theory."[18] Similarly, the citizens in Rawls's Well Ordered Society are "fully cooperating members of society over a complete life" (Rawls 1980: 546; 1996: 183).

Life, of course, is not like that. Real people begin their lives as helpless infants and remain in a state of extreme, asymmetrical dependency, both physical and mental, for anywhere from ten to twenty years. At the other end of life, those who are lucky enough to live on into old age are likely to encounter another period of extreme dependency, either physical or mental or both, which may itself continue in some form for as much as twenty years. During the middle years of life, many of us encounter periods of extreme dependency, some of which involve our mental powers and some our bodily powers only, but all of which may put us in need of daily, even hourly, care by others. Finally, and centrally, there are many citizens who never have the physical and/or mental powers requisite for independence. In short, any real society is a caregiving and care-receiving society, and must therefore discover ways of coping with these facts of human neediness and dependency that are compatible with the self-respect of the recipients and do not exploit the caregivers. This, as I have said, is a central issue for gender justice.

In this area a Kantian starting point, favored by Rawls and other modern contractarians, is likely to give bad guidance. For Kant, human dignity and our moral capacity, dignity's source, are radically separate from the natural world. Morality certainly has the task of providing for human neediness, but the idea that we are at bottom split beings, both rational persons and animal dwellers in the world of nature, never ceases to influence Kant's way of thinking about how these deliberations will go.

What is wrong with the split? Quite a lot. First, it ignores the fact that our dignity is just the dignity of a certain sort of animal. It is the animal sort of dignity, and that very sort of dignity could not be possessed by a being who was not mortal and vulnerable, just as the beauty of a cherry tree in bloom could not be possessed by a diamond. Second, the split wrongly denies that animality can itself have a dignity; thus, it leads us to slight aspects of our own lives that have worth, and to distort our relation to the other animals.[19] Third, it makes us think of the core of ourselves as self-sufficient, not in need of the gifts of fortune; in so thinking we greatly distort the nature of our own morality and rationality, which are thoroughly material and animal themselves; we learn to ignore the fact that disease, old age, and accident can impede the moral and rational functions, just as much as the other animal functions. Fourth, it makes us think of ourselves as a-temporal. We forget that the usual human lifecycle brings with it periods of extreme dependency, in which our functioning is very similar to that enjoyed by mentally or physically handicapped people throughout their lives. Feminist thought has recognized these facts about human life more prominently, at any rate, than most other political and moral thought.

Political thought in the Kantian social contract tradition (to stick with the part of the tradition I find deepest and most appealing) suffers from the conception of the person with which it begins. Rawls's contracting parties are fully aware of their need for material goods. Here Rawls diverges from Kant, building need into the foundations of the theory. But he does so only to a degree: for the parties are imagined throughout as competent contracting adults, roughly similar in need, and capable of a level of social cooperation that makes them able to make a contract with others. Such a hypothesis seems required by the very idea of a contract for mutual advantage.

In so conceiving of persons, Rawls explicitly omits from the situation of basic political choice the more extreme forms of need and dependency that human beings may experience. His very concept of social cooperation is based on the idea of reciprocity between rough equals, and has no explicit place for relations of extreme dependency. Thus, for example, Rawls refuses to grant that we have any duties of justice to animals, on the grounds that they are not capable of reciprocity (*Theory of Justice* 17: 504–505); they are owed "compassion and humanity," but "[t]hey are outside the scope of the theory of justice, and it does not seem possible to extend the contract doctrine so as to include them in a natural way" (ibid.: 512). This makes a large difference to his theory of political distribution. For his account of the primary goods, introduced, as it is, as an account of the needs of citizens who are characterized by the two moral powers and by the capacity to be "fully cooperating," has no place for the need of many real people for the kind of care we give to people who are not independent (see Kittay 1999).

Now of course Rawls is perfectly aware that his theory focuses on some cases and leaves others to one side. He insists that although the need for care for people who are not independent is "a pressing practical question," it may reasonably be postponed to the legislative stage, after basic political institutions are designed:

> So let's add that all citizens are fully cooperating members of society over the course of a complete life. This means that everyone has sufficient intellectual powers to play a normal part in society, and no one suffers from unusual needs that are especially difficult to fulfill, for example, unusual and costly medical requirements. Of course, care for those with such requirements is a pressing practical question. But at

> this initial stage, the fundamental problem of social justice arises between those who are full and active and morally conscientious participants in society, and directly or indirectly associated together throughout a complete life. Therefore, it is sensible to lay aside certain difficult complications. If we can work out a theory that covers the fundamental case, we can try to extend it to other cases later.
>
> (Rawls 1980: 546)

This reply seems inadequate. Care for children, elderly people, and mentally or physically handicapped people is a major part of the work that needs to be done in any society, and in most societies it is a source of great injustice. Any theory of justice needs to think about the problem from the beginning, in the design of the most basic level of institutions, and particularly in its theory of the primary goods.[20]

What, then, can be done to give the problem of care and dependency sufficient prominence in a theory of justice? The first thing we might try, one that has been suggested by Eva Kittay in her fine book, is to add the need for care during periods of extreme and asymmetrical dependency to the Rawlsian list of primary goods, thinking of care as among the basic needs of citizens.

This suggestion, if we adopt it, would lead us to make another modification: for care is hardly a commodity, like income and wealth, to be measured by the sheer amount of it citizens have. As Sen has long suggested (see the first section of this chapter), we would do well to understand the entire list of primary goods as a list – not of things, but of central capabilities. This change would not only enable us to deal better with people's needs for various types of love and care as elements of the list, but would also answer the point that Sen has repeatedly made all along about the unreliability of income and wealth as indices of well-being. The well-being of citizens will now be measured not by the sheer amount of income and wealth they have, but by the degree to which they have the various capabilities on the list. A woman may be as well off as her husband in terms of income and wealth, and yet be unable to function well in the workplace because of burdens of caregiving at home (see Williams 2000).

If we accepted these two changes, we would surely add a third, relevant to our thoughts about infancy and old age. We would add other capability-like items to the list of basic goods – for example, the social basis of health, adequate working conditions, and the social basis of imagination and emotional well-being, items that figure on my list (Nussbaum 2000a: ch. 1).

Suppose, then, we do make these three changes in the list of primary goods: we add care in times of extreme dependency to the list of primary goods; we reconfigure the list as a list of capabilities; and we add other pertinent items to the list as well. Have we done enough to salvage the contract doctrine as a way of generating basic political principles? I believe that there is still room for doubt. Consider the role of primary goods in

Rawls's theory. The account of primary goods is introduced in connection with the Kantian political conception of the person, as an account of what citizens characterized by the two moral powers need. Thus, we have attributed basic importance to care only from the point of view of our own current independence. It is good to be cared for only because care subserves moral personality, understood in a Kantian way as conceptually quite distinct from need and animality. This seems like another, more subtle way of making our animality subserve our humanity, where humanity is understood to exclude animality. The idea is that because we are dignified beings capable of political reciprocity, we had better provide for times when we are not that, so we can get back to being that as quickly as possible. I think that this is a dubious enough way to think about illnesses in the prime of life; but it surely leads us in the direction of a contemptuous attitude toward infancy and childhood, and, a particular danger in our society, toward elderly disability. Finally, it leads us strongly in the direction of not fully valuing those with lifelong mental disabilities: somehow or other, care for them is supposed to be valuable only for the sake of what it does for the "fully cooperating." They are, it would seem, being used as means for someone else's ends, and their full humanity is still being denied.

So, I believe that we need to delve deeper, redesigning the political conception of the person, bringing the rational and the animal into a more intimate relation with one another, and acknowledging that there are many types of dignity in the world, including the dignity of mentally disabled children and adults, the dignity of the senile demented elderly, and the dignity of babies at the breast. We want the picture of the parties who design political institutions to build these facts in from the start. The kind of reciprocity in which we humanly engage has its periods of symmetry, but also, of necessity, its periods of more or less extreme asymmetry – and this is part of our lives that we bring into our situation as parties who design just institutions. And this may well mean that the theory cannot be a contractarian theory at all.

We thus need to adopt a political conception of the person that is more Aristotelian than Kantian, one that sees the person from the start as both capable and needy – "in need of a rich plurality of life-activities," to use Marx's phrase, whose availability will be the measure of well-being. Such a conception of the person, which builds growth and decline into the trajectory of human life, will put us on the road to thinking well about what society should design. We do not have to contract for what we need by producing; we have a claim to support in the dignity of our human need itself. Since this is not just an Aristotelian idea, but one that corresponds to human experience, there is good reason to think that it can command a political consensus in a pluralistic society. If we begin with this conception of the person and with a suitable list of the central capabilities as primary goods, we can begin designing institutions by asking what it would take to get citizens up to an acceptable level on all these capabilities. Although Sen refrains from specifying a political conception of the person, I believe that this suggestion is squarely in line with his ideas.

In *Women and Human Development* I propose that the idea of central human capabilities be used as the analogue of Rawlsian primary goods, and that the guiding political conception of the person should be an Aristotelian/Marxian conception of the human being as in need of a rich plurality of life activities, to be shaped by both practical reason and affiliation (Nussbaum 2000a: ch. 1). I argue that these interlocking conceptions can form the core of a political conception that is a form of political liberalism, close to Rawls's in many ways. The core of the political conception is endorsed for political purposes only, giving citizens a great deal of space in which to pursue their own comprehensive conceptions of value, whether secular or religious. Yet more room for a reasonable pluralism in conceptions of the good is secured by insisting that the appropriate political goal is capability only: citizens should be given the option, in each area, of functioning in accordance with a given capability or not so functioning. To secure a capability to a citizen it is not enough to create a sphere of noninterference: the public conception must design the material and institutional environment so that it provides the requisite affirmative support for all the relevant capabilities. Thus, care for physical and mental dependency needs will enter into the conception at many points, as part of what is required to secure to citizens one of the capabilities on the list.

Although Sen has not commented explicitly on issues of mental disability and senility, I believe that the view I have just mapped out is squarely in line with his emphasis on freedom as goal. We see, then, here again, that the capabilities approach solves some problems central to a theory of social justice that other liberal theories seem unable to solve well; the capability-based solution seems to be an attractive way of thinking about fundamental entitlements.

But now we must observe that the capabilities approach does these good things only by virtue of having a definite content. The capabilities approach provides us with a new way of understanding the *form* of "primary goods," and that is one part of the work that it does in providing a more adequate theory of care. But getting the *form* right was not all that had to be done: we also had to add the need for care in times of acute dependency to the existing list of primary goods.[21] And then, I argued, we would also need to add other capabilities as well to the list, in areas such as healthcare, work conditions, and emotional well-being. My own list of capabilities provides for these things already, in areas such as emotions, affiliation, and health. A shift from the space of resources to the space of capabilities would not go far in correcting the deficiencies of the Rawlsian framework unless we had a list with a definite content, one that prominently includes care. Moreover, I also argued that we need to associate the list with a specific political conception of the person, one that conceives of dignity and animality as related rather than opposed. This is another piece of definite content, one that suffuses the capabilities list as I conceive it.

The capabilities approach is a powerful tool in crafting an adequate account of social justice. But the bare idea of capabilities as a space within which comparisons are made and inequalities assessed is insufficient. To get a vision of social justice that will have the requisite critical force and definiteness to direct social policy, we need to have an account, for political purposes, of what the central human capabilities are, even if we know that this account will always be contested and remade. Women all over the world are making critical proposals in public discussion, proposals that embody their radical demand for lives with full human dignity. While we await the day when the world as a whole accepts such ideas, the capabilities list is one way of giving theoretical shape to women's definite, and justified, demands.

Notes

1 I develop related arguments similar to those developed in this chapter, but with a focus on constitutional and legal issues, in Nussbaum (forthcoming a).

2 Although Sen tends to treat this example as one of straightforward physical difference, it should not be so treated, since the reasons why wheelchair users cannot get around are thoroughly social: the absence of ramps, etc. (for elaboration, see Nussbaum 2001a). See also Nussbaum (forthcoming b), where I point out that all societies cater to the disabilities of the average person. Thus, we do not have staircases with steps so high that only giants can climb them. A further problem not mentioned by Sen, but relevant to his critique of Rawls: even if the person in the wheelchair were equally well off with regard to economic well-being, there is a separate issue of dignity and self-respect.

3 Obviously, the case for this depends very much both on what capability we are considering and on how we describe it. Thus, equality of capability seems to be important when we consider the right to vote, the freedom of religion, and so on; but if we consider the capability to play basketball, it seems ludicrous to suppose that society should be very much concerned about even a minimum threshold level of it, much less complete equality. With something like health, much hangs on whether we define the relevant capability as "access to the social bases of health" or "the ability to be healthy." The former seems like something that a just society should distribute on a basis of equality; the latter contains an element of chance that no just society could, or should, altogether eliminate. So the question whether equality of capability is a good social goal cannot be well answered without specifying a list of the relevant capabilities, another point in favor of the argument I advance in the section "Endorsing a list" (p. 51).

4 One way of using it, discussed elsewhere, is as a basis for constitutional accounts of fundamental entitlements of all citizens (see Nussbaum 2000a; forthcoming a).

5 See especially Eva Kittay (1999), Nancy Folbre (1999, 2001), Joan Williams (2000), and Mona Harrington (1999). Earlier influential work in this area includes that of Martha Fineman (1991, 1995), Sarah Ruddick (1989), Joan Tronto (1993), Virginia Held (1993), and Robin West (1997). For an excellent collection of articles from diverse feminist perspectives, see Held (1995). See also Nussbaum (2000b). And, finally, see *Human Development Report 1999*.

6 See his reply to letters concerning Amartya Sen (2001).
7 Not invariably: Art. 14, closely modeled on the equal protection clause of the US Fourteenth Amendment, reads: "The State shall not deny to any person equality before the law or the equal protection of the laws within the territory of India."
8 Of course, this account of both is in many ways too simple; I refer primarily to the wording of the documents here, not to the complicated jurisprudential traditions stemming from them.
9 On a difference with Sen concerning the role of rights as "side-constraints," see Nussbaum (1997).
10 For the relation of this idea to objectivity, see Nussbaum (2001c).
11 See my discussion of this issue in Nussbaum (2000a: ch. 1); and for a rejoinder to perfectionist critics, see Nussbaum (2000c).
12 I am very skeptical of attempts to add group cultural rights to the list, because every group contains hierarchy; see Nussbaum (2001c).
13 This is what Sen said in response to the present paper at the conference on his work at the Zentrum für interdiziplinarische Forschung in Bielefeld in July 2001, at which it was first presented.
14 Thus, I do not see that we can coherently frame the notion of an increase or decrease in freedom without specification of whose freedom, and freedom to do what. See John Rawls (1971: 202): "[L]iberty can always be explained by a reference to three items: the agents who are free, the restrictions or limitations which they are free from, and what it is that they are free to do or not to do."
15 Sen stated at the Bielefeld conference that this is not his concern.
16 For a detailed discussion, see Nussbaum (2000b).
17 For the idea of "overlapping consensus," see the discussion in the previous section: the idea is that the values in the political conception can be viewed as a "module" that can be attached to different comprehensive conceptions. Rawls's list of primary goods is actually heterogeneous, including liberties, opportunities, and powers alongside income and wealth; recently, Rawls has added still other capability-like items to the list, such as access to healthcare and the availability of leisure time.
18 David Gauthier (1986: 18), speaking of all "persons who decrease th[e] average level" of well-being in a society.
19 For one particularly valuable treatment of this theme, see Rachels (1990).
20 See Kittay (1999: 77): "Dependency must be faced from the beginning of any project in egalitarian theory that hopes to include all persons within its scope." For a remarkable narrative of a particular life that shows exactly how many social structures play a part in the life of a mentally handicapped child from the very beginning, see Berube (1996).
21 In terms of the capabilities list, I argue in current work-in-progress that both the capabilities of the cared-for and those of the caregiver are multiple, and should be understood to include many of the existing capabilities on the list. Getting care when one needs it is a "primary good" in Rawls's sense, in that it is one of the essential prerequisites for being able to carry out one's plan of life.

References

Agarwal, Bina (1994) A *Field of One's Own: Gender and Land Rights in South Asia*, Cambridge: Cambridge University Press.

Agarwal, Bina (1997) "'Bargaining' and Gender Relations: Within and Beyond the Household," *Feminist Economics* 3 (1): 1–51.

Anderson, Elizabeth (1993) *Value in Ethics and Economics*, Cambridge, MA: Harvard University Press.

Berube, Michael (1996) *Life as We Know It: A Father, a Family, and an Exceptional Child*, New York: Vintage.
Chen, Martha A. (1983) *A Quiet Revolution: Women in Transition in Rural Bangladesh*, Cambridge, MA: Schenkman.
Fineman, Martha (1991) *The Illusion of Equality*, Chicago: University of Chicago Press.
Fineman, Martha (1995) *The Neutered Mother, the Sexual Family and Other Twentieth Century Tragedies*, New York: Routledge.
Folbre, Nancy (1999) "Care and the Global Economy," Background paper prepared for *Human Development Report 1999.*
Folbre, Nancy (2001) *The Invisible Heart: Economics and Family Values*, New York: The New Press.
Gauthier, David (1986) *Morals by Agreement*, New York: Oxford University Press.
Harrington, Mona (1999) *Care and Equality*, New York: Knopf.
Held, Virginia (1993) *Feminist Morality: Transforming Culture, Society, and Politics*, Chicago: University of Chicago Press.
Held, Virginia (ed.) (1995) *Justice and Care: Essential Readings in Feminist Ethics*, Boulder, CO: Westview Press.
Kittay, Eva (1999) *Love's Labor: Essays on Women, Equality, and Dependency*, New York: Routledge.
Locke, John ([1698] 1960) *The Second Treatise of Government*, in *Two Treatises of Government*, ed. Peter Laslett, Cambridge: Cambridge University Press, 1960.
Marx, Karl (1844) *Economic and Philosophical Manuscripts of 1844*, in Karl Marx, *Early Writings*, trans. and ed. T. Bottomore, New York: McGraw-Hill, 1964.
Mill, John Stuart ([1859] 1977) *On Liberty*, reprinted in Mill, *Collected Works*, ed. J. Robson, vol. 18, Toronto: University of Toronto Press.
Nussbaum, Martha (1997) "Capabilities and Human Rights," *Fordham Law Review* 66: 273–300.
Nussbaum, Martha (2000a) *Women and Human Development: The Capabilities Approach*, Cambridge: Cambridge University Press.
Nussbaum, Martha (2000b) "The Future of Feminist Liberalism," Presidential Address delivered to the Central Division of the American Philosophical Association, *Proceedings and Addresses of the American Philosophical Association* 74: 47–79.
Nussbaum, Martha (2000c) "Aristotle, Politics, and Human Capabilities: A Response to Antony, Arneson, Charlesworth, and Mulgan," *Ethics* 111: 102–140.
Nussbaum, Martha (2001a) "Disabled Lives: Who Cares?" *The New York Review of Books* 48: 34–37.
Nussbaum, Martha (2001b) "The Costs of Tragedy: Some Moral Limits of Cost-Benefit Analysis," in Matthew D. Adler and Eric A. Posner (eds) *Cost–Benefit Analysis: Legal, Economic, and Philosophical Perspectives*, Chicago: University of Chicago Press, pp. 169–200.
Nussbaum, Martha (2001c) "Political Objectivity," *New Literary History* 32: 883–906.
Nussbaum, Martha (2002) "Women and the Law of Peoples," *Philosophy, Politics, and Economics* 1 (3): 283–306.
Nussbaum, Martha (forthcoming a) "Constitutions and Capabilities," in M. Krausz and D. Chatterjee (eds) *Globalization, Development and Democracy: Philosophical Perspectives*, Oxford: Oxford University Press.

Nussbaum, Martha (forthcoming b) *Hiding from Humanity: Disgust, Shame, and the Law*, Princeton, NJ: Princeton University Press.

Rachels, James (1990) *Created from Animals: The Moral Implications of Darwinism*, New York: Oxford University Press.

Rawls, John (1971) *A Theory of Justice*, Cambridge, MA: Harvard University Press.

Rawls, John (1980) "Kantian Constructivism in Moral Theory: The Dewey Lectures," *Journal of Philosophy* 77: 515–571.

Rawls, John (1996) *Political Liberalism*, expanded paperback edition, New York: Columbia University Press.

Ruddick, Sarah (1989) *Maternal Thinking*, New York: Beacon Press.

Sen, Amartya (1980) "Equality of What?" in S. M. McMurrin (ed.) *Tanner Lectures on Human Values*, Salt Lake City: University of Utah Press. (Reprinted in Sen 1982, pp. 353–369.)

Sen, Amartya (1982) *Choice, Welfare and Measurement*, Oxford: Blackwell.

Sen, Amartya (1985) *Commodities and Capabilities*, Amsterdam: North-Holland.

Sen, Amartya (1990) "Gender and Cooperative Conflicts," in Irene Tinker (ed.) *Persistent Inequalities*, New York: Oxford University Press, pp. 123–149.

Sen, Amartya (1992) *Inequality Reexamined*, New York and Cambridge, MA: Russell Sage and Harvard University Press.

Sen, Amartya (1995) "Gender Inequality and Theories of Justice," in M. Nussbaum and J. Glover (eds) *Women, Culture and Development*, Oxford: Clarendon Press, pp. 259–73.

Sen, Amartya (1997) "Human Rights and Asian Values," *The New Republic* (July 14/21): 33–40.

Sen, Amartya (1999) *Development as Freedom*, New York: Knopf.

Sen, Amartya (2001) "The Many Faces of Misogyny," *The New Republic* (September 17): 35–40.

Tronto, Joan (1993) *Moral Boundaries: A Political Argument for an Ethic of Care*, New York: Routledge.

West, Robin (1997) *Caring for Justice*, New York: New York University Press.

Williams, Joan (2000) *Unbending Gender: Why Family and Work Conflict and What to Do about It*, New York: Oxford University Press.

3 A sufficientarian approach?

A note

Alexander Kaufman

This note disputes the view that the character of the capabilities approach is unqualifiedly sufficientarian. The approach, I argue, neither limits its attention to securing threshold levels of capabilities nor assigns absolute priority to the goal of securing such thresholds.

Martha Nussbaum's extension of Amartya Sen's capabilities approach, Richard Arneson argues, is of "paramount importance" because it clarifies the *character* of the ideal of social justice that is implicit in Sen's approach (see Arneson 2000, this volume). And that character, Arneson argues, is sufficientarian. The basic tendency of the capabilities approach – a tendency made explicit in Nussbaum's extension – is to require that egalitarians must privilege above all other concerns the goal of guaranteeing to all persons the capability to realize a "good enough" level of all essential functionings. Acceptance of a capabilities account of egalitarian concerns would therefore require that egalitarians must focus their attention almost exclusively on the circumstances of persons whose conditions fall below the stated thresholds of functionings.

Nussbaum's writings on the capabilities approach, Arneson observes, provide a welcome acknowledgment that the capabilities approach requires an objective account of value in order to justify the comparative assessments of quality of life that are necessary to ascertain the justice or injustice of social arrangements. The sufficientarian character of the resulting theory, however, is – in Arneson's view – both seriously problematic and characteristic of the capabilities approach.

Arneson develops his objection to sufficientarian theories by criticizing the moral importance assigned to sufficiency thresholds in such theories. In a *strict* sufficiency account of distributive justice, Arneson notes, "trumping moral weight" is assigned to the goal of lifting persons above the sufficiency threshold (this volume, Chapter 1, p. 28). Yet no sufficiency threshold could justify such absolute concern. Strict sufficiency accounts of social justice must therefore be rejected as implausible. Indeed, Arneson asserts, sufficiency accounts of social justice become increasingly plausible as they are progressively modified *to weaken or eliminate their sufficientarian character*. The most reasonable approach, Arneson concludes, is to abandon sufficientarianism altogether and to acknowledge that an acceptable conception of social justice should be characterized by the continuity: "a small shift in the values of the factors that morally matter should not generate a large shift in what we morally ought to do" (this volume, Chapter 1, p. 30).

Arneson is certainly correct to note that the priority that Nussbaum assigns to securing threshold levels of basic capabilities has significant implications for the character of her theory. The commitment to thresholds does not, however, define the full scope of Nussbaum's account of the capabilities approach; moreover, that approach may assign a priority that is less absolute than Arneson's reading suggests to securing minimum thresholds of basic capabilities. Nussbaum's account of capabilities equality in fact explores a wide range of egalitarian concerns and commitments, some of which appear more or less consistent with the approach characterized by continuity that Arneson advocates.

Arneson's critique thus suggests the need for a thorough investigation of the status in Nussbaum's account of the commitment to securing threshold levels of basic capabilities. The purpose of this note, however, is more limited: simply to highlight strands of Nussbaum's theory which suggest that her account of the capabilities approach may be more flexible and less single-minded than Arneson suggests. In particular, I will suggest that Nussbaum's approach recognizes fundamental priorities that extend beyond the goal of securing threshold levels of capabilities.

Capabilities and necessary conditions of justice

Nussbaum argues that it is "a necessary condition of justice for a public political arrangement that it deliver to citizens a certain basic level of capabilities" (2000: 71). While this is *one* necessary condition of justice in Nussbaum's account, however, it is not the only such condition. Rather, Nussbaum argues only that "social and political institutions should be chosen, *at least in part*, with a view to promoting at least a threshold level of ... [basic] capabilities" (ibid.: 75; emphasis mine).

Nussbaum (1988, 1990, 2000) discusses three categories of capabilities that are particularly relevant to the justice of social relations, and proposes necessary conditions of justice relating to all three categories. Each such necessary condition is required to address a potential effect of natural and social endowments on life chances. First, severe deprivation may impair the person's innate cognitive equipment (e.g., the ability to see, speak, reason). Second, lack of access to resources may deny the person the opportunity to realize more developed capacities (e.g., the ability to practice a trade or to do research). Finally, lack of the proper social conditions may deny persons with fully realized developed capacities the opportunity to employ those capacities.

Nussbaum addresses these potential effects by distinguishing between (i) *basic capabilities*, defined as innate forms of cognitive equipment; (ii) *internal capabilities*, defined as developed states of the person necessary for the performance of important functionings; and (iii) *combined capabilities*, defined as internal capabilities combined with external conditions suitable for their realization. The realization of basic and internal capabilities combined with the presence of suitable external conditions provides the person with the freedom to realize the form of life he or she chooses to live.

Each category of capabilities performs an essential role in enabling the person to choose and realize the form of life she wishes to pursue, but the roles performed by the different categories are quite different. The egalitarian obligation to address deficits in each category is determined by the role performed by the particular category and the practical implications of a deficit in that category.

Basic capabilities perform an essential role in the realization of any human form of life; a person who is deprived of the capability to see, hear or reason has been deprived of one of the qualities that makes a life essentially human. An acceptable theory of equality must therefore aim to secure threshold levels of basic capabilities for all persons. Access to adequate nourishment, health care and education should, that is, be among the unconditional guarantees of an acceptable egalitarian theory.

Complete realization of *internal capabilities* is not the subject of a similar commitment. (To be more accurate, such a guarantee will follow only from the combination of the capabilities approach with other relevant principles of justice.) The capabilities approach, in itself, merely argues for the obligation to secure each person's capacity to choose, rather than a guarantee of the full realization of the person's set of internal capabilities. The egalitarian's obligation to assist is therefore limited to assuring *access* to the social bases of the internal capabilities (e.g. access to various forms of education) necessary to ensure that each person realizes the capacity to choose freely the kind of life that they wish to pursue. This obligation is, nevertheless, significant and substantial.

Finally, different sets of internal capabilities will require different kinds of external conditions to be realized as *combined capabilities*. Even if a person has completely realized his or her internal capabilities, that person will not possess the opportunity to employ them productively if he or she has internalized a norm that prevents the person from applying his or her capabilities practically (e.g. a norm requiring that a wife should sacrifice her career to that of her husband). Nussbaum is particularly concerned about this possibility, citing with emphasis representative cases of Indian women who were "relegated … to substandard lives" – who willingly suffered physical abuse, malnutrition and illiteracy – because they had internalized norms of modesty and purity (2000: 42–43). A distribution of social goods will not satisfy the necessary conditions of justice under the capabilities approach if the choices of many citizens are determined by habituated preferences that induce their bearers to suppress their genuine preferences to realize at least a threshold level of capabilities. The external conditions of preference formation must, therefore, be designed to secure social conditions that will not produce distorted or habituated preferences.

The capabilities approach thus argues in favor of necessary conditions of justice relating to: (i) threshold levels of basic capabilities; (ii) access to the social bases of internal capabilities; and (iii) external conditions that secure the integrity of the process of preference formation. Moreover, the capabilities approach does not claim to provide a complete account of the necessary conditions of justice (Nussbaum 2000: 75, 86). Rather, far from assuming that the egalitarian obligation to assist is exhausted by necessary conditions derivable from capabilities analysis, the capabilities approach encourages evaluation of equality in terms of the capabilities metric as a basis for judgments implementing the requirements of broader accounts of justice (ibid.: 86).

Among the necessary conditions that the capabilities approach does generate independent of such broader accounts of justice, the obligation to secure an environment in which persons may develop their abilities and the capacity for choice free from distortive influences upon preference formation is both substantial and independent of the obligation to secure threshold levels of basic capabilities. Nussbaum, in fact, argues that the commitment to realizing such an environment requires a reorientation of liberal theory (Nussbaum 1990: 216). While traditional liberal theory assumes the priority of the right to the good, Nussbaum argues for the priority of the good to the right. That is, she argues for the specification of an account of basic capability interests and needs that will operate to constrain and shape the terms within which meaningful deliberation about the nature of justice may be framed.

Such a reorientation is necessary because of the profound influence that basic institutions exert over the process of preference formation. If (i) the most basic commitments of justice require the guarantee to each citizen of the ability to choose freely what type of life to pursue; and (ii) the pervasive effects of basic institutions may distort the process of preference formation and thus undermine the faculty of free choice; then (iii) justice requires special and fundamental protections regulating the basic institutions of society in order to guarantee an environment free from habituating influences.

Expressed in terms of Rawls's account of fair deliberations about justice, such an approach would require that capabilities protections must be modeled as a feature of the original position itself. If a capabilities account of the good is accepted as prior to the right, then not only would basic capabilities displace primary goods as the metric by which choosers behind the veil of ignorance measure the well-being of persons in the dimension of distributive justice, but the minimum condition of acceptability for principles designed to guarantee *liberty interests* would include the satisfaction of the necessary conditions of liberty as set out in the capabilities account. In particular, if the capabilities approach holds that the liberty interests of citizens have been respected "only if they have been given the necessary conditions for the exercise of choice and practical reason" (Nussbaum 1990: 216), then an adequate system of liberties would necessarily guarantee the satisfaction of these conditions.

The Rawls analogy therefore suggests the full scope of the necessary conditions of justice for a capabilities account of social justice – conditions that extend beyond the goal of securing threshold levels of capabilities. The capabilities approach offers both a new necessary condition for the acceptability of principles of justice, and a metric which may enhance the applications of complementary social theories.

Flexibility and political reflection

While the ambitions of capabilities theory thus extend beyond the goal of securing threshold levels of capabilities, can the theory in fact accommodate its diverse goals? When policies necessary to secure (i) threshold levels of capabilities, (ii) the necessary conditions for free preference formation, and (iii) equal opportunity generate inconsistent recommendations, how would Nussbaum's theory resolve conflicts? Nussbaum offers an approach to political judgment to address potential conflicts of this type.

Nussbaum in fact argues for an approach to political justification that "lies close to the Rawlsian account of argument proceeding towards reflective equilibrium" (2000: 101). Working from considered judgments of justice, viewed as provisionally fixed points, such an approach first generates a theoretical position reflecting the more general intuitions underlying our more particular judgments. The resulting theory is then tested against the set of provisional considered judgments. "By going back and forth, sometimes altering [the theory], at others withdrawing our judgments and conforming them to principle" (Rawls [1971] 1999: 18), the procedure aims to generate conclusions that can accommodate both the set of initial considered judgments and the more general theory worked up from those judgments.

The three necessary conditions of just social relations discussed above are thus elements of a general theory of capabilities that are to be tested against each other and against the considered judgments that motivate acceptance of the capabilities approach. Conflicts, if they arise, are to be resolved through a process of reflection that aspires to identify all relevant considerations, to assign the proper weight to each consideration, and to resolve conflicts according to the most persuasive arguments.

Arneson will respond, plausibly, that such a deliberative approach will ultimately generate judgments that coincide with his account of prioritarianism and that reject the idea of special priority for the goal of securing threshold levels of capabilities. Whether considered judgments on due reflection would ultimately endorse prioritarianism or the capabilities approach is clearly a question that deserves further examination.

References

Arneson, R. (2000) "Perfectionism and Politics," *Ethics* 111: 37–63.

Nussbaum, M. C. (1988) "Nature, Function and Capability: Aristotle on Political Distribution," *Oxford Studies in Ancient Philosophy* suppl. vol.: 145–184.

Nussbaum, M. C. (1990) "Aristotelian Social Democracy," in R. B. Douglass, G. M. Mara and H. S. Richardson (eds) *Liberalism and the Good*, London: Routledge.

Nussbaum, M. C. (2000) *Women and Human Development: The Capabilities Approach*, Cambridge: Cambridge University Press.

Rawls, J. ([1971] 1999) *A Theory of Justice*, Cambridge, MA: Harvard University Press.

Part II

A clearly differentiated approach?

4 Capability versus opportunity for well-being

Peter Vallentyne

Distributive justice is concerned with the justice of distributions of benefits and burdens. A very basic question concerns the nature of the benefits and burdens that are the ultimate concern of distributive justice. This question is independent of the question of how these benefits and burdens should be distributed (e.g. equally, so as to maximize the value to the least advantaged, or so as to maximize the total). Probably the most natural view is to hold that the relevant benefits and burdens are captured by net well-being (quality of life; e.g. happiness). This view, however, does not allow individuals to be held accountable for their choices (since it is not sensitive to how their well-being was generated). Several theorists, notably, G. A. Cohen, Richard Arneson, and John Roemer, have therefore endorsed something like *opportunity for well-being* as the relevant net benefit of justice. Justice, they claim, is concerned with the distribution of the opportunity for well-being and not with the distribution of well-being.

Amartya Sen and Martha Nussbaum have defended an apparently alternative view according to which the relevant net benefits are *capabilities*, understood as opportunities to function in life. This appears to be different from the opportunity for well-being approach because it emphasizes the value of activity over passive enjoyment. I shall argue, however, that although some versions of the capability view are incompatible with some versions of the opportunity for well-being view, the most plausible version of the capability view is identical to a slight generalization of the opportunity for well-being view.

Introduction

Amartya Sen (1979, 1980, 1982, 1985a–c, 1992, 1993, 1997, 1999) and Martha Nussbaum (e.g. 1988, 1990, 1999) have argued that justice is concerned, at least in part, with the distribution of capabilities (opportunities to function). Richard Arneson (1989, 1990), G. A. Cohen (1989, 1990), and John Roemer (1993, 1998) have argued that justice is concerned with something like the distribution of opportunities for well-being. I shall argue that although some versions of the capability view are incompatible with some versions of the opportunity for well-being view, the most plausible version of the capability view is identical to a slight generalization of the opportunity for well-being view.

This thesis is not novel. The significant similarity of the two views is obvious and has been noted by Arneson (1989: 90–93), Cohen (1989: 941–944; 1990: 378–380), and Sen (1993: 42–46). There are, however, many different versions of the capability view, and many of these are radically different from the opportunity for well-being view. I shall identify each of the ways that the capability view could diverge from a generalization of the opportunity for well-being view, and argue that none of them is plausible.

Background

The issue that concerns us is the "distribution of what?" question in the theory of justice, and not the "what form should the distribution take?" question. Much of Sen's writing has rightly focused on criticizing views, such as utilitarianism, that are insensitive (except contingently) to issues of distributive fairness. In what follows I shall assume that justice is sensitive to distributive fairness, but I shall not be concerned with how it is so concerned. It might be sufficientarian (concerned that people get enough), prioritarian (concerned with giving people as much as possible, but with extra concern for benefits to those who have less), or egalitarian (concerned with giving people equal benefits), some combination of these, or other principles.[1] Our focus is on the nature of the benefits with which justice is concerned.

Below, we shall examine more carefully the nature of capabilities and of opportunities for well-being, but it will first be useful to compare them in broad terms with *the commodity view*, which holds that justice is ultimately concerned with the distribution of resources, either for their own sake (independently of their value) or for the general value. One version is *resourcism*, according to which justice is concerned with the distribution of the value of resources, where this value is determined by its competitive value (based on demand and supply) in society.[2] Another version is *the primary goods approach*, which holds that justice is concerned with the distribution of primary goods, where these are understood as resources that every rational person would want more of.[3] The commodity view agrees with the capability approach and the opportunity for well-being approach that: (i) Justice is concerned with distribution of certain kinds of opportunities rather than outcomes (as opposed, for example, to standard utilitarianism and outcome egalitarianism). (ii) Justice is, or at least may be, concerned with the distribution of both nonpersonal resources (money, material objects, etc.) and personal resources (abilities, etc.). (Of course, some commodity theorists may reject this claim, but the point is that it does not follow from resourcism or the primary goods approach as such.) (iii) Justice requires, at least in some cases, that people with inferior personal resources be given superior nonpersonal resources.

Sen criticizes resourcism and the primary goods approach for failing to recognize that resources and primary goods are but means to what ultimately matters for justice. Each fails to take into account that individuals vary in their ability to convert these means into what ultimately matters (e.g. the opportunity to have a good life). Both of these views take the value of a resource – relevant for the justness of distributions – to be determined by how people in general value it. They are thus relatively insensitive to how the recipient values it and what he on she can do with it. The opportunity for well-being view is not, at least not obviously, subject to this objection. It holds that resources matter because they provide opportunities to individuals to have a good life. The capability view and the opportunity for well-being view are thus similar in this respect.

Before considering the details of the capability view, we need to identify and set aside two ideas that are sometimes associated with it. First, the capability view is sometimes offered as a conception of *well-being* (good life) rather than as a specification of the goods with which justice is concerned. According to this view (roughly), the quality of one's life depends not only on one's functioning, but also on one's opportunity to function.[4] This is not an implausible view, but it is not our present topic. We are concerned with the "distribution of what?" question for justice, not the "what is well-being?" question. We shall leave open what the most plausible conception of well-being (quality of life) is, and focus instead on the currency of justice. Although I shall claim in what follows that justice is concerned with something like the opportunity for well-being, this does not commit us to any particular conception of well-being.

The second point to note is that both Sen and Nussbaum sometimes seem to give a mixed answer to the "distribution of what?" question. They both seem to think that there are at least some very basic functionings for which justice is concerned that these *functionings* – as opposed to merely the opportunity for those functionings – be adequate. Sen and Nussbaum, that is, sometimes suggest that justice is concerned both with functioning and with the opportunity to function (capabilities). Although I would argue against the outcome-based concern, it is beyond the scope of this chapter to do so. In what follows, I shall limit myself to *pure* capability views. These may not be the views of Sen and Nussbaum.[5]

We are finally ready to begin to examine the capability view in more detail. There are three main questions that I shall address: (i) Exactly what kinds of *functioning* are relevant for capabilities? (ii) Exactly what kinds of *opportunity* to function are included in capabilities? (iii) How is the *value* of opportunities to function assessed? Adequate answers to each of these questions will, I shall argue, leave us with a generalized version of the opportunity for well-being view.

The relevant functionings: the selection problem, part 1

Capabilities are opportunities to function, but what are functionings? Sen makes it clear that functionings include not only doings but also states of being.[6] Thus, physical and mental activities (running, playing piano, etc.), as well as physical and mental states (such as being adequately nourished, being in good health, being happy), count as functionings. The question that concerns us here is whether *all* functionings are taken into account or only a subset. An adequate view, I shall argue, must take all functionings into account (although, depending on the theory of value, not all functionings may be deemed valuable).

The first point to note is that functionings need to be understood as including both desirable functionings (e.g. states of pleasure) and undesirable functionings (e.g. states of pain). Any theory that considered only desirable functionings would be oblivious to possibly very important differences in people's lives on the negative side. People often write as if all functionings are desirable, but this is, I believe, only for the sake of brevity. It seems clear that both positive and negative functionings need to be considered.

Moreover, *all* functionings should be considered. None should be excluded from consideration. By way of contrast, consider, for example, the view that justice is concerned only with the distribution of *basic capabilities*, on some (nonempty) criterion of basicness. There are different criteria of basicness that might be invoked to select the subset of relevant functionings. One is the *species-normal adult criterion*, according to which the relevant functionings are those that are exercised by most adults of the species on a regular basis.[7] Another is the *basic needs criterion*, according to which the relevant functionings are those necessary for survival and nonpoverty (on some specified criterion). Another is the *human flourishing criterion*, according to which the relevant functionings are those that are necessary for a good human life. There are, of course, many other possibilities.

Each of these criteria has some problems specific to its content, but I shall not address these. Instead, I shall argue that, no matter what the criterion, it is a mistake to hold that there are some functionings (the nonbasic ones) the opportunities for which are irrelevant to justice. The crucial point is that, for any functioning, there are some circumstances in which it would affect the quality of one's life, and justice is concerned with the opportunities for a good life. There are, for example, lots of functionings that are not necessary for a good human life, but which can radically enhance one's life. Being able to sing beautifully can very much enhance the quality of one's life, but it is not necessary for having a good human life. Given that any functioning could, under some circumstances, enhance (or otherwise affect) the quality of someone's life, it is a mistake to exclude some functionings from consideration. To do so would leave out something that is relevant to justice.

The problem generated by excluding some functionings is especially powerful for criteria of basicness that exclude lots of functionings. The species-normal adult criterion, the basic needs criterion, and even the good human life criterion are highly exclusionary. The former restricts basicness to those functionings that *most* adults of the species exercise on a *regular basis*. The latter two restrict basicness to those that are *necessary* for a certain kind of life (respectively: survival and non-poverty, and a good human life), and there are many functionings that are not so necessary but have a significant impact on whether that kind of life is achieved. Other criteria may be less exclusionary, but any exclusion of functionings is problematic.

This criticism is based on the assumption that the justice of a distribution of capabilities is determined by the distribution of the *value* of those opportunities to function for individuals. Functionings matter, as Sen himself has emphasized, because they are either means to, or constitutive of, good lives or other things that agents have reason to value. Hence, it is arbitrary to exclude some functionings that can contribute to such value.

One might think that if justice is only concerned with getting people above a certain threshold (e.g. either nonpoverty or minimal flourishing), then certain functionings and the opportunities therefore do not matter. That, however, would be a mistake. What matters for justice is the *value* of a person's capabilities. Even if justice is only concerned with ensuring that the value of each person's capabilities is adequate, no capability that contributes to the value of a person's capabilities should be excluded. Instead, all capabilities should be included and their value assessed, and then, if appropriate, improvements beyond the specified threshold can be deemed irrelevant to justice. (We shall consider in what follows the question of how the value of capabilities is assessed.)

This is not to deny, of course, that, for the purposes of public policy, some selection of functionings and capabilities will be needed. Public policy will, of course, need to focus on the most important and most easily assessable capabilities. The point here is that the basic principles of justice do not exclude any capabilities.

The relevant opportunities: the selection problem, part 2

Capabilities are opportunities to function, but how are *opportunities* to be understood here? One aspect of this question, as Sen (e.g. 1985a) has emphasized, is whether the concern is with *control freedom* only or, more broadly, with *effective freedom*. Control freedom to function is based on those possible functionings that one can bring about, or at least sufficiently influence the probability of coming about, through the appropriate exercise of one's will. Effective freedom to function includes all possible functionings independently of whether one's will (as opposed to nature and the choices of others) plays any role in bringing them about. Consider, for example, a person who is temporarily in a coma. Her freedom to be adequately nourished is in no way under her control, but if others are disposed to provide intravenous nutrition, she has effective freedom (but no control freedom) to be adequately nourished.

Sen sometimes writes as if he is concerned only with control freedom,[8] but, as he himself recognizes, this is not a plausible view. Control clearly is important, but it is not the only thing that matters for the purposes of justice. Consider two individuals who have the same control freedom to function, but for which one has a much greater effective freedom to function (e.g. to be adequately nourished). Justice is concerned with this difference. Indeed, suppose that they each have no control freedom (because they have lost volitional control), but one has effective freedom (because of nature and the choices of others) to have all basic needs met and to flourish, while the other has no effective freedom to have even basic needs met. It is quite implausible to think that justice is unconcerned with this difference. To do so, as Sen has emphasized, is to fail to recognize the extent to which economic, social, and political structures (as well as natural structures) can significantly affect one's opportunity to function. Hence, freedom to function must be construed as effective freedom. (Admittedly, it is misleading to call prospects to function that depend on the will of others, and not on one's will or interests, "freedoms," but I will simply follow Sen here and use "freedom" in this loose way.)

This conclusion has been challenged by Pettit (2001). He usefully identifies a third kind of freedom intermediate between control and effective freedom, and claims that justice is concerned with it. *Favor-independent freedom* includes control freedom, effective freedom provided by nature, and effective freedom provided by others when they have an enforceable obligation to provide it. It excludes, however, effective freedom provided by others when they have no enforceable obligation to provide it (i.e. when they are simply doing it as a favor).

Justice, we can grant, is concerned with favor-independent freedom to function, but it is not solely concerned with this freedom. It is, pace Pettit, also concerned with favor-dependent freedom. Consider, for example, the case (modified from an example of Sen 2001) of two mobility-disabled persons who are able to get out of their houses only with the help of others. Suppose that there is no enforceable obligation to provide such help, but one is able to get out because others are highly disposed to provide such help as a favor, and the other is not able to get out because others are highly disposed not to provide such help. Neither person has the favor-independent freedom to get out, since the outcome (getting out) is highly dependent on the favors of others. Justice, however, is surely concerned with the difference between the two individuals because the effective freedom to get out of one is significantly better than that of the other. (Sen 2001 makes roughly this reply.) Favor-independent freedom may be more valuable (even, perhaps, in a lexical way) than favor-dependent freedom, but that is not a reason for restricting capabilities to only those freedoms. All effective freedoms can be valuable, and all should be included in capabilities. The relative value of different kinds of effective freedoms should be addressed in the evaluation of capabilities, not in their definition.

The capabilities with which justice is concerned, then, are *effective* opportunities to function. One's capabilities at a given time, however, depend in part on one's past choices, and we now need to consider whether justice is concerned only with those capabilities that one has as a matter of brute luck or also with those that are the result of past option luck. A state of affairs is a matter of *brute luck* for an agent to the extent that the agent could not have (reasonably) deliberately influenced the possibility or probability of its occurrence or nonoccurrence. A state of affairs is a matter of *option luck* otherwise.[9] The effects on one's capabilities due to one's initial genetic endowment, one's early childhood environment, and unforeseeable adult events (e.g. being struck by an unforeseeable meteor) are a matter of brute luck. The effects on one's capabilities of one's past choices (e.g. whether to go mountain climbing) are a matter of option luck.

Consider two individuals, Diligent and Indolent, who start adult life (as a matter of brute luck) with identical capabilities. Suppose that Diligent wisely works very hard at developing her capabilities, while Indolent unwisely chooses short-terms pleasures over the significant long-term benefits of capability development. Now, after many years, Diligent's capabilities are significantly better than Indolent's. What does justice have to say about this situation? Does, for example, Indolent have a claim to more resources than Diligent because her current (as opposed to initial) capabilities are more limited?

The central point at issue is whether individuals can in principle be held accountable for their past option luck in the sense of having no claim against others to compensation when things turn out unfavorably. Brute luck theorists (whether egalitarian, prioritarian, or sufficientarian) claim – and I fully agree – that individuals can be so held accountable and that they have no valid claims to compensation for bad option luck.[10] More specifically, justice is only concerned with brute luck capabilities – that is, the capabilities that one has as a matter of brute luck (i.e. ignoring any impact from option luck).

The issue is, of course, complex. There are lots of important issues about the exact nature of brute luck, and it is controversial that justice is only concerned with the impact of brute luck. Furthermore, unlike my earlier claims about functionings and opportunities therefor, the present claim is exclusionary rather than inclusionary. My earlier claims were that all functionings (and not just basic functionings) and all opportunities (and not just control freedoms or favor-independent freedoms) should be included in the specification of capabilities. Those inclusionary claims are much easier to defend, since they do not require that the specified functionings or opportunities ultimately be relevant to justice (since the theory of value for capabilities may deem them irrelevant). The present claim, on the other hand, is exclusionary, and hence much more difficult to defend. If the relevant opportunities do not include option luck opportunities, then the latter are irrelevant to justice (no theory of value can make them relevant if they are not part of the thing being assessed).

Although the irrelevance to justice of option luck opportunities to function is not uncontroversial, it has been given strong defenses and is widely accepted.[11] I shall therefore assume that a plausible conception of the capability approach will limit capabilities to brute luck opportunities to function.

The evaluation of opportunities to function: the metric problem

Capabilities are opportunities to function, but how is the value of a capability set determined? There are at least two central issues here: (i) How is the value of functioning assessed? (ii) How is the value of a set of opportunities to function based on the value of the possible functionings?

How is the value of functioning assessed? Some of the main possibilities include narrow self-interest (i.e. self-regarding quality of life),[12] well-being (i.e. overall quality of life, including, for example, the impact on one's quality of life of other-regarding concerns), and overall agency goals (everything that the agent has reason to value, even if it does not affect the quality of his or her life). Furthermore, well-being can be interpreted subjectively (in terms of the agent's experiences; i.e. in welfare terms) or objectively (e.g. certain forms of perfectionism). Sen (e.g. 1985b, 1993) tends to favor, for the theory of justice, well-being evaluations, or perhaps both well-being and agency goal evaluations. He has also raised powerful objections against evaluating well-being as welfare (i.e. subjectively).

These are, of course, extremely important issues, but for the present purposes we can set them aside. The specification of the object of evaluation (capabilities) is independent of the specification of how that object is to be evaluated.[13] The generic capability approach could be combined with any theory of evaluation for capabilities, and for the present purposes there is no need to settle the evaluation issue. I shall return to this issue later, when I shall suggest that whatever theory of evaluation is adopted by the capability approach, this same theory can be adopted by a generalization of the opportunity for well-being view.

One might think that a fundamental difference between the capability approach and the opportunity for well-being approach is that the latter, but not the former, is committed to the commensurability in value of different functionings (and opportunities to function). This, however, is not so. First, any plausible view will recognize some commensurability. It will need to recognize, for example, that having severe multiple sclerosis and $40,000 is less valuable than being healthy and having $30,000 (with all else being equal). Functionings, that is, are not *radically incommensurable* in value: at least sometimes, an increase in one functioning combined with a decrease in another makes things better.

Perhaps, then, the difference is that the opportunity for well-being approach, but not the capability approach, is committed to functionings being *fully* commensurable in value in the sense that *any* decrease in *any* functioning can be compensated for by a sufficiently large increase in *any* other functioning. Admittedly, opportunity for well-being approaches are often presented as if well-being and the opportunities therefor are fully commensurable, but there is nothing in the approach that is committed to this claim. No amount of money, or other resource or functioning, may be able to fully compensate for having multiple sclerosis, but that does not invalidate the opportunity for well-being approach. It just means that the metric of value is less commensurable than might have been thought. Suppose, for example, that justice is concerned with *equality* of opportunity for well-being, and that the only relevant features of individuals are the presence or absence of multiple sclerosis and the amount of money that they have. Consider a two-person society in which one person has multiple sclerosis and the other doesn't. If multiple sclerosis is incommensurable with money, then justice will require curing the disease if possible. If that is not possible, then it requires giving all the money to the person with the disease. Given that the absence of multiple sclerosis is infinitely more valuable than any (finite) amount of money, this will (assuming interpersonal comparisons, which are granted by capability theorist) leave the disease-free poor person better off than the rich person with the disease. This is not perfect justice, but it is, by assumption, the most just feasible alternative, and capability reaches the same judgment. Hence, the issue of commensurability of functionings and opportunities therefor does not separate the two.

How, then, is the value of a set of *opportunities* to function based on the value of the possible functionings? One question here is whether opportunities are only instrumentally valuable for the functionings that they make possible. This seems implausible. Freedom (especially control freedom) sometimes matters for its own sake, and the value of opportunity sets should reflect this. Another question is whether (ignoring for the moment the intrinsic value of freedom) the value of an opportunity set is based on the expected (i.e. probability-weighted) value, the minimum (i.e. worst-case) value, or some other mathematical function of the value of the possible functionings – on the assumption, for example, that the agent chooses reasonably in some specified sense. These are very important issues, but fortunately we need not decide these issues either. We can allow all possible conceptions of the value of opportunities.

I am now finally ready to show that a plausible version of the capability approach is a version of a slight generalization of the opportunity for well-being approach.

Capabilities as opportunities for well-being

Capabilities are opportunities to function. Functionings include both doings and states of being, and no functionings are irrelevant to justice (justice is not concerned solely with basic functionings). Opportunities are to be understood as effective freedoms and not merely as control freedoms, but they include only brute luck opportunities and not the effect of past option luck on one's current opportunities. Opportunities to function can be evaluated many different ways as long as individual functionings (and hence capabilities) are not held to be radically incommensurable. With two qualifications, this gives us a version – indeed, a plausible version – of the opportunity for well-being view. The latter looks at one's effective brute luck opportunities for a good life, and, given the broad construal of functionings (all doings and states of being), this is just the effective brute luck opportunities to function – that is, capabilities.

One qualification concerns the evaluation of *functionings*. The opportunity for well-being approach evaluates functionings on the basis of the well-being of the agent. Some early versions of the opportunity for well-being view (e.g. Arneson 1989) assumed that well-being was *welfare* (i.e. some subjective conception of the quality of life). The opportunity for well-being approach, however, is not committed to this subjective method of assessment (and indeed Cohen (1989, 1990) rejects it). Strictly speaking, however, the opportunity for well-being approach is committed to evaluating opportunities on the basis of their contribution to *well-being* (quality of life, whether understood objectively or subjectively). An agent's well-being is based only on the quality of *his or her life*, and not on how well the world in general conforms to his or her desires and values. Sen (1985a) draws a useful distinction between *well-being freedom* – which is the freedom to achieve well-being (have a good life) – and *agency freedom* – which is the freedom to achieve that which one has reason to value. One has reason to value one's well-being, but one also can have reason to value many other things (e.g. the well-being of a loved one or the state of the environment).

If, as Sen tends to endorse, capabilities are assessed on the basis of their well-being freedom, then the capability view, so understood, is equivalent to a version of the opportunity for well-being view. If, however, capabilities are assessed on the basis of the agency freedom, then it is not so equivalent. A small generalization of the opportunity for well-being view, however, reintroduces the equivalency. Understand the *opportunity for value view* to be the same as the opportunity for well-being view, except that it does not require that functionings be assessed on the basis of well-being. It also allows that they be assessed on the basis of other agency goals (i.e. other states of the worlds that the agent has reason to value).

With one remaining qualification, the capability view is equivalent to the opportunity for value view.

The second qualification concerns the evaluations of *opportunities*. Opportunity for value (e.g. well-being) views have tended to assume that opportunities are only instrumentally valuable. They have tended to assume that freedom has no value except as conducive to achieving valuable functionings. We need not resolve this debate here. We need simply to ensure that opportunities may be evaluated in part on the basis of the freedom that they provide over and above the instrumental value that such freedom provides for obtaining valuable functionings. To make this explicit, we might better call it the *value of opportunity view*, which makes it clearer that opportunities may have intrinsic value.

A plausible version of the capability view, we can now see, is equivalent to a version of the value of opportunity view.

Conclusion

The capability approach and the opportunity for well-being view are not equivalent in general. First, the capability approach might limit functionings to doings (but not states of being), to basic functionings (on some criterion of basicness), or to control-freedom (rather than effective freedom) to function. The opportunity for well-being is incompatible with such restrictions, but such restrictions, I have suggested, are implausible. Second, the capability approach might include all opportunities to function, and not only brute luck opportunities to function. Although the opportunity for well-being approach could also make this move, it is implausible, and has not been made. Third, the capability approach might hold that functionings and capabilities are radically incommensurate. This is incompatible with the spirit of the opportunity for well-being view, but it is quite implausible (and makes the capability view an extremely weak view). Finally, the capability approach could adopt a theory of value for functionings that includes more than the impact on well-being (quality of life). It could, for example, hold that the relevant value is that which the agent has reason to value. Strictly speaking, the opportunity for well-being is incompatible with this view, but a slight generalization – the value of opportunities view – is not.

Although they are not in general equivalent, a plausible version of the capability view is equivalent to a version of the value of opportunities view. If this is right, the real work is in working out the appropriate theory of value for functionings and the opportunities therefor.[14]

Notes

1 Both Sen and Nussbaum seem to hold that ensuring that everyone's capabilities are at least adequate is an especially important (perhaps lexically primary) concern of justice.

2 See, for example, Dworkin (1981). For a defense of resourcism against Sen's criticisms, see Pogge (2003).
3 See, for example, Rawls (1971: 90–95) (where he limits his attention to social primary goods).
4 See, for example, Sen (1993). Sugden (1993: 6) notes that although Sen (1992: 50; 1993: 38) takes the capability set to include a specification of the actual functioning, it would be clearer to leave this out and simply claim that well-being is a function of both the capabilities and the actual functioning.
5 For penetrating discussions of Sen, see Cohen (1995), Alkire (2002), and Robeyns (2003). For an insightful analysis of the differences between the views of Sen and Nussbaum, see Crocker (1995).
6 In places, Sen writes as if functionings are restricted to doings (e.g. 1980, p. 218; parts of 1985b: 10–11). Cohen (1990) so interprets him, and criticizes him for ignoring states of being. Elsewhere (e.g. Sen 1985b: 10; 1985a: 197–198), however, Sen has made clear that functionings include states of being.
7 Something like this is advocated by Daniels (1990).
8 See, for example, Sen (1993: 31, 38, and the definition of F in 1985b: 11). Cohen (1990) criticizes him for the exclusive emphasis on what is under one's control. Sen elsewhere clarifies (e.g. 1993: 43; 1992: 64–66; 1985a), however, that he does not intend to limit capabilities to control freedom.
9 Dworkin (1981: 293) introduced the distinction between brute and option luck. For analysis thereof, see Vallentyne (2002).
10 In Vallentyne (2002), I argue that justice is only concerned with initial brute luck and not with (later) outcome brute luck. For simplicity, I here ignore this qualification.
11 See, for example, Dworkin (1981), Arneson (1989, 1990), Cohen (1989, 1990), and Roemer (1993, 1998).
12 Sen (1993: 37) calls this "standard of living."
13 Cohen (1990) has argued persuasively that metric of value issues (e.g. welfarism versus perfectionism) are independent of the outcome vs. opportunity issue.
14 For their helpful comments, I thank Dick Arneson, Ian Carter, Philip Pettit, Mathias Risse, Thomas Pogge, and Jo Wolff.

References

Alkire, Sabina (2002) *Valuing Freedoms*, Oxford: Oxford University Press.

Arneson, Richard (1989) "Equality and Equal Opportunity for Welfare," *Philosophical Studies* 56: 77–93.

Arneson, Richard (1990) "Liberalism, Distributive Subjectivism, and Equal Opportunity for Welfare," *Philosophy and Public Affairs* 19: 158–194.

Arneson, Richard (2000) "Perfectionism and Politics," *Ethics* 111: 37–63.

Cohen, G. A. (1989) "On the Currency of Egalitarian Justice," *Ethics* 99: 906–944.

Cohen, G. A. (1990) "Equality of What? On Welfare, Goods, and Capabilities," *Recherches Économiques de Louvain* 56: 357–382. Reprinted in Martha Nussbaum and Amartya Sen (eds) *The Quality of Life*, Oxford: Clarendon Press, 1993.

Cohen, Joshua (1995) "Amartya Sen: Inequality Reexamined," *Journal of Philosophy* 92: 275–288.

Crocker, David (1995) "Functioning and Capability: The Foundations of Sen's and Nussbaum's Development Ethic, Part 2," in *Women, Culture, and Development*, Oxford: Clarendon Press, 1995.

Daniels, Norman (1990) "Equality of What: Welfare, Resources, or Capabilities?" *Philosophy and Phenomenological Research* 50, supplement: 273–296. Reprinted in Norman Daniels (1996) *Justice and Justification*, New York: Cambridge University Press.

Dworkin, Ronald (1981) "What Is Equality? Part 2: Equality of Resources," *Philosophy and Public Affairs* 10: 283–345. Reprinted with minor changes in Ronald Dworkin (2000) *Sovereign Virtue*, Cambridge, MA: Harvard University Press.

Nussbaum, Martha (1988) "Nature, Function, and Capability: Aristotle on Political Distribution," *Oxford Studies in Ancient Philosophy*, suppl. vol. 145–184.

Nussbaum, Martha (1990) "Aristotelian Social Democracy," in R. Bruce Douglass, Gerald M. Mara, and Henry S. Richardson, (eds) *Liberalism and the Good*, New York: Routledge.

Nussbaum, Martha (1999) "Women and Cultural Universals," ch. 1 of *Sex and Social Justice*, New York: Oxford University Press.

Pettit, Philip (2001) "Capability and Freedom: A Defense of Sen," *Economics and Philosophy* 17: 1–38.

Pogge, Thomas W. (2003) "Can the Capability Approach Be Justified?" manuscript.

Rawls, John (1971) *A Theory of Justice*, Cambridge, MA: Harvard University Press.

Robeyns, Ingrid (2003) "Sen's Capability Approach and Gender Inequality: Selecting Relevant Capabilities," *Feminist Economics* 9 (2–3): 61–92.

Roemer, John (1993) "A Pragmatic Theory of Responsibility for the Egalitarian Planner," *Philosophy and Public Affairs* 22: 146–166.

Roemer, John (1998) *Equality of Opportunity*, Cambridge, MA: Harvard University Press.

Sen, Amartya (1979) "Utilitarianism and Welfarism," *Journal of Philosophy* 76: 463–89.

Sen, Amartya (1980) "Equality of What?", in S. McMurrin (ed.) *The Tanner Lectures on Human Values*, vol. 1, Salt Lake City: University of Utah Press. Reprinted in Amartya Sen (1982) *Choice, Welfare, and Measurement*, Oxford: Blackwell.

Sen, Amartya (1982) "Rights and Agency," *Philosophy and Public Affairs* 11: 3–37.

Sen, Amartya (1985a) "Well-being, Agency, and Freedom: The Dewey Lectures: 1984," *Journal of Philosophy* 82: 169–221.

Sen, Amartya (1985b) *Commodities and Capabilities*, Amsterdam: North-Holland.

Sen, Amartya (1985c) "Rights and Capabilities," in Ted Honderich (ed.) *Morality and Objectivity: A Tribute to J. L. Mackie*, London: Routledge and Kegan Paul.

Sen, Amartya (1990) "Justice: Means versus Freedom," *Philosophy and Public Affairs* 19: 111–121.

Sen, Amartya (1992) *Inequality Reexamined*, Cambridge, MA: Harvard University Press.

Sen, Amartya (1993) "Capability and Well-Being," in Martha Nussbaum and Amartya Sen (eds) *The Quality of Life*, Oxford: Clarendon Press.

Sen, Amartya (1997) *On Economic Inequality*, enlarged edition, Oxford: Oxford University Press. Original edition published in 1973.

Sen, Amartya (1999) *Development as Freedom*, New York: Alfred A. Knopf.

Sen, Amartya (2001) "Reply," *Economics and Philosophy* 17: 51–66.

Sugden, Robert (1993) "Welfare, Resources, and Capabilities: A Review of *Inequality Reexamined* by Amartya Sen," *Journal of Economic Literature* 31: 1947–1962.

Vallentyne, Peter (2002) "Brute Luck, Option Luck, and Equality of Initial Opportunities," *Ethics* 112: 529–557.

5 Capability and gender inequality

Timothy Hinton

Feminists are helping to reshape the research agenda of philosophical egalitarianism in many exciting ways. Consider two puzzles raised by feminist egalitarians. First, how should we think about gender inequality? Is inequality between men and women constituted by the unequal social and economic circumstances in which men and women find themselves, or is it constituted primarily by the relations of domination and subordination that exist between men and women? Second, what role, if any, should a normative conception of human nature play in our thought about gender relations?

Nussbaum's development of the capabilities theory intersects directly with these two puzzles. Nussbaum sees gender inequalities as inequalities in circumstance and functioning, rather than primarily as inequalities in social power. On the question of the place of a normative idea of human nature in accounting for the wrongs of gender inequities, Nussbaum feels that the human personality cannot be entirely the creature of power or the outcome of social construction, because capabilities are grounded in a substantive human nature that we all share.

In this chapter I intend to argue that Nussbaum's analysis of gender overlooks crucial elements of the feminist analysis of women's experience. By taking on board certain feminist insights that present gender inequality as primarily a matter of relations of power between men and women, the theory of capabilities emerges considerably strengthened.

On the other hand, I shall suggest that Nussbaum's naturalistic approach to justification in political philosophy can be of great use to radical feminists, for it enables us to provide an especially clear answer to the question of why oppression is bad for women: it prevents them from living lives that are (as Nussbaum puts it) "truly human."

Introduction

Feminists are helping to reshape the research agenda of contemporary political philosophy in many exciting ways. Consider two puzzles raised by feminist philosophers. One concerns the most plausible way to think about gender inequality. Using somewhat oversimplified categories, we can distinguish between the approaches of liberal and radical feminists respectively. The former see inequality between men and women as a matter of the unequal social and economic circumstances in which men and women are placed. In consequence, liberal feminists tend to think of the wrongs visited upon women in terms of the unjustified discrimination they suffer on grounds of gender. Radical feminists, on the other hand, see gender inequality as a matter of relations of domination and subordination that exist between men and women. On their view, men as a social group dominate women as a social group. For these feminists, unequal circumstances are symptoms or evidence of domination; they are not what inequality consists of. So we have a puzzle: is gender basically a matter of inequality in things like rights or access to goods, or is it, in addition, a matter of asymmetrical relations of group power? The second puzzle concerns the role, if any, that a normative conception of human nature should play in our thought about gender relations. Again using simplified categories, we can distinguish between ethical naturalists and ethical constructivists. The former maintain that there is something significant to be said about the role of human nature in accounting for the wrongs of gender inequality, while the latter maintain that there is no room for a normative idea of human nature in grounding our rejection of gender inequalities.

In *Women and Human Development: The Capabilities Approach*, Martha Nussbaum brings the theory of capabilities to bear on the problem of gender relations. Nussbaum proposes a theory of justice that weaves together three different strands of thought: her theory seeks to be at once liberal, feminist, and capability-based. Since each of these strands requires some explanation, I shall take them in turn. First, the theory is meant to be a form of political liberalism: it is supposed to provide support for traditional liberal principles and institutions. Nussbaum argues for a familiar array of individual rights and liberties, including freedom of religion, association, and speech. In addition, her approach is avowedly individualistic: she focuses throughout the book on the position of each person considered as a separate individual, an end in his or her own right. It is *politically* liberal because it seeks to justify these principles and institutions without appealing to any controversial metaphysical premises and because its concern is with specifically political goals. Nussbaum's theory is *feminist* because it focuses primarily on the plight and interests of women. In fact, she argues that feminism ought to show special concern for the needs and conditions of women in the developing world. She says that the material and social circumstances these women confront must be understood by engaging in dialogue with them before any proposals can be made about how to improve those circumstances (2000: 7). For this reason, much of the book focuses on Indian women in particular. Finally, Nussbaum's theory is capability based because its fundamental framework involves a concern with what people are "actually able to do or to be" (ibid.: 12) Unlike utilitarians, who focus on people's welfare (understood, say, in terms of preference satisfaction), or Rawlsians, who focus on people's shares of primary goods, Nussbaum is interested in the levels and kinds of functioning that people are effectively in a position to achieve.

Nussbaum's extension of the capabilities approach to the case of gender intersects directly with the two puzzles with which I began. On the question of the nature of gender injustice, Nussbaum affirms a version of what I characterized as the liberal feminist position. On her view, gender inequalities are inequalities in circumstance and functioning. They are not primarily inequalities in social power. On the question of the place of a normative idea of human nature in accounting for the wrongs of gender, Nussbaum falls squarely in the ethical naturalist camp. On her view, the human personality cannot be entirely the creature of social power or the outcome of social construction because capabilities are grounded in a substantive human nature that we all share.

In this chapter, I intend to argue that Nussbaum's capability-based account of women's situation overlooks certain crucial elements of the feminist analysis of women's experience. In particular, her account of the subjective effects of gender on people's sense of their own identity strikes me as inadequate. I shall argue that this is partly due to her conception of the nature of gender relations. This fault in Nussbaum's analysis – her failure to account for gender inequality in terms of relations of power between men and women – affects her use of capability theory. The result is an account of capability inequality less thoroughgoing than it otherwise might be. By taking on board some of the insights of radical feminists, I suggest, Nussbaum's theory of capabilities emerges considerably strengthened. For doing so enables us to raise questions about the extent to which gendered differences in capability are a result of underlying inequalities in social power.

On the other hand, I shall argue, at least some of the radical feminists who write about gendered power relations lean too far towards a constructivist conception of human identity. Accordingly, I shall argue that Nussbaum's naturalistic approach to justification in political philosophy can be of great use to radical feminists, for it enables them to provide an especially clear answer to the question of why oppression is bad for women, namely, that it prevents them from living lives that are (in Nussbaum's words) "truly human."

The chapter unfolds as follows. I begin with a discussion of Nussbaum's account of capabilities, connecting that account with her conception of human nature in particular. From there, I move to examine her analysis of gender relations. In particular, I focus on her use of Elster's model of preference malformation. I then discuss the radical feminist analysis of gender, pointing out how gender is construed in that analysis in terms of inequalities in social status and power. In the penultimate section I show how Nussbaum's approach can be enriched by incorporating this analysis of gender. I close by suggesting how the radical feminist account of power can draw from Nussbaum's naturalistic conception of capabilities.

Nussbaum on capabilities

There are two main parts to Nussbaum's theory of capabilities. The first involves distinguishing between three types of capabilities. At the ground level, Nussbaum places *basic capabilities*: these are innate abilities on the basis of which people develop more advanced capacities. Examples include the ability to see and hear, the capacity to speak and to master a language, and the capacity for love and gratitude. Next she identifies *internal capabilities*: these are developed states of the person that are, from the person's own point of view, sufficient conditions for exercising the relevant functions. As Nussbaum puts it, internal capabilities are "mature conditions of readiness." (2000: 84) To possess them is to be in a position to achieve the associated levels of functioning. Examples include the capacity for sexual pleasure in adults and the ability to make self-determining religious decisions. Note that some internal capabilities develop naturally – provided that their development is not impeded – while others require suitable education and training in order to come to fruition. Third, Nussbaum suggests, there are *combined capabilities*, which are internal capabilities in tandem with appropriate external conditions for exercising the relevant function (ibid.: 85). One has a combined capability to φ when there is nothing to impede one's achieving the functionings associated with φ-ing.

It is worth pointing out that this classification could do with some fine-tuning. For one thing, it is not obvious that there is such a thing as *the* capability to φ, if that is meant to denote a single ability a person possesses. Even in the case of an innate capacity for love, it is obvious that there is no single capability in question here: it a question of commanding a whole repertoire of abilities. Some of the abilities in the repertoire have to do with a person's emotional responsiveness: one has to be able to feel a certain kind of affection and warmth for others in order to be able to love them. Other related abilities are more matters of judgment and responsiveness to reasons of the right kind. To love someone, one has to be able to make judgments about how to treat that person and about what kind of treatment to expect from him or her in turn. Still others are a matter of the disposition of the will, a question of how one cares for others, what one is willing to do and say to them and for them.

Notice that it usefully follows from Nussbaum's analysis that a person can lack a combined capability to do a thing for two distinct kinds of reasons. Someone might be in the right set of internal states but lack the external wherewithal to exercise the internal capability those states make possible (as black South Africans under apartheid were fully capable of voting but lacked the right to do so). One might equally well be in the right external conditions while lacking the abilities to take advantage of them (as a tone-deaf owner of a Stradivarius might be incapable of playing a violin concerto).

The second part of Nussbaum's account involves the provision and defence of a detailed list of combined capabilities. Her point here is that governments have a duty to provide all of their citizens with each of the capabilities on the list. Securing any one of the items on the list involves ensuring both that each citizen is able to develop the relevant internal capabilities and that the external environment is conducive to their proper exercise. Nussbaum (2000: 78) believes that all citizens must be capable of

1. living to the end of a human life of normal length;
2. enjoying bodily health;
3. enjoying bodily integrity, freedom of movement and sovereignty over their bodily boundaries;
4. exercising their senses, imagination, thought and reason in searching for meaning in life;
5. forming emotional attachments to things and people free from fear, abuse and neglect;
6. forming and reflecting critically on a conception of the good and a plan of life;
7. being affiliated with other people and developing compassion and the virtues of justice and friendship while enjoying the social bases of self-respect and non-humiliation;
8. showing proper concern for other species;
9. engaging in play and recreation;
10. commanding a degree of political and material control over their environment.

For Nussbaum, two of these clusters of abilities are of paramount importance: the capabilities connected with practical reason and affiliation respectively (6 and 7). This is because, on her view, practical reason and affiliation give structure to and suffuse the rest of the capacities.

How is the list to be justified? According to Nussbaum, the primary weight of justification for the list of capabilities is carried by "the intuitive conception of truly human functioning and what that entails" (2000: 76) The basic appeal, then, is to a rich ideal of what it is to live a truly human life: to live as a human being should live is to be in a position to exercise this set of capabilities. Secondary weight is borne by an argument from actual consensus: the list has evolved over the course of several years of cross-cultural discussion (ibid.: 76). So, as I read Nussbaum, the heart of her case for the list of capabilities is a kind of reflective equilibrium argument. She starts from an ideal of properly human functioning, makes inferences from that ideal to a set of capabilities needed to secure such functioning, and then tests the results against (i) the considered convictions of a cross-cultural group of reflective people, and (ii) the ideal itself.

The ideal of functioning is nicely illustrated by the following passage from Marx that Nussbaum finds especially significant:

> It is obvious that the *human* eye gratifies itself in a way different from the crude, non-human eye; the human *ear* different from the crude ear, etc. … The *sense* caught up in crude practical need has only a *restricted* sense. For the starving man, it is not the human form of food that exists, but only its abstract being as food; it could just as well be there in its crudest form, and it would be impossible to say wherein this feeding activity differs from that of *animals*.
>
> (Karl Marx, quoted, in Nussbaum 2000: 34)

Nussbaum enters two main claims about the ideal. First, certain functions ("beings and doings") are held to be especially important in human life, such that their presence or absence fixes whether or not we have human life at all. Second, there is a way of performing these functions that is distinctively or properly human. The human eye gratifies itself by gazing at beautiful things and by being used in performing higher-level functions such as reading or interpreting the look on a person's face.

This ideal gives rise to a picture of what it is to be human, a picture of the value or dignity associated with the members of our species. As Nussbaum puts it,

> The core idea is that of the human being as a dignified free being who shapes his or her own life in cooperation and reciprocity with others, rather than being passively shaped or pushed around by the world in the manner of a "flock" or "herd" animal. A life that is really human is one that is shaped throughout by these human powers of practical reason and sociability.
>
> (2000: 72)

So, each human being, merely by virtue of being human, commands a certain ethical status, the status of someone entitled to shape his or her own life on decent terms with those around. Basic to the enjoyment of such a status is the possession of practical reason and the capacity for humiliation-free social relations with others. But because our ethical status is natural to us, rather than being the outcome of social conventions, all social relations have to show proper respect for our basic dignity as self-determining beings.

Nussbaum's analysis of gender relations

Nussbaum appears to think of gender inequality as consisting of two basic evils. The first is unequal social and political circumstances. These include sharply different levels of access to education, healthcare, and jobs for men and women. They also involve differences in access to the legal and political system and distinct kinds of cultural demands. Men and women are often expected to do different kinds of paid labour, while certain unpaid activities, such as housework and childrearing, are thought of as distinctively feminine tasks. These inequalities in circumstance give rise to quite disparate day-to-day experiences and treatment in the home, in the workplace, and in civil and political society. They are connected with the second main form of inequality between men and women that troubles Nussbaum. This has to do with grave differences in the levels of human functioning which men and women actually achieve. These include things like the fact that women are often less well nourished than men, their health tends to be worse, they are more vulnerable to domestic violence and rape, their imaginative and cognitive faculties are less well developed, and they are unable to enjoy rewarding types of love. Nussbaum thinks that gendered inequalities in circumstances give rise to gendered inequalities in human functioning, there being a fairly straightforward causal relation between these two kinds of evils. In summarizing her basic analysis of gender inequality, she says that

> all too often women are not treated as ends in their own right, persons with a dignity that deserves respect from laws and institutions. Instead, they are treated as mere instruments of the ends of others – reproducers, caregivers, sexual outlets, agents of a family's general prosperity.
>
> (2000: 1)

What women lack, on Nussbaum's view, are the elements necessary to lead "fully human" lives: in short, they suffer from unequal capabilities for being and doing the sorts of things that are worthy of human dignity.

In her discussion of the lives of Vasanti and Jayamma, the two Indian women whose stories she tells in some detail, Nussbaum traces the evils of unequal circumstance and unequal functioning back to two fundamental wrongs perpetrated against them. The first is the systematic discrimination that these women have experienced on account of their gender. As Nussbaum puts it,

> Both have been raised in a nation in which women are formally the equals of men, with equal political rights and nominally equal social and employment opportunities. ... Both, however, have also suffered from deprivations that do arise from sex discrimination, and sex discrimination is such a pervasive factor in these women's experience of poverty that it would be wrong to say that any aspect of their poverty is fully understandable without taking it into account.
>
> (2000: 20)

Nussbaum is here identifying the basic injustice perpetrated against Vasanti and Jayamma in civil society as taking the form of unfair discrimination against them. She does not think of their situation primarily in terms of relations of subordination to men. To be sure, Nussbaum is keenly aware of their heavy reliance on men in their domestic lives. This dependence on men is the source of the second way in which Nussbaum thinks that these women have been wronged. All too often, the men in their lives have simply failed to act on their responsibilities to Vasanti and Jayamma: they have simply taken their duties too lightly (ibid.: 21). So, Nussbaum finds these men to blame for failing to do what they ought to do. What this shows is that Nussbaum is not conceptualizing the dependence of women on men in terms of asymmetrical power relations. Instead, she sees it as making possible a host of ways in which men can be in dereliction of their duties.

It is a familiar feminist claim that gender inequalities have profound and pervasive subjective effects on people. The idea is that both men and women internalize norms associated with their respective genders, and this has deeply disfiguring effects on their psychology. Nussbaum is by no means insensitive to these subjective effects of gender inequalities. As she sees it, the unequal social and political circumstances of men and women affect both their "external options" and their "inner lives" (by which she means "what they hope for, what they love, what they fear, as well as what they are able to do" (2000: 31)). She sometimes puts the point by saying that one ought not to underestimate the extent to which differences in external options "construct differences in thought" (ibid.: 31). Indeed, on her view, a person's external options are often profoundly shaped by tradition and social context. As a result, Nussbaum argues, tradition and context play an equally important role in "constructing desire and preference" (ibid.: 32). In the course of telling the stories of Vasanti and Jayamma, Nussbaum describes some of these subjective effects of gender inequality on the two women:

> [W]e find it odd that Jayamma seems to accept this [sex discrimination in employment] as the way things are, and yet we know that women suffering from discrimination have not always been able to organize to fight against inequality. … The fact that [Vasanti] does not even seem to want to go to school is not so surprising either, or the sign of an alien consciousness, given that she does not see any signs of a better way of life that she could enjoy by becoming educated.
>
> (ibid.: 23)

When it comes to offering a theoretical analysis of the subjective effects of gender, Nussbaum appears to construe those effects as a matter of "preference-deformation." The main theoretical model she has in mind is Jon Elster's explanation of malformed desires in terms of the mechanism of adaptive preferences (Elster 1982). The paradigm, for Elster, of adaptive preference change is provided by the fox's desires in Aesop's fable. The fox begins by wanting the grapes; but then, seeing them become unavailable, he forms the belief that they are sour. Owing to this belief, the fox finds himself no longer desiring the grapes.

Elster distinguishes between adaptive preferences like this and several other ways in which preferences are responsive to changes in the feasible set with which the agent is confronted. First, they differ from preferences that come about through learning and experience, in that adaptive preferences are always more or less reversible as the feasible set changes. Second, they differ from preferences arising from prior commitments the agent has made. If the agent prefers something in the feasible set and would continue to prefer it in a much larger set of alternatives, that might be because he or she has bound herself to that preference by a precommitment. Ulysses prefers not to give in to the sirens' song, so he deliberately structures the feasible set in such a way that giving in to it is no longer an option for him. Here the preference in question itself gives rise to the restricted feasible set. In the case of adaptive preferences, it is the shrinking feasible set that gives rise to the preference. Third, Elster distinguishes between preferences formed by adaptation and those that come about through manipulation by someone else's deliberate agency. Someone whose desires and wants are shaped by another agent has exogenously arising preferences, while adaptive preferences are endogenous. Fourth, adaptive preferences are to be distinguished from preferences that arise from deliberate efforts to shape one's own character. The difference here turns on whether or not the change in preference is intentionally induced by the agent, as opposed to taking place "behind his or her back," as it were. Finally, they differ from preferences connected with wishful thinking, because in cases involving the latter, we have a desire that gives rise to a change in belief about the situation, rather than a belief that causes a change in desire. Someone whose team fails to win the game might come to believe that this was a result of cheating by the other side, rather than coming to think that victory is not such a great thing anyway.

At the core of Elster's analysis is a kind of ideal conception of what it is to be a free person. This seems plausible, since, after all, adaptive preferences are morally troubling because they seem in some way to be nonautonomous: they arise behind the back of the person whose preferences they are. Elster proposes that we explicate what it is to be a free person in terms of "being free to do all the things one autonomously wants to do" (1982: 228). He frankly admits to having no general criterion for distinguishing between autonomous and nonautonomous desires, but he is happy to classify adaptive preferences as one instance of the more general class of wants lacking in autonomy. He then suggests that we can screen these preferences out by adopting a certain conceptual condition. This specifies that for a preference to be autonomous, the agent must be free to satisfy the preference and free to do otherwise. As he puts it, "If I want to do x, and am free to do x, and free not to do x, then my want cannot be shaped by necessity." (ibid.: 228).

The radical feminist analysis of gender relations

In my discussion of the ideas of radical feminist writers, I want to pick up on two main themes. One is the account of gender as involving domination; the other is their analysis of the subjective effects of that domination. I shall call the first the domination thesis and the second the distortion thesis.

The domination thesis says that gender relations are social relations in which men dominate women. There are at least two different aspects to the thesis, as I understand it. One is that a person's gender identity is created socially rather than being a matter of brute natural fact. The suggestion is that the character traits, expectations, and ideals having to do with being a man or being a woman, at least as we understand these roles, are largely the result of social convention. In order to clarify the claim that gender is socially constructed, I shall follow those feminist philosophers who distinguish between sex and gender. In drawing this distinction, such writers identify sex as a way of classifying human beings according to their anatomical characteristics, so that, in consequence, there are two main sex classes, namely, those of male and female. (We can leave it open at this stage whether or not these categories are natural kinds or are themselves socially constructed.) Gender, on the other hand, is taken to be a system of social roles that is socially constructed, with its two main classes being the roles of men and of women.

What is it for roles to be socially constructed? I take the basic idea to be that some or other system of social norms constitutes the roles in question. Were it not for that system of norms, such roles would not exist. For instance, a system of constitutional and political norms defines what it is to occupy the role of President of the United States. Something similar is being claimed for the role of being a man or a woman. Informal social rules and expectations define what it is to be and to behave like a man or a woman. Sally Haslanger suggests that the set of social norms that constitutes the gender system comprises "clusters of characteristics and abilities that function as a standard by which individuals are judged to be 'good' instances of their gender; they are the 'virtues' appropriate to the gender" (1993: 89). To be a good man or a good woman is to live one's life in accordance with those norms.

The second aspect of the domination thesis is that the social positions (or "social labels," as MacKinnon sometimes calls them) of being a man and being a woman involve asymmetrical relations of power (MacKinnon 1987: 164). It is not simply that men and women occupy different social roles or that what distinguishes these roles is simply a difference in social function. Rather, the point is that men have power over women in ways that women are lacking in power over men. Being a woman in a sexist society means occupying a social role that is subordinate to the position of men because men have the power to define the social position of women.

In addition, men can make women do things like yield to sexual advances, or put up with sexual harassment or remain silent about domestic violence, while women cannot do these things to men. Notice that men's having power is not necessarily a matter of their actually treating women badly, but rather of their having the ability to determine whether or not women are so treated.

Tying the two parts of the domination thesis together, MacKinnon defines gender as "a nonnatural characteristic" that arises out of or is constituted by a certain "division of power in society" (1989: 95).

What, then, of the distortion thesis? This has to do with the subjective effects of the gender system. It says that as a result of growing up in a gendered society, people acquire deeply distorted identities. I shall discuss three different aspects of this thesis. The first is the idea that gender enters very deeply into people's sense of their identity, and of what matters most to them. At one point, MacKinnon describes the domain of gender as having to do with how the distinct social positions of men and women are lived out in day-to-day life. She mentions various dimensions of this process:

> Gender and sexuality, in this view, become two different shapes taken by the single social equation of male with dominance and female with submission. Feeling this as identity, acting it as role, inhabiting it and presenting it as self, is the domain of gender.
>
> (1989: 143)

MacKinnon is here identifying several closely related aspects of the lived experience of being gendered. There is, to begin with, a sense of inner identification with one's socially imposed gender. One sees oneself as being a man or a woman, and that fact about oneself is fundamental to one's sense of who one is. Gender positions are lived out by people as though they are (at least partially) constitutive of their identity. But this identification is not simply an inner process: its outer criteria are deeply ingrained forms of behavior. It shapes how one dresses, speaks, carries one's body and responds to other people. The point is that in behaving in these ways – in playing these roles – people see themselves as inhabiting and presenting aspects of themselves. They are not external social functions but deeply embedded in our consciousness and conduct.

Marilyn Frye offers a very insightful account of the pervasiveness of gender identification in our lives and language. For instance, what she calls "sex-marking behavior" commonly occurs in informal social interactions of the kind that occur in restaurants and churches (Frye 1983). If a man and a woman enter a restaurant together, for instance, the man is likely to be greeted first, or eye contact will be made with him before the woman. We have elaborate repertoires of behavior that differ according to the gender of the person we are interacting with: whether one shakes hands, or slaps someone on the back or offers the "high five" gesture, for instance. The genders of the people interacting will often determine such matters as

> frequency and duration of eye contact, frequency and type of touch, tone and pitch of voice, physical distance maintained between bodies, how and whether you smile, use slang or swear words, whether your body dips into a shadow curtsy or bow.
>
> (ibid.: 20)

A second aspect of the distortion thesis is that the subjective effects of gender are the result of inequalities in social power. The crucial point about sex-marking behavior is that it enables a person's gender identity itself to be a source of power or weakness. Consider something as simple as taking a walk at night. If one announces oneself as a man in such a situation, that makes one less likely to be a target for assault, since one of the signals one is sending is that one is better able to fight off any would-be attackers. If one announces oneself as woman, then would-be assailants take one to be less capable of fighting them off. As Frye puts it, "though both men and women must behave in sex announcing ways, the behavior which announces femaleness is in itself both physically and socially binding and limiting as the behavior which announces maleness is not" (1983: 32). Identifying as a woman means engaging in behavior that is "physically and socially" constraining. It constrains people socially because any female who behaves differently has to put up with severe social pressure to "act like a woman." It constrains people physically because the clothing one is expected to wear restricts one's movements and because one's body itself becomes deeply habituated to certain kinds of movements. A body that has never learned to throw a punch is unlikely to be capable of landing a good blow. In sum, Frye concludes:

> Constant sex-identification both defines and maintains the caste boundary without which there could not be a dominance–subordination structure. The forces which make us mark and announce sexes are among the forces which constitute the oppression of women, and they are central and essential to the maintenance of that system.
>
> (ibid.: 33)

In similar vein, MacKinnon suggests that the pervasiveness of gender relations understood in terms of unequal relations of power is revealed by systematically reflecting on ordinary experiences of ordinary women. For instance, one of the discoveries of women's consciousness-raising groups is that these relations of domination are manifested even in casual encounters between men and women. She gives an example of a woman who, during a group discussion, mentioned being upset by the leering way a man on the subway had looked at her (MacKinnon 1989: 89). For many women, such treatment leads to feelings of degradation and depression. It also seems to them to highlight their relative powerlessness, in that men have the power to affect women in this way, but women do not have the power to reciprocate. As a result of reflecting on their experiences, MacKinnon says, "Women learn that the entire structure of sexual domination, the tacit relations of deference and command, can be present in a passing glance" (ibid.: 89).

The final aspect of the distortion thesis is that the identity women come to acquire as a result of growing up in sexist conditions is a distortion of who they really are. For MacKinnon, women inhabit a social world in which they are "systematically deprived of a self" (1989: 89). The process in which this is enacted and lived out is what it amounts to to be socialized as a woman. Like Frye, MacKinnon finds the results of male domination to be pervasive. She suggests that it is particularly as a result of consciousness raising that feminism

> has grasped the completeness of the incursion into who one really becomes through growing up female in a male-dominated society. This effect can be understood as a distortion of self. It is not only one's current self one is understanding, but the self that understands what one has become *as* a distortion.
>
> (ibid.: 103)

In referring to "the incursion into who one really becomes," I take MacKinnon to mean that women's deepest sense of themselves is shaped in oppressive ways by their formation in a society organized along gender lines. But notice that if a distortion of self occurs as a result of growing up in oppressive conditions, it must be possible to identify some aspect of the self that is not distorted. Consider a comparison with a distorted message. If I distort what you say, then there is a difference between what I claim you have said and what you really said. If women suffer from a distortion of self, there must be a difference between the identity they take up and the identity they authentically possess.

What consciousness-raising groups do for women, on this account, is to provide them with conditions under which they can come to identify who they really are. For MacKinnon, reflecting on the process of how one becomes who one is in gender terms has a dual aspect to it. It is both sobering to see the depths of the grip of one's "imposed status" and liberating to begin to see how to rid oneself of it:

> Realizing that women largely recognize themselves in sex-stereotyped terms, really do feel the needs they have been encouraged to feel, do feel fulfilled in the expected ways, often actually choose what has been prescribed, makes possible the realization that women at the same

> time do not recognize themselves in, do not feel, and have not chosen this place.
>
> (1989: 103)

Reflection on how they have become who they are enables women to acknowledge the fact that many of their desires seem to come from authentic depths within them. Reflecting critically on the process enables them to see that who they have been shaped to be is a distortion. In fact, the mere experience of reflecting in this way enables them to stand back from that identity and no longer to feel compelled to identify with it.

Capabilities, power, and gender

Nussbaum holds that to ask about a person's capabilities is to ask about what she is "actually able to do and to be" (2000: 12). I think she is quite right that this is a much more fruitful way of asking about the situation of women than asking about their levels of preference satisfaction or about the resources to which they have access. But Nussbaum's liberal feminism prevents her from making fully effective use of the capabilities approach in her examination of gender. This is so for three reasons.

The first is that, as we have seen, Nussbaum thinks of gender inequality not primarily as an inequality in social power, but as an inequality in treatment. On her view, women suffer from sex discrimination, and that is at the root of the different levels of functioning women and men are able to achieve. Second, Nussbaum's ethical individualism seems to go hand in hand with a kind of explanatory individualism that causes her to misdiagnose the nature of women's oppression. From the plausible ethical claim that our ethical and political focus must always be on the functioning of each distinct person considered as an end in her own right, Nussbaum seems to infer that the only factors we can appeal to in explaining the plight of women are individualistic factors such as people's beliefs and desires. This overlooks a key insight of radical feminists, namely, that women's oppression is a matter of men as a social group exercising domination over women as a social group. Finally, Nussbaum's use of the deformed preferences model renders her unable to recognize the full range of subjective effects of gender domination.

In what follows I want to consider these objections in greater detail. In the course of doing so, I shall be suggesting ways in which the insights of radical feminists can deepen and extend the capabilities approach to gender inequality that Nussbaum has pioneered.

If to ask about capabilities is to ask about what people are able to do and to be, capabilities need to be situated in the context of the social relations in which people actually live out their lives. To be sure, unequal treatment or gender discrimination is one kind of barrier preventing people from doing and being what they might otherwise do and be. It seems plausible to think that gender discrimination affects capabilities in the following way: men often enjoy a certain combined capability (say, that of being kiln operators), while women do not. The reason for such an inequality in capability is that women suffer from informal discrimination in civil society. Although they possess the internal capability to perform the task, there are barriers in the form of social expectations that make it impossible for them to exercise that capability.

But so far we have not gone deeply enough into the underlying factors shaping women's combined capability situation. The first thing we need to ask is: to what extent are gendered differences in capability a result of underlying inequalities in social power?

Nussbaum tells us that Vasanti's husband began taking the household money and using it to buy alcohol. In other words, he was in a position to steal her share of resources without fear of recrimination. When he had run out of that money, he took advantage of a local government policy offering cash payments to men willing to have a vasectomy. All the while, presumably, he was getting Vasanti to do the reproductive work in their home. Eventually he began to take out his frustrations on Vasanti: he was able to inflict physical violence on her. Note that his behaving in these ways – stealing money with impunity, depriving Vasanti of the possibility of children, beating her – was made possible by an inequality in power between him and his wife. His status as a man gave him the power to do these things.

This raises an important question: what explains this profound asymmetry in power? Here the explanation that radical feminists would offer is that men as a group have power over women as a group. It is not just that men are better-circumstanced than women, but that there are relations of domination and subordination between these social groups. In brief, these relations can be thought to work as follows.

Men have the power to impose a certain social status on women, while women lack the power to impose any kind of social status on men. Nussbaum in fact offers a very accurate description of the status that men impose on women, although she does not describe it in those terms. In situations of profound inequality, she tells us, women become "mere instruments of the ends of others – reproducers, caregivers, sexual outlets, agents of a family's general prosperity" (2000: 2). This is exactly what it is to suffer an imposed status: one becomes a mere instrument of the ends of others. But in bearing the imposed status of being reproducers, caregivers, and so forth, women are not merely instruments of anonymous others. They are instruments, precisely, of men.

The effect of men as a group having exercised their power to impose that status on women is that women are socially inferior to men. Norms of behavior and social expectations that shape how people see themselves enable men to do things to women that women are incapable of doing to men. Assume that Vasanti had the internal capability of stealing from her husband and was even capable of using physical violence against him. Nevertheless, her subordinate social status deprived her of the combined capability of exercising those capabilities. There was no symmetry in social power; consequently, they did not have the same combined capabilities.

Once we move to thinking of gender inequality in these terms, we have to ask questions about what the members of the social category *men* are capable of doing to members of the social category *women* or about what members of the social category *men* are capable of getting members of the social category *women* to do.

If this is along the right lines, we should note two mistakes in Nussbaum's way of thinking about gender and capability. The first is that she understands capability as fundamentally a two-place relation between a person and an activity. Ascriptions of capability in her analysis seem always to take the basic form "x is capable of φ-ing" where "x" names an individual and "φ-ing" stands for an active verb. Once we are properly sensitive to the existence of inequalities in social status, we have to allow that at least some capability ascriptions are more accurately to be thought of in terms of three-place relations between two people and an activity: "x is capable of getting y to φ" or "x is capable of φ-ing (from or over) y." Accordingly, the capability questions we must ask have to be not only of the form "what is x able to do and to be?" but also of the form "what is x able to get others to do and to be?"

Nussbaum's second mistake is to overlook the fact that, in the case of gendered inequalities in capability, it is in virtue of the social properties of being a man or being a woman that people have these unequal capabilities. Correcting this problem necessitates rethinking the explanatory individualism that seems to pervade much of Nussbaum's analysis of the situation of women. Consider the following passage, in which Nussbaum reflects on the fact that Vasanti stayed for years in an abusive marriage. Nussbaum tells us that Vasanti did not value her bodily integrity

> especially before her husband's vasectomy, when she thought she might still have children. Like many women, she seems to have thought that abuse was painful and bad, but still a part of women's lot in life, just something women have to put up with as part of being women dependent on men, and entailed by having left her own family to move into a husband's home. That idea that it was a violation of rights, of law, of justice, and that she herself has rights that are being violated by her husband's conduct – these ideas she didn't have at that time, and many women all over the world don't have them now.
>
> (2000: 112–113)

This explanation for Vasanti's staying in the marriage appeals only to facts about Vasanti's beliefs and desires. Her desire to have children with her husband and her belief about what women must put up with are the only explanatory factors Nussbaum invokes here. But this seems to me to overlook what is really fundamental in accounting for Vasanti's situation. We need to know where these beliefs and desires come from. And part of the answer, surely, must lie in the fact that her social position was such that she simply lacked the power to stand up to her husband. The status that had been imposed on Vasanti as a woman was that of a person who could be treated in these ways. In her society, being a woman means being someone who is fundamentally lacking in social standing. The fact that she lacked such standing helps to explain why she might have formed the belief that domestic abuse is "a part of women's lot in life." Those who are comparatively powerless must resign themselves to the inevitable results of lacking power. In this way, a person's gender itself is revealed to be a capability-shaping asset or liability. Men are capable of doing things to women that women are incapable of doing to men.

Notice that in rejecting Nussbaum's explanatory individualism, I am not attributing any kind of mysterious explanatory power to groups as entities over and above the individuals comprising them. The appeal is, instead, to the social properties that membership in groups confers on people. In certain societies, having the social property of being a man gives one the power to do certain things, while having the social property of being a woman does not. Recall Haslanger's definition of gender norms as "clusters of characteristics and abilities that function as a standard by which individuals are judged to be 'good' instances of their gender; they are the 'virtues' appropriate to the gender." Being a good or a true man in India appears to involve exercising domination over women, while being a good or a true woman in that society involves being the passive recipient of such treatment.

The last of my general criticisms of Nussbaum has to do with her reliance on the deformed preferences model in accounting for the subjective effects of gender. How useful is this account in trying to make sense of the lived effects of gender as many women encounter them? There can be no denying that some preferences of some women could be explained by using Elster's model. Many women, for example, rank staying at home to look after children above having or continuing a career of their own. But that preference could well have the kind of genesis that ensures its conformity to the sour grapes paradigm. Such women would prefer to work outside the home, but because of the norms shaping workplace expectations, that option is no longer available to them once they have children. As a result, they come to believe that work is in some way undesirable – too stressful and demanding, perhaps – and this in turn leads to the formation of their preference for staying at home.

However, the sour grapes model seems to be inadequate in one important respect that Nussbaum appears not to notice. We have seen that radical feminists argue that what happens to women under conditions of subordination is that their very sense of self comes to be fundamentally distorted. To use MacKinnon's term, women's identities are imposed on them: their basic self-image qua inhabitants of the role of women in sexist societies is formed under conditions of unequal power. But the conditions of unequal power can seem to the agents involved to be perfectly natural and beyond challenge. This makes their resulting desires seem to be autonomous, for they are desires that spring from the self that comes into being under these conditions. But given the conditions under which women's identity is formed, their desires are not in fact autonomous.

Elster's analysis seems to presuppose a very simple distinction between a person and her wants. The idea, apparently, is that a person's identity is fixed independently of the wants she happens to have. To be a free person, on this view, is to be in a position to act on one's autonomous wants. But what if the way one conceives of oneself is itself a kind of distortion? To get at the kind of situation I'm thinking of, consider an imaginary case based on the example of what happens during a typical Self-Employed Women's Association (SEWA) education program. Nussbaum tells us that these meetings involve

> getting each woman to look straight at the group leader and say her name. The process is videotaped, and women grow accustomed to looking at themselves. Eventually, though with considerable difficulty, they are all able to overcome norms of modesty and deference and to state their names publicly.
>
> (2000: 17 n. 20)

Assume that prior to taking part in such a session, a certain Indian woman is deliberating about whether or not she should try to become more self-assertive. Curiosity about what this would mean leads her to a SEWA meeting. On the first day of the program she has to decide whether she will go along with the exercises – whether or not to make eye contact with the group leader, for instance. Given the environment she is in, let us think about her situation in the light of Elster's condition on autonomous wants. It appears to be true that the woman is free to be assertive and free to be deferential. But when her turn comes to say her name, she finds herself, on reflection, unable to do so. The norms of modesty she has internalized make this impossible. Instead, she feels compelled to exhibit the deferential behavior expected of a woman of her social station. Now consider this desire to exhibit deference. It appears to satisfy Elster's condition. She is free to exhibit deference and also free not to. Is it the case that this want is not shaped by necessity? It seems to me that the answer has to be in the negative.

In my judgment, Elster's model is incapable of fully grasping what MacKinnon describes as "the completeness of the incursion into who one really becomes through growing up female in a male-dominated society" (1989: 103). Recall the two capabilities on her list that Nussbaum takes to be fundamental. One is the capacity to form and reflect critically on a conception of the good. The other is the capacity to affiliate with other people while enjoying the social bases of self-respect and nonhumiliation. We have seen that, on Nussbaum's view, what makes these powers especially important is that they give structure to and suffuse the rest of the capabilities.

Consider what is involved in forming a conception of the good and relating to other people on terms that are mutually respectful and free of humiliation. To form a conception of the good presupposes an ability to adopt a reflective stance toward one's beliefs, values, and preferences. One assesses those beliefs, values, and preferences in the light of one's basic or most fundamental values, one's deepest sense of who one is. Relating to other people without self-abasement, on the other hand, presupposes an ability to set an appropriate value on oneself. One has to see oneself as worth being valued by other people, as a source of claims that they ought to respect. In the case of both of these crucial capacities, then, what is needed is a certain kind of reflective self-understanding. In order to be able to form a conception of the good, I have to see myself as an agent, as having the deliberative capacity to decide how I shall live, and what I shall make of the questions that my life poses for me. In order to relate to others on mutually respectful terms, I have to see myself as a locus of value: I must see my agency as something valuable in its own right. Call what is needed here a proper conception of the deliberating and interacting self. What seems fundamental to the exercise of both capacities is that the deliberating and interacting self be in some sense authentic, a self that one can reflectively endorse. But if the radical feminists are right, then under conditions of gender inequality women are deprived of the conditions in which an authentic self can emerge.

Capabilities, power and human nature

In this final section of the chapter I want to point out some of the ways in which Nussbaum's naturalistic construal of the foundations of capability theory can be a useful corrective to the constructivist tendencies of certain radical feminists. Here my point is that Nussbaum is right to insist that a normative conception of human nature is fundamental to the justification of claims about capabilities.

This is not to deny that invocations of the category of the natural are fraught with difficulties in this area. I want to mention two such difficulties: one having to do with explanations of the situation of women, the other to do with appeals to natural rights or natural law. MacKinnon (1989: 54) offers a very plausible critique of those forms of feminism that advance theories that implicitly or explicitly give explanatory primacy to biological factors. What MacKinnon objects to is the various ways in which women's biology is construed as the source of their subordination. For instance,

Simone de Beauvoir apparently traces the situation of women back to the reproductive functions of women's bodies. The functions themselves, on de Beauvoir's view, rather than the social meanings attributed to those functions, are responsible for women's oppression. What MacKinnon finds objectionable about such naturalistic explanations of unequal social status

> is that the characteristic that the members of the dominant group share is [said to be] the inherent cause of and continuing justification for their dominance, and the characteristics shared by the subordinate groups [is said to] cause and justify their subordination.
>
> (1989: 55)

Her worry, I take it, is that there is a decisive explanatory objection to this kind of naturalism. Any remotely plausible account of how women have come to occupy the position they do must include some reference to the role of social factors in this process.

Similarly, appeals to biology are often held to justify women's inferior social position. For instance, at least some ways of appealing to the natural law are straightforwardly and incorrigibly sexist. In his notorious concurring opinion in *Bradwell* v. *Illinois*, Justice Bradley wrote:

> [N]ature herself, has always recognized a wide difference in the respective spheres and destinies of man and woman. Man is, or should be, woman's protector and defender. The natural and proper timidity and delicacy which belongs to the female sex evidently unfits it for many of the occupations of civil life. The constitution of the family organization, which is founded in the divine ordinance, as well as in the nature of things, indicates the domestic sphere as that which properly belongs to the domain and functions of womanhood. The harmony, not to say the identity, of interests and views which belong, or should belong, to the family institution is repugnant to the idea of a woman adopting a distinct and independent career from that of her husband.

The position that radical feminists are rejecting could be summarized in the following claim:

1 The differential status of men and women is explained and justified by natural differences between males and females.

It is obviously in reaction to claims like this that MacKinnon wants to argue that "gender has no basis in anything other than the social reality its hegemony constructs" (1987: 173). It is natural to take her in passages like this to be endorsing a thoroughgoing social constructionist account of power. On that account, men's power in society enables them to fashion social reality, including the gender system, in their interests. Because gender is social "all the way down," there is no basis to it in anything other than social relations. The conclusion appears to be that not only does power produce the categories of man and woman, but it produces the very categories of male and female. So, against claim 1, MacKinnon might be read as affirming the suggestion that:

2 Nothing justifies the differential status of men and women and only social factors have any part to play in explaining it.

But 2 seems to be mistaken. It is surely more plausible to think that there are indeed certain natural differences between males and females, differences that are not in any way socially constructed. What power does is to take natural features that are, in themselves, morally neutral and make them the basis for justifying the subordinate status of women and the dominant status of men. In place of 2, then, we might consider:

3 Nothing justifies the differential status of men and women, and, while natural differences between males and females have some part in explaining it, social factors have explanatory primacy.

There are two reasons for preferring 3 over 2. The first is that until the difference between them is pointed out, it looks easy to endorse 2 because one might well confuse it with something more like 3. In one's desire to deny 1, one might feel compelled to affirm 2 without noticing the possibility of affirming 3 instead. The second reason for this preference is that, as I have suggested, natural differences between males and females surely do have some explanatory part to play in the etiology of women's oppression. Consider the fact that female human beings have the capacity to lactate. That fact in itself is surely morally neutral on the question of the social status that women should occupy. It is fully consistent with acknowledging that women should command the same status as men. But if men have the power to define the status of women, then they have the power to make the natural capacity to lactate a socially salient ground for discriminating against women or for getting women to do things such as shouldering greater responsibilities for childrearing. What this reveals is that the power to impose a status is, in part, the power to make some facts about people more salient than others. But such an explanation presupposes a distinction that 2 simply denies, namely, a distinction between natural facts and the social power to make such facts salient.

Indeed, it seems to me that this distinction between the natural and the social is necessary for making sense of the idea that sexist social norms are bad for people. Consider MacKinnon's claim that "Men are damaged by sexism. (By men I mean the status of masculinity that is accorded to males on the basis of their biology but is not itself biological)" (1987: 170). If, as I have suggested, the category of being a man is a social category (that is to say, its content is given by a set of social norms and ideals), then men qua men could not be damaged by sexism. For sexist norms are precisely those norms that help to create and sustain men's domination over women. The claim has to be that among those who are damaged by sexism are the people who bear the roles of men; that is to say, male human beings. But if the individuals who occupy the social position of men are damaged by sexism, then obviously those who occupy the social position of women are even more profoundly damaged by it. Indeed, this is one of MacKinnon's frequently repeated claims: sexism and gender inequality cause profound damage to women. But these claims raise a crucial question: what is it about gender inequality that makes it harmful to men and women? MacKinnon's answer, in the case of women, is that there are certain basic goods that women need but are "socially prevented from having on the basis of a condition of birth: a chance at productive lives of reasonable physical security, self-expression, individuation, and minimal respect and dignity" (1987: 32). But this drives the question of the harmfulness of sexism to a deeper level. What makes these goods worth having? Surely it cannot simply be that men have them while women lack them. The most plausible answer has to be that they are good for us, given the kind of creatures we are. But that is exactly the kind of answer that Nussbaum's approach to women's capabilities enables us to supply.

As we have seen, Nussbaum's justification for her list of capabilities makes crucial use of a normative conception of human nature. At the core of that conception, as I read it, is the idea of each human being as possessing a pre-political or natural ethical status. Each of us enjoys the moral status of being someone entitled to shape our lives on reasonable terms in cooperation with the people around us. Two capabilities are fundamental to that status as Nussbaum construes it: the capacity to shape our life in accordance with practical reason, and the capacity to relate to others in ways that are free of domination and humiliation. This allows us to say that gender inequality is harmful to people because it deprives women (to a great extent) and men (to a lesser extent) of what they need in order to achieve the functioning of which the members of our species are capable. Given the sort of creatures we are, being able to exercise our capacities for bodily integrity, self-expression, individuation, and self-respect enables us to flourish.

In the previous section I examined what may be called the distortion thesis: the claim that under conditions of gender inequality, women are not in a position to develop an authentic sense of their own identity. I noted that the idea of suffering from a distortion of self presupposes the idea of a person's authentic self. But in order to make best sense of the idea of a person's authentic self, so it seems to me, we need to invoke an idea of natural human development. In the absence of oppressive social relations, we must say, each person's identity would emerge free from distortions and inauthentic elements (or at any rate, free from those distortions and inauthentic elements that are plausibly traceable to oppresive conditions). In a society free from domination, we could each be truly ourselves.

Conclusion

I have argued in this chapter that Nussbaum's capabilities approach to gender inequality could be enriched by the incorporation of some of the social analysis presented by radical feminists. Thinking of a person's capabilities as being profoundly shaped by the social relations in which she stands seems to me to be a much more comprehensive way of coming at the capabilities question. I have also suggested that the normative underpinnings for Nussbaum's view of capabilities are eminently well suited to correcting the social constructionism apparently favored by some radical feminists. Social relations that include the distortions of gender domination are bad for us because they prevent us all from being fully human.

Of course, my argument raises many questions. Of these many questions, I shall end by mentioning just two. One concerns the plausibility of the domination thesis: how credible is the claim that relations between men and women in liberal democracies are best explained in terms of a basic asymmetry of social power? While that thesis seems to hold true for societies in which women really are treated as the chattels of men, there is surely room for skepticism about the suggestion that something similar is true in the contemporary United States, for example.

What I would say in response is that the domination thesis, presumably, has to be taken as a species of inference to the best explanation. This means that we have to consider it in the context of other purported explanations for facts like the levels of violence against women and the persistence of social and political inequalities between men and women in liberal democracies. Doing so raises unavoidably large and difficult questions about explanation. But it strikes me that the thesis is likely to fare reasonably well in such an exercise.

The other question I have in mind is rather in the spirit of Rousseau. It is this: how reliable are claims about human nature – such as those underlying Nussbaum's theory of capabilities – given the fact that we only ever know of human beings who have been profoundly shaped by social relations? After all, if the feminists are right, those relations have distorted people's identities in pretty radical ways. How can anything plausible be said about what is good for animals like us?

I would be inclined to say in reply that the conception of human nature that is in play in an account like Nussbaum's is one that sees human beings as social by nature. What a purely presocial human being would look like is irrelevant to determining what kinds of social relations might be best for creatures like us. What we have to do, then, in order to justify our claims about what is good for animals like us, is to look at how well people do in various kinds of society. The working hypothesis of someone who takes Nussbaum's approach is that people do best when they live in societies that affirm an equal standing for all and that guarantee decent functioning for everyone. While that hypothesis is not obviously correct, it can be thought of as a broadly empirical claim whose evidential support would have to come from the findings of the social sciences and history. Understood in this way, it seems to me, the hypothesis is at least in the running for being true.

References

Elster, J. (1982) "Sour Grapes – Utilitarianism and the Genesis of Wants," in Amartya Sen and Bernard Williams (eds) *Utilitarianism and Beyond*, Cambridge: Cambridge University Press.

Frye, M. (1983) *The Politics of Reality: Essays in Feminist Theory*, Trumansburg, NY: Crossing Press.

Haslanger, S. (1993) "On Being Objective and Being Objectified," in Louise M. Antony and Charlotte Witt (eds) *A Mind of One's Own: Feminist Essays on Reason and Objectivity*, Boulder, Co: Westview Press.

MacKinnon, C. A. (1987) *Feminism Unmodified: Discourses on Life and Law*, Cambridge, MA.: Harvard University Press.

MacKinnon, C. (1989) *Toward a Feminist Theory of the State*, Cambridge, MA: Harvard University Press.

Nussbaum, M. C. (2000) *Women and Human Development: The Capabilities Approach*, Cambridge: Cambridge University Press.

6 What goods do to (and for) people

Duality and ambiguity in Sen's capabilities approach?

Alexander Kaufman

While Amartya Sen's identification of the previously neglected "capabilities dimension of assessment" was a significant contribution to egalitarian thought, G. A. Cohen argues, Sen has obscured the nature of this contribution by employing the term "capability" to refer to two different aspects of advantage. Because of this "confusing duality," Cohen argues, Sen fails to provide a clear account of "the aspect(s) of a person's condition that should count as fundamental for egalitarians." I argue, however, that Sen's account is not characterized by motivational confusion or conceptual inadequacy; rather, Sen's pluralistic view of advantage in fact expands the descriptive and analytic range of egalitarian thought.

Amartya Sen's capabilities approach offers an account of the aspects of a person's condition that should count in a fundamental way in assessing the well-being that persons experience. Two aspects of the person's condition, Sen argues, are most fundamentally important to his or her well-being: what the person is able to *be* and what the person is able to *do*. Goods enhance well-being precisely to the extent that they enhance these abilities. Moreover, Sen argues, each of these abilities is of *equally fundamental* concern. The capabilities approach therefore "sees persons from two different perspectives" (Sen 1985b: 169).

Gerald Cohen enthusiastically endorses what he views as Sen's effort to specify "a metric of well-being which measure[s] something falling *between* primary goods and utility." Sen's attempt to provide an account of what goods do to people, Cohen argues, constitutes a major advance in the study of quality of life (1989: 943). But, Cohen argues, Sen has obscured the character of this contribution because of his dual focus on (i) "what goods do to (or for) human beings in abstraction from the utility they confer," and (ii) the ability to do certain things that is conferred by the possession of goods (ibid.: 942–943). This dual focus, Cohen argues, introduces "substantial ambiguity" into his account, "mak[ing] it hard to be sure exactly what his conception of equality implies" (ibid.: 942).

Because of this "confusing duality" (Cohen 1989: 943), Cohen argues, Sen fails to provide a clear account of "the aspect(s) of a person's condition that should count as fundamental for egalitarians" (Cohen 1993: 9). If correct, Sen concedes, Cohen's criticisms would identify "major motivational confusion as well as conceptual inadequacy" in his account of the capabilities approach (Sen 1993: 42). I will argue, however, that Sen's account is not characterized by motivational confusion or conceptual inadequacy; rather, a coherent structural relation unites the two aspects of advantage to which the account assigns fundamental importance.

In order to develop this argument, I will first outline the basic elements of Sen's capabilities approach. Second, I will evaluate Cohen's objection that Sen's dual focus introduces confusion and ambiguity into the approach. After rejecting this argument, I will argue that in adopting such a heterogeneous account of fundamental egalitarian concerns, the capabilities approach expands the descriptive and analytic range of egalitarian thought.

The capabilities approach

The capabilities approach argues that how well a person is doing is a function of what the person is able to be (e.g. well or poorly nourished) and do (e.g. perform more or less meaningful work). The ability to be or do various fundamentally important things is therefore constitutive of well-being. Sen refers to the various states of being and doing relevant to the assessment of well-being as *functionings* (1985a: 10; emphasis mine).

Sen defines capabilities as the various combinations (or vectors) of functionings that the person can achieve (1993: 40). A person's capability set contains the alternative vectors of functionings that the person can achieve with the resources available to him or her. An affluent person, for example, possesses not only the capability to be well nourished, but also the capability to "starv[e] out of choice because of his religious beliefs" (Sen 1985b: 201). If he chooses to starve, his actual functioning may be identical to that of a person who is starving due to poverty. His capability set, however, is quite different: he has the capability to choose to be well nourished, while the poor person does not.

Persons who possess different capabilities sets may achieve functionings that are similar or identical. Conversely, persons may possess similar or identical capabilities sets and choose quite dissimilar levels of functionings. This would be the case if, for example, identical twins raised in the same environment achieved different levels of material success. While the less successful twin might achieve a less desirable level of functioning, her capability set would remain similar or identical to that of her more successful sibling, since both enjoyed the same effective freedom to choose the functionings that they wished to achieve.

Confusing duality

While Sen's identification of the previously neglected "capabilities dimension of assessment" was a significant contribution to egalitarian thought,

Cohen argues (1994: 119), Sen has obscured the nature of this contribution by employing the term "capability" to refer to two different aspects of advantage. First, Sen uses the term to refer to an aspect of advantage or well-being falling *between* primary goods and utility. Cohen refers to this first aspect, which he views as attuned "to the true shape of … egalitarian concern" (1993: 28), as 'midfare." Sen, Cohen argues, conflates this first – and in Cohen's view much more significant – aspect of advantage with a second aspect that involves the person's ability to do certain basic things. In defining capabilities so broadly, Cohen claims, Sen fails to notice that he has brought together "two distinct aspects of the person under a single name" (Cohen 1993: 17).

In his definition of "functionings," Cohen claims, Sen exhibits the "imprecision" of his understanding of the capability dimension. Sen employs the term "functioning," Cohen notes, to refer to both (i) states of being, and (ii) capacities that the person possesses to do certain things. In this definition, then, Sen again combines "incompatible broad and narrow definitions" of advantage (Cohen 1993: 21).

Cohen's critique of the capabilities approach, however, exhibits an ambiguity of its own. Sometimes Cohen describes the "confusing duality" that he diagnoses in Sen's approach as an "unnoticed" and accidental feature of Sen's account (Cohen 1989: 942); but at other points he discusses this dual focus as a conscious and intentional feature of Sen's approach. In responding to Cohen's objection, I will first examine Cohen's claim that Sen's dual focus is an unnoticed confusion. After rejecting this claim, I will assess the degree to which ambiguity may be introduced into the capabilities approach by the three aspects of Sen's account that directly reflect his dual focus: (i) the assessment of quality of life in terms of what people are able to *be* and *do*; (ii) the examination of the person's concerns in the dual dimensions of *achievement* and *freedom to achieve*; and (iii) the assignment of intrinsic importance to two distinct aspects of the person.

An unnoticed confusion?

Sen's early work on the capabilities approach, Cohen claims, identified, but failed to distinguish carefully, "two ways of assessing a person's condition." Rather, Sen treated both as different ways of describing the same phenomenon; and this "unnoticed and confusing duality has persisted in his subsequent writings" (Cohen 1989: 942).

While Cohen claims that the dual focus of Sen's approach is unnoticed, however, Sen notes explicitly that his analysis requires a "plural informational base" that takes account of two "distinct" aspects of the person (well-being and agency), each of which is of intrinsic importance (Sen 1985b: 204–205).[1] Nor does Sen ignore the implications of such a "nonintegrated" approach (ibid.: 176): Sen concedes the possibility that such an approach may leave "a large subset" of significant issues unresolved.[2] Moreover, Sen argues that well-being and agency concerns must each be examined in two dimensions: (i) achievement; and (ii) freedom to achieve (ibid.: 203–208). As a result, Sen assigns equally fundamental status to *four* distinct "concepts of advantage": (i) well-being achievement; (ii) well-being freedom; (iii) agency achievement; and (iv) agency freedom (Sen 1993: 35).

Beings and doings

The capabilities approach assesses quality of life in terms of what people are able to be and do. As a result, Cohen argues, the approach conflates "incompatible broad and narrow definitions" of advantage (1993: 21), introducing ambiguity into its assessments of well-being.

While Sen's account does focus on both *beings* and *doings* in its assessments of well-being, however, this dual focus does not introduce ambiguity into his account of the capabilities dimension of assessment. Capabilities, Sen emphasizes, are neither beings nor doings. Rather, capabilities are the person's freedoms to choose over sets of possible functionings. Beings and doings are *functionings*, which are not constitutive of the standard of advantage employed to assess a person's well-being (Sen 1993: 43).

But since capabilities are "defined in terms of the *same* focal variables as functionings" (Sen 1992: 50), is the observation that doings and beings are merely functionings responsive to Cohen's criticism? The observation *is* responsive, because, in defining capabilities as freedoms to choose over various capabilities sets, Sen confines duality to the class of functionings. Capabilities, which define the standard of advantage employed to assess a person's condition, therefore constitute a homogeneous and unambiguously defined category of freedoms. While assessment of the person's ability to be and do various things *provides information for the assessment of a person's condition*, then, one clear and unambiguous standard of advantage is employed to assess that information.

Cohen concedes that by defining capabilities as merely freedoms to choose over capabilities sets, Sen may avoid conflating broad and narrow concepts of advantage in his account of functionings. This achievement, Cohen claims, is nevertheless costly. Freedom "obtains only when it is the agent who secures the conformity of the world to its will" (Cohen 1994: 124). By limiting egalitarian concerns to capabilities defined as freedoms, then, Sen appears to exclude from central concern states of the person "which he neither brought about nor was in a position to bring about" (Cohen 1993: 28). That is, Cohen claims, the definition of capabilities as freedoms would limit the concern of the capabilities egalitarian to objects over which the person can exercise control.

Sen, however, argues persuasively that his account does not limit fundamental egalitarian concerns in this way: "As long as the levers of control are systematically exercised in line with *what I would choose*" Sen argues, "my 'effective freedom' is not compromised" (1992: 64–65). Central to this view is Sen's claim that it is not an essential element of freedom that the person's choices must control what actually happens (Sen 1985b: 208; see also Pettit 2001: 13–17). Rather, a person's freedom may reasonably be assessed in terms of that person's power to achieve certain results, regardless of whether the person controls the process generating those results. According to this view, a policy that enhances the person's ability to lead a form of life that he or she prefers – for example, by reducing the incidence of malaria, or by improving air quality – enhances freedom, even if the person exercised no influence in causing the policy's enactment.[3]

Sen therefore avoids substantial ambiguity in his account of functionings without unduly limiting the scope of egalitarian concerns.

Achievement and freedom to achieve

Sen argues that capabilities must be examined in two dimensions: (i) achievement; and (ii) freedom to achieve. Does this dualistic division justify Cohen's charge of fundamental ambiguity? The short answer is *no*. Achievement and freedom to achieve are merely *dimensions* in which the agent's realization of capability goals is measured. The *achievement* dimension identifies the vector of goals actually realized, while the *freedom* dimension provides information about the set of vectors from which the person could choose. As a result, alterations in the agent's position in either of these dimensions can be properly evaluated according to a common metric: contribution to the agent's fundamental capability goals. If the necessary conditions of achievement and of freedom to achieve are in conflict, no serious tension necessarily results. This common metric provides a criterion adequate to determine which of the conflicting necessary conditions should be satisfied.

An example from Sen's Dewey Lectures illustrates the degree to which this underlying common metric unifies the apparently heterogeneous dimensions of freedom and achievement (Sen 1985b: 207). In Sen's example, someone who is enjoying lunch on the banks of a river becomes aware of a second person who is drowning in the river. As Sen notes, awareness of the drowning person (i) diminishes the picnicker's well-being freedom;[4] but (ii) increases her agency freedom (since she is presented with an opportunity to act in the service of a "goal in line with … her conception of the good" (1985b: 206). Thus, Sen demonstrates the independence of well-being freedom and agency freedom.

The example also, however, illustrates the practical implications of the distinction between achievement and freedom to achieve. Awareness of the drowning second person reduces the picnicker's well-being in both dimensions: (i) her well-being *achievement* is diminished because the satisfaction she can take in her lunch is reduced;[5] and (ii) her well-being *freedom* is diminished because she is no longer free to eat without anxiety. The appropriate response will vary, depending upon which dimension we privilege. We could redress the loss in well-being achievement by supplying compensatory satisfaction;[6] the loss in well-being freedom, however, requires active intervention (we could save the second person ourselves, restoring the picnicker's freedom to eat without anxiety). The important point is that in either case, the intervention will be motivated by the aim of addressing a deficit in well-being, not a deficit in freedom or achievement *per se*. If we address the loss in well-being achievement by supplying the picnicker with compensatory satisfaction, our intervention addresses a *well-being* deficit (lack of satisfaction), not an *achievement* deficit (the failure to achieve satisfaction through picnicking). Compensatory satisfaction cannot restore the lost achievement, since that achievement could derive only from a specific activity in a context that is no longer available. Similarly, if we address the picnicker's loss in well-being freedom by saving the drowning person, our intervention is designed to remedy a *well-being* deficit (the reduction in well-being resulting from anxiety), and not a *freedom* deficit (lack of freedom from anxiety). Thus, the dualism of freedom and achievement does not provide a basis for Cohen's charge that capabilities theory suffers from fundamental ambiguity.

Well-being and agency

Sen's account of the capabilities approach, Cohen suggests, suffers from confusing duality because it specifies two independent and equally fundamental egalitarian concerns. I have argued that neither the dualism of *beings* and *doings*, upon which Cohen focuses, nor the dualism of *achievement* and *freedom* to achieve supports such an argument. Sen *does*, however, acknowledge that his theory recognizes *agency* and *well-being* as equally fundamental concerns. Does Sen's dualism of agency and well-being reintroduce the danger of significant ambiguity? I will argue that a coherent structural relation unites agency and well-being interests in capabilities theory.

Unlike the relation between freedom and achievement, the relation between agency and well-being is not mediated by a common metric. Rather, agency and well-being interests are "quite distinct from each other" (Sen 1985b: 208n.). Well-being interests involve the assessment of the individual's advantage, where advantage refers to valuable states of being (e.g. being healthy or well nourished). Agency interests involve "what the person is free *to do and achieve* in pursuit of whatever goals or values he or she regards as important" (Sen 1985b: 203; emphasis mine). Such interests may reflect elements of the person's conception of the good, or they may express unreflective tastes. As long as an aim is the object of the person's conscious choice, it constitutes an agency interest.

The two sets of concerns differ principally with respect to the perspective from which the person's interests are assessed. The perspective of agency views the agent as an active chooser ("a doer and a judge"), while the perspective of well-being views the person as a "beneficiary"[7] (Sen 1985b: 208). Agency and well-being interests are of equally fundamental status for egalitarian theory, Sen argues, because the agency and well-being perspectives each provide information that is equally fundamental to the egalitarian assessment of the quality of life. Moreover, Sen explicitly contemplates the possibility of conflicts between interests viewed from these two perspectives, noting that "[t]he ability to do more good need not be to a person's advantage" (ibid.: 206).

Is problematic duality therefore built into capabilities equality? One way of addressing the issue of duality would be simply to reject Sen's claim that agency and well-being interests are essentially distinct forms of capabilities interests. Martha Nussbaum takes this approach, arguing that agency and well-being interests are both best understood as consisting of functionings that are both *chosen* and valuable (Nussbaum 1990: 226; see also Crocker 1995: 166). If Nussbaum's argument is persuasive, then both the agency and well-being perspectives view the person as an active chooser, rather than a recipient; and the potential dualism dissolves.

Sen nevertheless resists dissolving the distinction between agency and well-being interests, because evaluating the person's position from the perspectives of agency and well-being provides different kinds of information: "the well-being aspect and the agency aspect of the person have dissimilar roles in moral accounting" (1985b: 206). In Sen's picnic example, discussed in the previous section, the existence of a drowning person constitutes a positive opportunity for the person to realize agency interests while simultaneously reducing his or her ability to further well-being interests.

If the duality of Sen's account *is* problematic, the problem must derive either from the fact that a theory with such a heterogeneous focus (i) offers a confused interpretation of egalitarian concerns; or (ii) is necessarily indecisive over a wide range of practical questions. Sen addresses the first concern persuasively: the assignment of fundamental status to both sets of interests is necessary to reflect the fact that the agency and the well-being perspectives each provide information that is equally fundamental to the egalitarian assessment of the quality of life. Quality of life is, in fact, a complex and ambiguous notion; and "if an underlying idea has an essential ambiguity, a precise formulation of that idea must try to *capture* that ambiguity rather than hide or eliminate it" (Sen 1993: 33–34).

What about the concern that heterogeneity regarding fundamental values could lead to practical indecisiveness? Sen simply dismisses the idea that indecisiveness should be regarded as a serious theoretical defect. Decisiveness over all possible cases, Sen argues, cannot be an a priori requirement of a theory of distributive justice.[8] In fact, imposing completeness as a necessary condition for the acceptability of a moral theory reverses the proper order of priorities: the question of whether a complete ranking of states of affairs is possible can only be determined *after* the nature of an acceptable moral theory has been determined.[9]

Sen's discussion of this issue, however, concedes that his account of capabilities theory will necessarily leave significant issues unresolved. This is not a concession that a defender of Sen's conception needs to make. Heterogeneity in an account of fundamental value may take two forms: (i) informational pluralism, and (ii) principle pluralism. If the heterogeneity in question takes the form of equally fundamental *principles*, practical indecisiveness is likely to constitute a significant problem, since no privileged authority will generally be available to resolve conflicts among equally fundamental principles. Even in the case of principle pluralism, however, indecisiveness may be avoided if one principle is assigned the status of umpire with the authority to resolve conflicts among other equally fundamental principles.

Sen's theory suggests a plausible basis for such an umpire principle, since the theory views agency and well-being interests as of fundamental concern *because* they are constitutive of the person's freedom to lead one form of life or another.[10] It is therefore plausible to suggest that an appropriate umpire principle would resolve conflicts between principles relating to agency and well-being interests by requiring the resolution that would most effectively advance such freedom. Even if the heterogeneity of Sen's account involved principle pluralism, then, practical indecisiveness would not necessarily be unavoidable.

Sen's account of capabilities equality, however, is not characterized by principle pluralism. Rather, the heterogeneity of his account derives from the pluralism of its *informational base*. Sen distinguishes the agency and well-being perspectives not because they ground competing principles, but because each of these perspectives provides *information* that is of fundamental importance to egalitarians.

Unlike principle pluralism, informational pluralism is not inconsistent with practical decisiveness. For example, while a physician requires a heterogeneous information set (including information regarding nutritional intake, organ function, physical performance status) in order to provide medical care, the weight and significance of each item of information is determined by the principles of medical practice. A theory employing a plural informational base may therefore remain practically decisive as long as the theory specifies the weight to be assigned to particular kinds of information.

Sen's account of capabilities theory sets out at least a rough framework specifying the relative weight to be assigned to well-being and agency interests. Well-being interests, Sen argues, should be assigned priority in the consideration of claims relating to the distribution of basic and essential resources – "in such matters as … poverty alleviation [and the] removal of gross economic inequality" – while agency interests should be privileged in the evaluation of "the person's actual *use* of her well-being freedom" (1992: 71–72).

Sen does not develop the justification for this division of theoretical labor, but the relation to the distinct contributions of each category of interest to the realization of the freedom to choose a valued form of life seems clear. Well-being constitutes the standard for assessing the distribution of essential resources because the capabilities approach's concern to assure adequate access to such goods reflects a concern to ensure the realization of states of being (e.g. being healthy or well nourished) that are necessary conditions for the realization of a valued form of life. Agency constitutes the standard for assessing the use of well-being freedom because the quality of the person's employment of his or her freedom reflects the degree to which the person has realized the capacity to form and pursue ends – a capacity that the agent must realize before he or she can choose a form of life freely.[11] Thus, Sen's understanding of the distinct roles performed by well-being and agency interests in furthering the individual's freedom to choose a valued form of life allows him to specify principles determining the weight to be assigned to claims reflecting each set of interests, thus potentially avoiding the problem of practical indecisiveness.

Informational pluralism

The dual focus of the capabilities approach thus reflects Sen's insistence that an acceptable approach to the assessment of well-being requires a pluralistic informational base incorporating information regarding both well-being and agency interests. The value of such a pluralistic informational base for egalitarian judgment is suggested in the recent exchange between Ronald Dworkin and Andrew Williams. Dworkin argues that egalitarian justice requires only a monistic informational base focused on the distribution of resources.[12] To the extent that capabilities equality attempts to define a metric of egalitarian justice that incorporates information relating to both well-being and agency concerns, Dworkin argues, the theory will either (i) focus on personal and impersonal *resources* necessary for the realization of elementary capabilities; or (ii) focus on more "complex" functionings, such as happiness and self-respect (2000: 299–303). In the former case, capabilities equality collapses into resource equality. In the latter case, capabilities equality collapses into a form of welfare equality, and is therefore vulnerable to the compelling objections offered by Dworkin (2000: 11–64) and Sen (1985b: 169–184).

In response, Andrew Williams argues that it is possible to identify inequalities in capability which generate inequalities in the person's agency freedom – what the person is free to do in pursuit of goals that he or she regards as important – that neither (i) derive from inequalities in personal or impersonal resources; nor (ii) focus on complex, welfare-generating functionings (2002: 23–39).

Williams discusses two examples. I will focus on the first of these and on Dworkin's response. In this example, Anne and Bob are twins with similar endowments of talent, education, health, and ambition. They will not enjoy equal opportunity to satisfy their ambitions, however, because they are members of a society in which career preferences are asymmetrically distributed between men and women. Men generally prefer to devote their time to paid employment, while women generally prefer to devote their time to childcare and parenting. Under these conditions, Williams notes, Anne will find it harder than Bob to find a partner who is willing to share equally in childcare. She will have either to make larger career sacrifices than Bob in order to have children or to abandon the idea of having children.

If we assume that Anne and Bob begin with equal resources and ultimately realize equal happiness from the lives that they achieve, then Anne does not suffer from a welfare or resource deficit. Nevertheless, Williams argues, Anne's capabilities set is inferior to Bob's because her freedom to choose one form of life or another is constrained in a way that his is not. Anne therefore suffers from an inequality of capabilities that does not derive from an inequality in resources or welfare, but which leaves her less free than Bob to choose what to do in pursuit of goals she regards as important (2002: 30–34).

The example is problematic, Dworkin responds, on two grounds (2002: 136–140). First, equality of resources *does* require compensation for remedial measures to address the effects of unjust patterns of discrimination. Since, Dworkin asserts, the difference between Anne's and Bob's expectations is likely to result, at least in significant part, from the long-term effects of such discrimination, resource equality is likely to require the same remedial measures as capabilities equality (ibid.: 136–137).

This response, however, seems to misunderstand Williams's example. Williams is not arguing that Anne is a victim of the after-effects of the subjugation of women. Her problem does not result from discrimination in the workplace against women who fail to conform to the customary career track; nor is her problem that employers are unwilling to grant appropriate leaves for pregnant mothers. Anne's disadvantage, rather, results from the influence of the free preferences of men and women on the freedom of members of each group to pursue their life-plans. Since the preponderance of men in her society prefer to devote their time to paid employment, Anne is unlikely to find a partner who is willing to devote significant time to childcare. Bob will not face the same problem, because the preponderance of women prefer to devote significant time to childcare. Even if social legislation ensures fair treatment by employers, then, Anne will not enjoy freedom similar to Bob's to combine a rewarding career with family life.

Anne therefore enjoys less freedom to choose what form of life to lead than Bob as a result of the asymmetric distribution of preferences among men and women. Since Dworkin argues that inequalities that derive from the effects of preferences of other members of the market are not a matter for political concern (2000: 287), resource equality will, contrary to

Dworkin's assertion, necessarily fail to provide remedial measures comparable to those that will be required by capabilities equality.

Nor does Dworkin's argument for assistance to persons whose preferences constitute the equivalent of handicaps ground an obligation to assure equal freedom to choose a form of life to women in Anne's society. Dworkin does concede that certain involuntary preferences ("cravings") are so similar to physical handicaps that persons subject to them should not be held responsible for their effects. Victims of such cravings, Dworkin argues, possess tenable claims for compensation if their cravings deprive them of equal opportunity to choose what form of life to lead. It is characteristic of a craving, however, that the person who is subject to it "wishes he did not have [the craving] … it is a 'preference' … that he does not want" (Dworkin 2000: 82). Women in Anne's society do not resist their preferences to devote their time to childcare; rather, women in that society identify with those preferences and make free choices to compromise their careers in order to satisfy them. As a result, the compensatory assistance that Dworkin would make available to persons with cravings will not be available to women in Anne's society whose freedom to choose a form of life is diminished as a result of their preference to devote their time to family life.

Dworkin's second ground for objecting to Williams's example is his rejection of Williams's view that the inequality of capabilities between Anne and Bob is morally relevant. Why, Dworkin asks, should we assume that a capability set that includes childrearing and domestic responsibilities, but not an active career, is less valuable than a capability set that includes an active career and less involvement in childrearing? What objective basis could we have for such a claim (2002: 137)? Dworkin treats this rhetorical question as though it settles the issue of whether Anne suffers a morally relevant inequality in capability.[13] But the relevant question, for an account of egalitarian justice, is not whether Bob's capability set is more valuable than Anne's, but whether Anne and Bob have been treated as equals. And clearly they have not, even by the standards of Dworkin's account of equality of resources. Both desired a particular set of goals, but Bob enjoyed a much greater opportunity to realize that set than Anne. In terms of Dworkin's theory of resource equality, the arrangement fails the envy test: because the social distribution of preferences generates circumstances that impose a real constraint on Anne's options, she will legitimately envy Bob's otherwise identical resource distribution which did not leave him subject to a similar constraint.

Dworkin's exclusive focus on the distribution of resources, then, leads him to overlook the failure of equal treatment in such a case. Sen's employment of a plural informational base allows him to diagnose Anne's relative deficit of freedom to choose a form of life, a failure of equal concern and respect sufficient to justify an egalitarian obligation to assist.

Williams's example therefore appears to confirm Sen's claim that his theory's expansion of egalitarian justice's informational base extends the descriptive and analytic range of egalitarian theory. Sen's heterogeneous account of fundamental egalitarian concerns allows the capabilities approach to identify inequalities in the person's freedom to pursue goals that she regards as important that neither (i) derive from inequalities in personal or impersonal resources, nor (ii) focus on complex, welfare-generating functionings.

Conclusion

The capabilities approach is oriented by Sen's view that the ability to do and be various things is constitutive of well-being. The dual nature of these constitutive elements does not, I have argued, justify Cohen's claim that the theory suffers from substantial ambiguity. Rather, in adopting such a heterogeneous account of fundamental egalitarian concerns, the capabilities approach expands the descriptive and analytic range of egalitarian thought.

Notes

1 "It is hard to see how any part of this plurality (involving both the well-being aspect and the agency aspect of persons) can fail to have some intrinsic importance" (Sen 1985b: 204–205).
2 "The need to consider both the agency and the well-being aspect of persons is not compromised by the possibility that the combined structure may leave a large subset of unordered pairs" (Sen 1985b: 205). "[A] non-integrated moral structure could leave many moral issues unresolved" (ibid.: 176).
3 See Cohen (1994) for a critique of Sen's account of freedom without control. See Kaufman (forthcoming) for a response to that critique.
4 She is no longer free to eat without anxiety. Rather, she must either risk saving the second person or endure the discomfort of failing to undergo that risk.
5 "[T]he quiet lunch being replaced by a ducking in the chilling river" (Sen 1985b: 207).
6 Presumably we could supply comparable satisfaction by providing a similar picnic under less stressful conditions.
7 "Persons must enter moral accounting by others not only as people whose well-being demands concern, but also as people whose responsible agency must be recognized" (Sen 1985b: 208).
8 "Yielding complete orders cannot be an a priori requirement of the legitimacy of a moral principle. … It is not a matter of getting metamoral passmarks" (Sen 1985b: 180).
9 Incompleteness is not, in fact, a special problem associated only with heterogeneous moral theories; homogeneous theories (e.g. utilitarianism) often produce incomplete rankings. For example, since interpersonal utilities cannot be fully compared, "a pure utilitarian would have to *assert* the incompleteness of moral rankings as the correct moral position" (Sen 1985b: 179).
10 The "underlying idea of the [capability-based] conception of justice" is that "individual claims are … to be assessed in terms of … the freedoms [persons] actually enjoy to choose lives that they have reason to value" (Sen 1992: 81).
11 This distinction between (i) access to resources, and (ii) the choice to employ

those resources becomes important in cases such as Sen's example of a person fasting out of religious (or political) conviction. The person clearly suffers from a lack of an essential resource (adequate nutrition); but because this condition is freely chosen, the capabilities egalitarian would judge that the faster's agency achievement should be assigned greater weight than his or her well-being deficit, and would recognize no obligation to coerce the person to eat.

12 "Under equality of resources ... people decide what sort of lives to pursue against a background of information about the actual cost their choices impose on other people" (Dworkin 2000: 69). The level of opportunity to implement these decisions is defined by the share of resources available to the person; and the shares of resources available to each person as he or she takes part in this "institutionalized form of the process of discovery and adaptation ... should be equal" (ibid.: 70).

13 Dworkin also rejects the argument that Bob has "a greater second-order or 'complex' capacity" than Anne (2002: 137) on the grounds that such a claim must rely on a welfare metric. Yet this claim is not obviously decisive. Rawls argues plausibly, on nonwelfarist grounds, for the claim that persons who achieve more complex careers achieve a greater good.

References

Cohen, G. A. (1989) "On the Currency of Egalitarian Justice," *Ethics* 99: 906–944.

Cohen, G. A. (1993) "Equality of What?" in M. C. Nussbaum and A. Sen (eds), *The Quality of Life*, Oxford: Clarendon Press, pp. 9–29.

Cohen, G. A. (1994) "Review: Amartya Sen's Unequal World," *New Left Review* (January): 117–129.

Crocker, D. A. (1995) "Functioning and Capability: The Foundations of Sen's and Nussbaum's Development Ethic," in M. Nussbaum and J. Glover (eds) *Women, Culture and Development: A Study of Human Capabilities*, Oxford: Oxford University Press.

Dworkin, Ronald (2000) *Sovereign Virtue*, Cambridge, MA: Harvard University Press.

Dworkin, Ronald (2002) "*Sovereign Virtue* Revisited," *Ethics* 113 (1): 106–143.

Kaufman, A. (forthcoming) "Capability and Freedom," *Journal of Political Philosophy*.

Nussbaum, M. C. (1990) "Aristotelian Social Democracy," in R. B. Douglass, G. R. Mara, and H. S. Richardson (eds) *Liberalism and the Good*, New York: Routledge.

Pettit, P. (2001) "Capabilities and Freedom: A Defense of Sen," *Economics and Philosophy* 17: 1–20.

Sen, A. (1985a) *Commodities and Capabilities*, Amsterdam: North-Holland.

Sen, A. (1985b) "Well-Being, Agency and Freedom," *Journal of Philosophy* 82 (4): 169–221.

Sen, A. (1992) *Inequality Reexamined*, Cambridge, MA: Harvard University Press.

Sen, A. (1993) "Capability and Well-Being," in M. C. Nussbaum and A. Sen (eds) *The Quality of Life*, Oxford: Clarendon Press.

Williams, Andrew (2002) "Dworkin on Capability," *Ethics* 113 (1): 23–39.

Part III

Issues in implementation

7 Public debate and value construction in Sen's approach

Sabina Alkire

A central proposition of the capability approach is that social arrangements should be assessed according to the capability sets enjoyed by those who are affected by them. However, this proposition assumes that individuals and groups are able to identify *valuable* capabilities.

The proposition implies that in economic planning and decisions, more attention should be given to the role of public deliberation and debate. But can public deliberation fulfill this role in practice? One way in which it might do so is by "participatory planning." Participatory planning exercises that intentionally catalyze discussion on values and use those values to inform priorities may provide a way for people to make certain value judgments directly, provided power imbalances are not allowed to distort the process.

Form and judgment

When talking with Charles Juliet, Samuel Beckett agreed that artistic enterprise was impossible without rigorous ethical standards. But, he complained,

> moral values are not accessible and not open to definition. To define them, you would have to make value judgements, and you can't do that. That's why I have never agreed with the idea of the theatre of the absurd. Because that implies making value judgements. You can't even talk about truth. That is part of the general distress.
>
> (Juliet 1995: 149)

Certainly the value judgments individuals or groups make can be disquieting. But somewhat more disconcerting is Beckett's assertion that value judgments cannot be made well. For a central proposition of the capability approach – that social arrangements should be assessed according to the capability sets enjoyed by those who are affected by them – rests on the argument that individuals and groups are able to identify *valuable* capabilities. A further and related assessment is that the capability to make value judgments can in some instances itself be valuable (Sen 1982, 1983, 1985, 1987, 1993, 1999b, 2002b).

When the implications of this core proposition of the capability approach are traced through economic thinking, they turn out to be quite significant. In particular, the proposition implies that the border between decisions made on technical grounds of optimization, and decisions made in view of public deliberation and debate, should shift. Public debate and deliberation – which draws on ethical and normative considerations including efficiency and equity, as well as culture and values, and feasibility considerations – should shape economic decisions to a greater extent.

Can public deliberation fulfill this role in practice? Many have debated the possibility of making value judgments, and those who advance the capability approach regard this enterprise rather more positively than Beckett.[1] Yet it is one thing to demonstrate the philosophical coherence and normative importance of a position; it is quite another enterprise to create and instantiate that possibility using complex and fallible human processes. The practical considerations of the second enterprise may also be quite important.

Just after his comment on "general distress," Beckett continued the conversation by saying, "Paradoxically, it's through form that the artist can find a kind of solution – by giving form to what has none. It is perhaps only at that level that there may be an underlying affirmation" (Juliet 1995: 149).

After sketching out the concepts and relationships of interest, the second half of the chapter engages with the dusty rooms, local groups, and facilitators who together implement some of these august concepts, and whose experience raises important questions for both practical and theoretical response. In particular, it explores one set of "forms" by which people might make value judgments in public debate: "participatory planning." It argues that at certain junctures, participatory planning exercises that intentionally catalyze discussion on values – for example, using a set of dimensions akin to those Nussbaum proposes – and use those values to inform priorities provide an avenue along which to explore how people might make certain value judgments directly.[2] The chapter also explores common distortions to value judgments that arise from power imbalances.

Capabilities and value judgments

Capabilities are people's freedoms to enjoy valuable beings and doings. The definition of capability does not delimit a certain subset of capabilities as of peculiar importance. Rather, the *selection* of capabilities on which to focus is a value judgment (one that also depends partly on the purpose of the evaluation), as is the *weighting* of capabilities relative to each other, and the *comparison* of different groups' capability sets in order to set distributional priorities (Sen 1992, 1999b). In expanding capabilities, such value judgments will be required on an ongoing basis in order to identify what capabilities are valuable enough that they should be given priority. As Sen writes in *Inequality Reexamined*,

> The primary claim is that in evaluating well-being, the value-objects are the functionings and capabilities. That claim neither entails that all types of capabilities are equally valuable, nor indicates that any capability whatsoever – even if totally remote from the person's life – must have some value in assessing that person's well-being. ... The relative valuation of different functionings and capabilities has to be an integral part of the exercise.
>
> (1992: 46)

It may therefore be important to identify and explore the public processes by which value judgments can be made and communicated; by which the "relative valuation of different functionings and capabilities" might proceed.

Democracy, discussion, and value construction

The focal decisions of interest are not value judgments made by an individual or family: which person might be suitable to marry, for example, or whether to pursue lucrative career options in a firm, or downscale the family dwelling and cast out toward a different lifestyle. Rather, they are priorities that affect a larger group – whether that be a neighborhood and local community, a region, or a nation. Many have written on the role of deliberation in such decisions with penetrating depth (Bohman 1996; Bohnet and Frey 1994; Elster 1998; Escobar 1995; Finnis 1999; Forester 1999; Fung and Wright 2003; Gutmann and Thompson 1996; Koh and Slye 1999; Macedo 1999; Paul *et al.* 2000; Richardson 1997, 2002; Sunstein 2001, 2003; Young 2000). With respect to these decisions, Sen argues that "the process of generating informed and considered choices" regarding which capabilities are valuable and should be publicly provided (for example) entails "open discussion, debate, criticism and dissent."[3] Furthermore, he argues that "These processes are crucial to the formation of values and priorities, and we cannot, in general, take preferences as given independently of public discussion" (1999a: 253). Thus, when judgments as to which capabilities are valuable must be made, and when these judgments affect wider groups of people, procedural considerations enter. At a national level, and in a well-functioning democratic system, the procedures of interest may be closely tied to the formal political processes of democracy (election campaigns, lobbying, voting behavior, etc.). At other levels or in other contexts, procedures include indigenous institutions, or *ad hoc*, short-term "participation" in development planning. In either case the selection and prioritization and distribution of valuable capabilities draw on collective deliberation, and current priorities should be able to be influenced in some way by it.

As others have discussed, Sen proposes that democracy should be understood to be more complex than merely majority rule, and that it should entail the protection of liberties and freedoms, including the media and public discussions. Sen identifies diverse ways in which democracy "enriches the lives of citizens": the *intrinsic* value of political and social participation and decision making; the *instrumental* value of democracy in communicating people's demands effectively to political leaders; and the *constructive* value, mentioned earlier, of providing a forum in which people exchange information and analyses, modify their own views, and together influence the society's values and priorities (see Sen 1999a, b). It is the constructive value upon which this chapter focuses.

Technical and moral reasoning in economics

The "constructive" use of democratic action is important in society in general as a counterweight to imbalanced political priorities. It is also pertinent in relation to economic priorities. For example, in considering economics, Sen (1987) has suggested that the type of reasoning exemplified in much of economics – the rationality of Walras or Kautilya or Robbins, for example – is important but incomplete. Their "engineering" rationality, as he terms it, is technical. "The ends are taken as fairly straightforwardly given, and the object of the exercise is to find the appropriate means to serve them" (ibid.: 4). The value of a deeper understanding of efficient means is undeniable. Needed to complement and supplement the engineering approach is an ethical approach that considers the intrinsically valued goals, procedures, and side effects of an activity. This wider approach employs a wider rationality, which is at its font an ethical rationality. Sen argues that the monopolization of economics by the engineering approach has been misplaced. Ethical rationality is required to generate appropriate responses to many recurrent social ills.

Clearly, the capability approach challenges the existing border between engineering forms of economics, and ethical forms of public discussion and debate (whether one considers these to be part of economics or not is a secondary matter). It implies that some decisions currently made exclusively on the basis of efficiency considerations should be considered on additional ethical grounds such as desirability or equity.

In passing, it might be worth noting that if value judgments indeed become an "integral part of the exercise," this will affect the decision-making processes, and – on the assumption that value judgments are made by a different process and perhaps also a different group of decision makers than would be required by engineering approaches – the configuration of power. I will argue in the last section that this awareness is important because not all who engage the public debate may guide their debate by values alone.

Dimensions, forms, and value construction

In her chapter in this volume (Chapter 2), Martha Nussbaum argues convincingly for the need to identify and prioritize certain valued capabilities over others (see also Nussbaum 2000, 2003 among many others). She writes, "some freedoms limit others" (p. 55) and "some [freedoms] are central and some trivial, some good and some actively bad" (p. 56) She has for quite some time supported and advocated a set of "Central Human Capabilities" that are "open-ended and subject to ongoing revision and rethinking," but that can inform political principles. Furthermore, she argues that the dimensions can support plural specifications, and that they are framed in a general way

> in order to leave room for the activities of specifying and deliberating by citizens and their legislatures and courts that all democratic nations contain. Within certain parameters, it is perfectly appropriate that different nations should do this somewhat differently, taking their histories and special circumstances into account.

It might be heartening to note that many have already developed and used lists of well-being in their work precisely to spark the kind of reflection that Nussbaum proposes (for a survey of these lists, see Alkire 2002b; Qizilbash 2002). For example, Manfred Max-Neef (1992, 1993) has used ten very similar domains in participatory planning exercises (for another example see Alkire 2002a ch 6–7).

An appropriate question to explore, therefore, might be how dimensions might catalyze constructive deliberative discussion. The process in which communities consider a dimension or general category of valued capabilities and specify which capabilities within that dimension are most valuable (and whether there are other dimensions or categories they prefer) seems to be an important step. It is also limited, for a focus on the "ends" or an identification of valuable capabilities would need to be complemented by other equally important discussions – of distributional issues, efficiency, or procedures, for example.

Participatory planning

There are many potential processes by which to make collective value judgments, ranging from institutional mechanisms to executive committee decisions to participation to public debate.[4] The "form" this chapter explores is participatory planning, which is extensively employed in poverty reduction activities at diverse levels from the local to the national.

Participatory planning is an informal procedure in which "focus groups" of women and men from the community analyze the local situation and, on the basis of this analysis, set priorities and generate plans to address varieties of deprivation – sometimes (but not always) relying partially on external resources of technical assistance or finance (see Alkire and Mathai 2003; Bamberger 1988; Blackburn and Holland 1998; Blair 2000; Carmen 2000; Cernea 1991; Chambers 1993, 1997; Cooke and Kothari 2001; Drèze and Sen 2002; Edwards and Hulme 1992, 1995; Ellerman 2001; Jasek-Rysdahl 2001; Khan 1995; Max-Neef 1992; Narayan-Parker 1993, 1995; Oakley and Marsden 1984; Rahman 1993; Salmen 1987, 1995, 1999; Uphoff 1998; Wade 1988). Of course, there are many techniques and methods for participatory planning that influence its outcomes directly – for example, the choice of who participates in these groups (e.g. whether men and women, rich and poor, do the analysis together or whether some analysis is done in small groups), how the conversations are structured, how the analyses of different groups are combined, and what tone is set. Participatory planning techniques purport to offer a form of informed and deliberate decision making in which prospective value judgments may be made explicitly by the group(s) concerned, rather than relegating these judgments to a market mechanism, formal democracy, or leadership by committee by NGO staff or by dictator.[5]

Participatory planning processes (which vary tremendously in depth, mechanism, and duration) are becoming increasingly widespread in activities funded by the local community, NGOs, governments, development agencies, and donors. For example, World Bank lending to participatory or "community-driven development" activities, many of which are open menu, exceeded US$2 billion in 2003, (Mansuri and Rao 2003). Participatory planning methods are also used in national-level planning exercises. Significantly, many developing countries use participation as part of the inputs into their national "poverty reduction strategy" or a "comprehensive development framework" that sets priorities and guides interventions by a range of national and international institutions.[6] Participatory local and national plans are also constructed in industrialized countries.[7]

In the late 1980s and the 1990s, many participatory methods arose out of development activities in different places. One methodology is PRA (Participation, Reflection, and Action), which its initial architect, Robert Chambers, described as a "growing family of approaches and methods to enable local people to share, enhance and analyze their knowledge of life and conditions and to plan, act, monitor and evaluate" (1997: 102; see also Chambers 1993, 1994). It is but one of many approaches.[8] Development initiatives conceived, executed, and monitored in a deeply participatory, open-ended fashion were argued to be superior on intrinsic grounds – because the process enabled the poor to exercise self-determination. On instrumental grounds, the resulting sense of ownership was demonstrated in some cases to contribute to the long-term effectiveness and sustainability of the project (Isham *et al.* 1995). Participatory processes were quick to spread across sectors and geographies, and the rhetoric of participation pervades poverty-reduction activities.

The methodologies of participatory planning vary considerably and no effort is made here to summarize the diverse approaches. Many involve a sequence of activities similar to those described in deliberative democracy, and many are accompanied by educational activities and the exchange of salient information. Participants (who these are depends upon the exercise) generate a set of different possible activities they might undertake in common – sometimes as a group and sometimes individually. The suggestions are compiled or synthesized (sometimes by a computer; sometimes as a group) and some, on reflection, are discarded. A preliminary prioritization is made that is, at least in part, based on needs and values. Finally, the feasibility and sequencing of options are discussed, and last, a concrete plan is agreed that includes a set of priorities, together with steps toward their attainment. In what circumstances the resulting plan reflects the capabilities of all of the participants in a meeting, or of the community from which they are drawn, more adequately than plans generated by other processes, and when this planning process is in fact empowering, are questions under investigation. A possible hypothesis is that participatory planning processes, if adequately implemented, could both empower people and use deliberation to generate plans to expand capabilities people most value. Thus, participatory planning provides a possible venue for, as Henry Richardson (1997) so aptly titled it, practical reasoning about final ends.

Participation deliberation and capability

Participatory planning processes were selected for further exploration because of the following affinities with Sen's capability approach. Such links could also be made with the literature on deliberative democracy.

1 The purpose of participation planning is both (a) to create outcomes that people value and choose, and (b) to support a planning process that may be intrinsically valuable or "empowering", giving people voice and the ability to shape the decisions that will shape them. Sen (1982, 1983, 1999c) has identified and affirmed both of these types of freedom.
2 Participatory planning exercises implicitly view well-being and participation as inherently connected. In decisions made by this mechanism it is recognized that "who decides" is important, and "what is decided" is also important. In Sen's conception of capability, the "freedom to" pursue valuable beings and doings is not a separate functioning that can be fulfilled by certain freedoms such as voting and negative liberties. It is also important that people be able to have a say in common decisions.
3 Participatory planning processes presume underdetermination – that there may be no best choice, but that discussion and consideration can work out grounds for separating the "better" from "worse" choices.

Sen likewise recognizes incompleteness and identifies decision-making processes that may be adequate in these cases, such as partial orderings.

4 Participatory planning and the capability approach both positively recognize the fact of human diversity. Thus, they presume that some choices must be made or modified at the local level to take into account specifics of the circumstance(s).

Potential partly unrealized

Thus far, the synergies between participation – which is increasingly required in poverty-reduction activities – and democratic practice as advocated by Sen, Nussbaum, and the deliberative democracy writers, among many others, seem plenteous; however, they remain unrealized to a surprising extent. A thorough review of the existing white and gray literature on participatory planning, as well as interviews with practitioners and a review of the "training of trainers" courses offered by NGOs and international development banks, suggests that while open-ended participatory planning processes are increasingly widespread, many do not encourage explicit discussion of value judgments and trade-offs (Mathai 2002). Rather, they allow the range of capabilities to emerge organically from "brainstorming" sessions, claiming that brainstorming and other open-ended discussion forms will be sufficient – a claim many have challenged, as this chapter will discuss shortly.

For example, in the US$110 million Madhya Pradesh District Poverty Investment Project (MPDPIP) in India, World Bank staff and government worked together to develop a project in which the government agreed to on-grant the loan for productive activities undertaken by five-person "common interest groups," so long as these groups always included a majority of poor or marginalized people. Some village-wide activities would also be funded. The project was "open menu," which means that subgroups within targeted communities could submit any income-generating proposal, with a few exceptions (liquor stores, arms, religious dwellings, direct purchase of supplies for sale, etc.), and receive a small grant. This project design seems to provide communities and their subgroups with the capability to pursue valuable work-related functionings, thus providing an ideal setting in which to observe the value judgments.

To execute this project, MPDPIP planned to hire and train a total of 800 facilitators (called PFTs) over five years to assist communities in developing proposals that address poverty in their villages (other World Bank projects involve up to 2,500 such facilitators). Drawn from NGOs and the civil service, the 800 facilitators were trained to spread information, to manage financial contributions, to organize and support groups, and to access technical assistance as needed. Because of these responsibilities, the recruitment and selection procedures were stringent. Candidates attended a residential weekend where assessors selected those who demonstrated a willingness to learn, who seemed self-motivated and independent, and who were likely to develop rapport with the communities.[9] Successful candidates received an increase in salary and a promotion, although their circumstances became more difficult because they and their families relocated to the village cluster where they worked, without support staff and with only a motorcycle for transportation. Subsequently, facilitators regularly gathered as a group for a series of residential week-long training courses in topics such as orientation, entering a village and start-up activities, accounting, micro-planning, group formation, village development plans, and common project types (lift irrigation, goats, wells).

But they received no specific training in how to facilitate an efficient, flexible, systematic discussion of values the communities want to retain and enhance in their lives. Nor did facilitators receive training in how to address value conflict (facilitators are made acutely aware of power issues. Their training focuses on attitudes that empower, and how to manage relationships with both village leaders and marginalized groups, which are necessary but insufficient skills). Given that the facilitators may be veterinarians or horticulturalists or irrigation engineers or block development officers, their previous training and experience may not equip them to address these issues. And MPDPIP is only one example of a community-driven development project – of which there are several in India. Although the scale is very different indeed, the responsibilities of facilitators in MPDPIP and of field staff for NGOs such as Oxfam and ActionAid are quite similar.[10]

Facilitators and catalysts

This discrepancy between an inadequate "form" and an ambitious desired "outcome" is in part due to the fact that the shape of participation – during the deliberative planning exercises as well as the link between the exercises and the final decisions – often depends heavily upon the "facilitator(s)" of the planning. In many areas, participatory processes are an innovation rather than an established cultural or social practice that is used by many institutions. In these cases, facilitators form the hub of participatory activities – whether planning or implementation or monitoring and evaluation. Through conversations, discussions, and example, they communicate an alternative way of making collective decisions. The power of these persons is considerable. Thus, creating sound operational forms of participatory planning entails some engagement with these agents, to assure they have the skills required to facilitate the "value judgments" inherent in this work, and are rewarded for using them. Yet, as was mentioned earlier, these facilitators may not be trained in "forms" by which to guide value judgments, so rely on their innate aptitude and skills, which vary.

For in this setting, as in so many others, group responses (even to well-trained facilitators) may not reflect people's individual or shared values – or even their views – exactly. One reason for this is a power imbalance vis-à-vis the facilitator him- or herself. Chambers observed a decade or so ago that there is a regular pattern of beneficiaries ("lowers") reflecting back what they expect facilitators ("uppers") wish to hear:

> It has been a sobering experience to observe a charismatic outsider interrogate farmers who strain their minds and imaginations to say what they think he wants. Again and again they found the right words. The intelligent prudence of the lowers confirmed the conviction of the upper, unaware of his inadvertent ventriloquism.
>
> (1994)

This occurs in practice even with facilitators who have been trained to avoid this problem. The facilitators of the MPDPIP project were trained intensively and mentored repeatedly in best-practice PRA in 1999 and 2000. To avoid "inadvertent ventriloquism," they learned how to put others at ease, how to listen well, and how to create a "safe" and creative setting where (it is hoped) people will speak their mind. Yet by a remarkable coincidence, the projects facilitated by irrigation engineers tended to be lift irrigation projects; veterinarians' communities tended to "demand" livestock projects – and so on. Of course there were some sterling exceptions, but the "ventriloquist" trend was noticeable to those managing and monitoring the project.[11] As this example suggests, even when facilitators are well trained in PRA, "open-ended" questions may produce "inadvertent ventriloquism" where respondents say what the questioner hopes to hear. Thus, the capabilities this project was designed to produce were somewhat contrived.

Perhaps if facilitators also were familiar with a set of "forms" or participatory exercises by which they could facilitate the priority-setting exercises at key junctures, this might help to structure the dialogue more systematically, and decrease reliance on their individual skills in inspiring trust and creating deliberative moments.

Values exercises

Anisur Rahman, while discussing what development might mean to people who have not lost their sense of identity and continue to express themselves through authentic collective endeavors, noted that the challenge to social scientists is to "articulate an alternative development paradigm in which the evolution of popular life is not to be distorted and abused by paternalistic 'development' endeavours with alien conceptions but may be stimulated and assisted to find its highest self-expression which only can make a society proud of itself" (Rahman 1995: 153).

This difficult challenge of trying to achieve "highest self-expression" within the context of open-menu participatory activities is increasingly being recognized. In order to learn from these experiences, we surveyed many descriptions of open-menu participatory practices, the well-known methods such as PRA as well as alternative methods. We identified, from these sources, those exercises that specifically raised the values issue mentioned above (Alkire *et al.* 2003; Alkire and Mathai 2003). We found that in addition to the requisite attitudinal training (focusing on the facilitator, and attuning him or her to the attitudes of humility, listening, open-mindedness, creativity, and so on), the exercises or techniques fell broadly into three categories: (i) longitudinal exercises – for example, where a group creates a timeline to identify changes, then sketches a future timeline; (ii) interior exercises, in which, through meditation or direct personal reflection on their own experiences, people clarify the values individually before bringing them to the group; and (iii) exercises that evoke discussion around different dimensions of human development. I will introduce the first two of these briefly, and concentrate on the third.

Attitude and competence

"Attitudinal change and support measures" is arguably a *sine qua non*, for without it, facilitators may impose their own values for many reasons. Training programs commonly devote considerable time and energy to the cultivation of appropriate attitudes. For example, attitudes are cultivated in very preliminary PRA training exercises such as "handing over the stick" – in which the facilitator learns to hand the pointing stick over to the local community so that they can point to a chart and explain – or "not dominating" – in which the facilitator learns what it feels like to sit on the floor and talk to someone sitting on a chair, and learns to avoid this and other, often unconscious, ways of dominating others.

As the expanding body of studies are making clear, the practical effect of these attitudinal change exercises is mixed. Some people become enthusiastic "converts"; others do not. Furthermore, attitudes do not provide concrete exercises or forms to facilitate value judgments.

Longitudinal exercises

The key insight of this first set of exercises is that people are able to reflect constructively on valued capabilities when they reflect on concrete capability changes – whether these are changes that they have witnessed in their own lifetimes, or changes that they contemplate will occur in the lives of their children and grandchildren. Such historical reflection can seem lively to participants, and is relatively easy to facilitate in comparison, for example, with dimensions that can seem "abstract" if not done well.

These exercises proceed by participants first identifying a capability change (we opened a girls' school; we rebuilt our mosque after the floods) and subsequently assessing the change – what was good and what was bad; how important this event was, relative to others; who else was affected. In this way, "wider" or "big-picture" values can be discussed in a thoroughly instantiated rather than abstract manner.

For example, in one common PRA exercise the community together develops a "timeline" of significant events that tell their history – signal events might be natural (a hot, dry summer; a bumper crop of sugarcane) or political (a coup) or personal (an epidemic came and six people perished). These corporate timelines – which are familiar – can then be used subsequently. Variations include a "personal life events" activity in which people share and reflect on significant life events in different segments of life. The segments vary by culture but might include childhood, student or unmarried life, marriage, or the years with small children (for those without children this is done differently), etc. In a future longitudinal exercise called the "Grandchildren" exercise, members identify changes that are happening currently in their community or other communities, reflect on what they know about other cultures (positive and negative), then identify key capabilities they would like to pass on to their grandchildren.

Interior exercises

Some people can better identify and articulate to one another their values in the context of silence, of introspection, and of tranquility. Whereas many group exercises tend to generate a certain amount of nervous energy and focus on developing group dynamics, introspective and meditative energies turn the eyes of the imagination within. In situations where meditation/introspection is a welcome practice, facilitators can lead a "personal life events" exercise as an individual rather than a group exercise, or pose a question then schedule a time of silent meditation, prior to a discussion of valuable capabilities in the future.

Dimensions exercises

The third approach tries to deepen the discussion by mentioning dimensions of value in which human communities globally have expressed values. The real use of this "tool" is to make sure that some dimension that the community really values is not left out, either because people forget about it in the heat of discussion or because they presume that the facilitator is not interested (as in matters of faith or family), or because they are not used to talking about these issues in a group (such as culture or inner peace). I have tried to elaborate these methods elsewhere, with respect to ex-post evaluation or impact assessment procedures (Alkire 2002a); here, they are discussed in the context of participatory planning (on which see Max-Neef 1993).

The set of dimensions facilitators might use was based on rather extensive research on lists that have been developed by activists, basic needs theorists, human development psychologists, cross-cultural psychologists, philosophers, and values survey tools (Alkire 2002b). Of course it can be modified locally – for example, one group modified it to include gender relations as a distinct category of relationships; many groups change the wording so that the concepts resonate in their language. The dimensions are as follows.

Dimensions

1 *Life* – its maintenance and transmission; health and safety.
2 *Knowledge* – practical and useful education, understanding, wisdom.
3 *Aesthetic experiences* – beauty and whatever intensely engages our capacities to know and feel.
4 *Meaningful work*.
5 *Recreation/play* – relaxation, resting, entertainment, etc.
6 *Relationships* – harmony between and among individuals and groups; friendship, living at peace with others, neighborliness, social capital.
7 *Inner peace* – the harmony of one's inner feelings with one's judgments and choices.
8 *Participation* – the ability to make decisions that matter, to plan and shape one's life.
9 *Religion* – harmony with some more-than-human source of meaning and value, etc.

The dimensions can be introduced in planning exercises in different ways. For example:

- The facilitator begins by remembering concrete changes in the community over time, perhaps using the "impact tree" of PRA. Then as the conversation evolves, the facilitator will gradually introduce, and inquire about, dimensions that have not yet been mentioned. In that way, people can clarify their values about the past, and the facilitator generates the "language" and concrete examples that are needed in order to think about the values in the future. As far as possible, participants should play leading roles in the exercise by drawing or writing, facilitating, providing input on how to change or modify the exercise, etc.
- When the conversation is vigorous, then turn to the future and explain the planning exercises – as well as the follow-up. Of course, to do this

exercise also requires concrete information – regarding the expectations of and commitments by different external institutions as well as expectations concerning local people – but we focus only on the aspects pertinent to constructive deliberation.

- When the various key projects have been tentatively identified, the facilitator might double-check, using the "dimensions," that the potential set of capabilities is relatively complete, or whether there are any additional capabilities that they wish to add.

A related prospective systematic planning was vigorously developed by Manfred Max-Neef and spread into many communities through the Human Scale Development work. It conducts two-day participatory planning workshops employing a similar matrix of dimensions.

Limitations and timing of constructive discussion

While greater attention to the selection and prioritization of capabilities may greatly enrich a participatory planning process, this is obviously not sufficient for well-functioning social changes, as has been stressed previously.

For example, in the context of open-menu activities discussed earlier, facilitators need to be comfortable with proposals that arise outside their area of competence, and a separate issue is how they can access the assistance needed to facilitate creative proposals successfully, so that poverty is actually reduced, rather than groups being further disheartened by a failed attempt. Otherwise, naturally a veterinarian will (and should) prefer a livestock problem on the pragmatic grounds that he or she is more likely to be able to troubleshoot any difficulties and bring about a successful outcome that effectively reduces poverty. Facilitators also need supervision systems that reward the extra effort needed to facilitate unusual requests. Such very practical institutional flexibilities, capacities, and incentives are required in order to support "open-menu" projects, and respond to a variety of capability sets.

Beyond this, it is not necessary that all instances of participatory planning engage in extensive constructive discussion before selecting a capability set to pursue. In newly formed groups that have coalesced in the face of urgent and visible needs, the appropriate focus for planning is issues of implementation and problem solving only. Only later, when the group has experienced some progress and addressed the most urgent need, and its members have gained confidence in their ability to work together, will wider discussions appear useful to participants. For example, in MPDPIP the first project would be conceived and implemented quickly; its aim was to create a visible and valuable common good, but also to gain the trust of the community that the institution was able to deploy resources swiftly and to effect.

A different example arises from a case study in Washington DC in the Anacostia neighborhood, which roughly corresponded to the city designation of ANC 8A (Ward 8, Subsection A). The neighborhood is visibly deprived, with 30 percent of dwellings being abandoned, often piled with waste and uncut grass. Residents complain of drug rings, regular gun violence, lack of police support (the police take hours to respond to emergency calls), crime, unsafe driving practices exacerbated by a dearth of stop signs and traffic lights, and poor educational facilities. The household poverty rate is 49.9 percent, the highest in the district; the child poverty rate was 62.2 percent, whereas the average in Washington DC was 31.7 percent. Unemployment rates were 30.5 percent in 2000 (and in fact only 34.2 percent of the population were employed), and 25.5 percent of households were on public assistance, the highest in the district (US Census Bureau figures for 2000). While life expectancy is not computed by ANC subdivisions, the life expectancy for African American males in Washington DC is 57.5 years (and ANC 8A is over 98 percent African American) (Mayor's web page 2003).

A group of residents came together from local churches to begin to address the most visible of these common problems. They were very much at the initial stages of formation as a group, being unaccustomed to participatory methods and having never worked together before. Thus, although the meetings were conducted with the set of "dimensions" posted on the wall, and although these were explained briefly in the second meeting (and led to a new stream of conversation about how the churches could take actions – both religious and social – on their own, without city support), no attempt was made to discuss them systematically because it became rapidly apparent that the impatience for action was great. Instead, in this case study facilitators merely supported the community in the clear first steps of organizing, identifying three "feasible" goals,[12] having a large public event with city representatives answering key demands, and holding the representatives accountable for their promises afterwards. The energies of participatory planning are often best focused on concrete tasks rather than the making of value judgments.

But at some junctures, communities do pause either to reflect on a troubling trade-off or to make an integrated longer-term strategic plan. For example, Sungi, an NGO working in Hazara, Pakistan, developed a Village Development Plan (VDP) process to combine social development with community mobilization. Using PRA, Sungi staff facilitated a process of reflection and analysis by women and men in a village, in a number of meetings over a period of several months. Through this process, villagers identified and analyzed local issues. At the end of this process, program and field Sungi staff came together for one day. They examined the charts and diagrams, which were made by both men and women, to recall all the issues. On the basis of analysis, they decided on a flexible range of support that Sungi as an institution could offer to that village if requested to do so.

The next day, staff facilitated a "VDP closing" process in the village. During this process, women and men separately viewed the charts and diagrams (made by both men and women), revisited the local issues (water supply, road, deforestation, health, etc.) and prioritized capabilities. Men and women did this activity in separate groups working in separate locations. This allowed differences in gender perspective to emerge visibly. Subsequently, each group identified key actors who could oversee progress, such as individuals, local institutions, Sungi, government agencies, etc. The women's and men's groups then traded their draft plans, discussed discrepancies, and formed a five-year VDP. Sungi's tasks under this plan became the basis for a Partnership Agreement between Sungi and its local partner. The agreement acted as a tool for mutual accountability. When necessary, Sungi facilitated meetings with other institutions to explore additional partnerships.

Similarly, in the MPDPIP project it was envisaged that after a village had been engaged as a partner for six to twelve months, and after a number of common interest groups had completed small activities, they would undertake a "Village Visioning Process." This process would plan more comprehensively the village's relations with the project as well as with other government agencies and institutions. Again in the Aga Khan Rural Support Project in Pakistan, all of the villages along a valley would gather together in a summit from time to time, to consolidate their requests and inform AKRSP (the NGO) of the kinds of support they would require in the upcoming time period. During this valley summit the facilitator explained the meeting to new representatives, using an apt image. He said, "We [AKRSP] are like a camel. The camel has a ring in its nose. There is a rope slipped through the ring. You are holding that rope. You can lead us where you want us to go." In that discussion many issues arose, ranging from fear that development would bring unwanted values (high divorce rates, a lack of care for aging parents, a decline in religious devotion) to the need for all-weather roads.

It is at these kinds of junctures that value judgments of the sort that the capability approach advocates may be made: when many disparate functionings are under consideration at the same time – ranging from very tangible and concrete projects (roads, cemeteries, school buildings) to the more elusive cultural or intangible functionings (relationships to parents, religious devotion, dress customs).[13] And when the community can make judgments with some confidence that they will result in action.

Power imbalances

Participatory planning and approaches recognize that human diversity includes diversity in power – ranging from the power of verbal expression in a group to social, economic, political, or moral powers. Most commonly recognized, of course, is the power of the landlord(s) or the local elite.

Facilitators are thus schooled in different techniques to manage these power differentials in the course of a constructive discussion regarding values and priorities (by having the quiet speak more, or by managing the tendency of the powerful to dominate the discussion). They also learn other techniques such as having meetings of only poor persons, or only women, or only young people, or only a particular professional group, so as to make sure their views are fully heard. They struggle with decisions of how or when to use their credibility and power to confront rather than cajole the local elite into cooperation with activities that empower the poor relatively more than the elite. But is managing the composition of focus groups, and the environment of group discussions, sufficient to compensate for the power of the landlord over others, or of men over women, or of one caste or class or occupational group over others? Hardly (see Appadurai 1996; Blackburn and Holland 1998; Chambers 1994; Cooke and Kothari 2001; Crush 1995; Deneulin 2002a, b; Dore n.d.; Ellerman 2001; Escobar 1984; Guijt and Kaul Shah 1998; Goulet 1992; Khwaja 2001; Max-Neef 1989; Michener 1998; Nandy 1994; Narayan-Parker *et al.* 2000a; Narayan-Parker *et al.* 2000b; Nelson and Wright 1995; Rahman 1995; Sachs 1992; Stiefel and Wolfe 1994; Streeten 1984; Vivian 1994; Vivian and Maseko 1994).

Participatory development usually involves episodic encounters with a facilitator, and in some cases the power of this person creates an imbalance. This person may visit the community once every few weeks for a few hours or, occasionally, several days. In contrast, the power differentials are constant and ongoing. Time hangs between the "facilitator" visits in which prior power differentials can be emphatically reinserted – the poor persons instructed in what to say or bullied into promises of submission. Violence is regularly a threat.

When several field studies were undertaken in three provinces of India, the problem of facilitator power was raised repeatedly. Facilitators themselves stressed that every attempt should continue to be made to train facilitators in conflict management so as to prevent outbreaks of violence. They should also consider how project activities appropriately benefit the local elite so that the project is at once poverty focused and politically viable within the local context. Yet the periodic visits by such trained facilitators were unlikely to be sufficient safeguards for more equitable development in the long term, and in some cases in the short term. It could be equally important to strengthen other protective mechanisms such as legal and judicial systems, indigenous and religious institutions, political processes, or relationships with outside agencies that might counterbalance the force of the local elite.

Thus, even when activities are designed to "expand capabilities" and enable requisite value judgments to be made locally, two kinds of "power imbalances" regularly divert these projects from their design. The first, as discussed earlier in this chapter, emanates from the "facilitators" of the participatory process not having a "form" by which to raise value judgments explicity. The second is the very familiar issue of opposition to poverty activities by local elites. Participation, as a test case of a collective form or process for making value judgments (such as public debate, democratic practice, deliberative democracy, and other similar processes) cannot fulfill its function as providing a space for value judgments without direct attention to the long-term and nonviolent management of local power differentials.

Conclusion

This chapter and the studies upon which it draws explored the potential that "forms" of participatory discussion have for enabling communities – including communities riven by power and value conflicts – to identify common value judgments and priorities. It draws together the experience indicating that the forms of participatory planning do indeed have the potential for creating deliberative moments.

Notes

1 See, for example, Nussbaum and Sen (1993) and Nussbaum (1994, 2000).
2 On this and related proposals, see also David Crocker's chapter in this book (Chapter 8), which discusses Sen's capability approach as it relates to both deliberative democracy (especially the work of Richardson, Bowman, Gutmann, and Thompson) and participation.
3 For a survey of Sen's writings on public debate beginning with *poverty and famines*, see Alkire (forthcoming).
4 For a description of some of these mechanisms, see Sen (1970: 192–193).
5 Note that I refer to participatory planning as planning of activities by the people who will be involved and affected by the activity. Some development institutions such as the World Bank would refer to this as participation during project implementation (because planning, for them, refers to planning of the World Bank loan rather than local subcomponents of it).
6 For a description of how these are undertaken, see World Bank (1996). For one description of some of the shortcomings of a CDF exercise, see Deneulin (2002a).
7 For example, the annual "citizen's summit" in Washington DC or the popular forum in New York after September 11 regarding the use of the grounds upon which the World Trade Center towers had stood.
8 For overviews of participatory methodologies, see, for example, Blackburn and Holland (1998), Cooke and Kothari (2001), Guijt and Kaul Shah (1998), Oakley and Marsden (1984), Rietbergen-McCracken and Narayan-Parker (1997), Stiefel and Wolfe (1994), and Uphoff (1998).
9 These "Guidelines for Staff Recruitment and Selection" were developed in partnership by the staff of an NGO called SRIJAN.
10 This is based on fieldwork in 2001, and subsequent correspondence with field staff.
11 Observation, and interviews with the MPDPIP project director in her Bhopal office and with Mr. R. K. Tiwari, monitoring and learning officer, MPDPIP.
12 In this case, the three priorities were: addressing the unkempt appearance of

abandoned housing, installing traffic calming devices around schools and along the worst road, and providing summer recreation activities for children (which one of the churches undertook voluntarily because the City did not).

13 The other case where this kind of discussion may be timely is a more closely defined situation in which a decision must be made about a possible intervention (e.g. a new factory, a first paved road) that will fundamentally alter many capabilities – expanding some and contracting others – and some public consideration of these trade-offs, and of how to manage negative impacts, is appropriate.

Bibliography

Alkire, S. (2002a) "Dimensions of Human Development," *World Development* 30 (2): 181–205.

Alkire, S. (2002b) *Valuing Freedoms: Sen's Capability Approach and Poverty Reduction*, Oxford: Oxford University Press.

Alkire, S. and Mathai, M. (2003) "Empowering Values: A Review of Participatory Processes Designed to Identify and Clarify Values," mimeo.

Alkire, S. *et al.* (2003) "Responding to the Values of the Poor: A Training Module on Culture, Values, and Conflicts," mimeo.

Alkire, S. (forthcoming) "Structual Injustice and Democratic Practice: The trajectory in Sen's writings," in S. Deneulin, M. Nebel and N. Sagovsky (eds) *Capability and Justice*, Kluwer Academic Press.

Appadurai, A. (1996) *Modernity at Large: Cultural Dimensions of Globalization*, Minneapolis: University of Minnesota Press.

Bamberger, M. (1988) *The Role of Community Participation in Development Planning and Project Management: Report of a Workshop on Community Participation*, held in Washington DC, September 22–25, 1986, Washington, DC: World Bank.

Blackburn, J. and Holland, J. (1998) *Who Changes? Institutionalizing Participation in Development*, London: Intermediate Technology Publications.

Blair, H. (2000) "Participation and Accountability at the Periphery: Democratic Local Governance in Six Countries," *World Development* 28 (1): 21.

Bohman, J. (1996) *Public Deliberation: Pluralism, Complexity, and Democracy*, Cambridge, MA: MIT Press.

Bohnet, I. and Frey, B. S. (1994) "Direct Democratic Rules: The Role of Discussion," *Kyklos* 47: 341–354.

Carmen, R. (2000) "Prima mangiare, poi filosofare," *Journal of International Development* 12: 1019–1030.

Cernea, M. (1991) *Putting People First: Sociological Variables in Rural Development*, New York: University Press.

Chambers, R. (1993) *Challenging the Professions: Frontiers for Rural Development*, London: Intermediate Technology Publications.

Chambers, R. (1994) "All Power Deceives," *IDS Bulletin* 25 (2).

Chambers, R. (1997) *Whose Reality Counts? Putting the First Last*, London: Intermediate Technology Publications.

Cooke, B. and Kothari, U. (2001) *Participation: The New Tyranny?*, London: Zed Books.

Crush, J. S. (1995) *Power of Development*, London: Routledge.

Deneulin, Severine (2002a) "Responding to the Values of the Poor through Participation: The Case of the Dominican Republic," mimeo.
Deneulin, S. (2002b) "Perfectionism, Paternalism and Liberalism in Sen and Nussbaum's Capability Approach," *Review of Political Economy* 14 (4): 497–518.
Dore, R. (n.d.) "Sixth Dudley Seers Memorial Lecture: Why Visiting Sociologists Fail," IDS Discussion Paper 341.
Drèze, J. and Sen, A. K. (2002) *India, Development and Participation*, New Delhi: Oxford University Press.
Edwards, M. and Hulme, D. (1992) *Making a Difference: NGOs and Development in a Changing World*, London: Earthscan.
Edwards, M. and Hulme, D. (1995) *Non-governmental Organisations: Performance and Accountability beyond the Magic Bullet*, London: Earthscan.
Ellerman, D. (2001) *Helping People Help Themselves: Towards a Theory of Autonomy-Compatible Help*, Washington, DC: World Bank.
Elster, Jon (ed.) (1998) *Deliberative Democracy*, Cambridge: Cambridge University Press.
Escobar, A. (1984) "Discourse and Power in Development: Michel Foucault and the Relevance of His Work to the Third World," *Alternatives* 10: 377–400.
Escobar, A. (1995) *Encountering Development: The Making and Unmaking of the Third World*, Princeton, NJ: Princeton University Press.
Finnis, J. (1999) "Natural Law and the Ethics of Discourse," *Ratio Juris* 12 (4): 354.
Forester, J. (1999) *The Deliberative Practitioner: Encouraging Participatory Planning Processes*, Cambridge, MA: MIT Press.
Fung, A. and Olin Wright, E. (eds) (2003) *Deepening Democracy: Institutional Innovations in Empowered Participatory Governance*, London: Verso.
Guijt, I. and Kaul Shah, M. (eds) (1998) *The Myth of Community*, London: Intermediate Technology Publications.
Goulet, D. (1992) "Development: Creator and Destroyer of Values," *World Development* 20 (3): 467–475.
Gutmann, A. and Thompson, D. (1996) *Democracy and Disagreement*, Cambridge, MA: Belknap Press.
Isham, J., Narayan, D. and Pritchatt, L. (1995) "Does Participation Improve Performance? Establishing Causality with Subjective Data," *World Bank Economic Review* 9 (2): 175–200.
Jasek-Rysdahl, K. (2001) "Applying Sen's Capabilities Framework to Neighbourhoods: Using Local Asset Maps to Deepen Our Understanding of Well Being," *Review of Social Economy* 59 (3): 313–329.
Juliet, C. (1995) *Conversations with Samuel Beckett and Bram van Velde*, trans. Janey Tucker, Leiden: Academic Press.
Khan, M. (1995) "Participatory Approaches in Rural Development Planning in Pakistan," *Journal of Rural Development and Administration* 27 (1).
Khwaja, A. I. (2001) "Can Good Projects Succeed in Bad Communities? Collective Action in the Himalayas," Annual Bank Conference on Development Economics, Washington, DC.
Koh, H. H. and Slye, R. (1999) *Deliberative Democracy and Human Rights*, New Haven, CT: Yale University Press.
Macedo, Stephen (ed.) (1999) *Deliberative Politics: Essays on Democracy and Disagreement*, Oxford: Oxford University Press.
Mansuri, G. and Rao, V. (2003) "Evaluating Community-Based and Community-

Driven Development: A Critical Review of the Evidence." The World Bank, September 2003.

Mathai, M. (2002) "Case Studies: Observations on Operationalizing Sen's Capability Approach," mimeo.

Max-Neef, M. (1989) "Human Scale Development: An Option for the Future," *Development Dialogue* 1: 5–81.

Max-Neef, M. A. (1992) *From the Outside Looking In: Experiences in "Barefoot Economics,"* London: Zed Books.

Max-Neef, M. (1993) *Human Scale Development: Conception, Application and Further Reflections*, London: Apex Press.

Michener, V. J. (1998) The participatory approach: contradiction and co-option in Burkina Faso.

Nandy, A. (1994) "Culture, Voice and Development: A Primer for the Unsuspecting," *Thesis Eleven* 39: 1–18.

Narayan-Parker, D. (1993) *Participatory Evaluation: Tools for Managing Change in Water and Sanitation*, Washington, DC: World Bank.

Narayan-Parker, D. (1995) *Designing Community Based Development*, Washington, DC: World Bank.

Narayan-Parker, D., Chambers, R., Shah, M. and Petesch, P. (2000a) Crying Out for Change: Voices of the Poor, Washington, DC: World Bank Publications/Oxford University Press.

Narayan-Parker, D., Patel, R., Schafft, K., Rademacher, A. and Koch-Schulte, S. (2000b) Can Anyone Hear Us? Voices of the Poor, Washington, DC: World Bank.

Nelson, N. and Wright, S. (1995) *Power and Participatory Development: Theory and Practice*, London: Intermediate Technology Publications.

Nussbaum, M. (1994) "Skepticism about Practical Reason in Literature and the Law," *Harvard Law Review* 10: 714–744.

Nussbaum, M. (2000) *Women and Human Development: The Capabilities Approach*, Cambridge: Cambridge University Press.

Nussbaum, M. (2003) "Capabilities as Fundamental Entitlements: Sen and Social Justice," *Feminist Economics* 9 (2/3): 33–59.

Nussbaum, M. and Sen, A. (1993) *The Quality of Life*, Oxford: Clarendon Press.

Oakley, P. and Marsden, D. (1984) *Approaches to Participation in Rural Development*, Geneva: International Labour Office.

Paul, E. F., Millar, F. D., and Paul, J. (eds) (2000) *Democracy*, Cambridge: Cambridge University Press.

Qizilbash, Mozaffar (2002) "Development, Common Foes and Shared Values," *Review of Political Economy* 14: 463–480.

Rahman, M. A. (1993) *People's Self Development: Perspectives on Participatory Action Research: A Journey through Experience*, London and Dhaka: Zed Books and Dhaka University Press.

Rahman, M. A. (1995) "Toward an Alternative Development Paradigm," in Richard Morse, Anisur Rahman, and Kersten L. Johnson (eds) *Grassroots Horizons: Connecting Participatory Development Initiatives East and West*, London: Intermediate Technology Publications.

Richardson, H. (1997) *Practical Reasoning about Final Ends*, Cambridge: Cambridge University Press.

Richardson, H. (2002) *Democratic Autonomy: Public Reasoning about the Ends of Policy*, Oxford: Oxford University Press.

Rietbergen-McCracken, J. and Narayan-Parker, D. (1997) *Participatory Tools and Techniques: A Resource Kit for Participation and Social Assessment*, Washington, DC: World Bank.
Sachs, W. (1992) *The Development Dictionary: A Guide to Knowledge as Power*, London: Zed Books.
Salmen, L. F. (1987) *Listen to the People: Participant-Observer Evaluation of Development Projects*, New York: Oxford University Press.
Salmen, L. F. (1995) *Beneficiary Assessment: An Approach Described*, Washington, DC: World Bank.
Salmen, L. F. (1999) *Beneficiary Assessment Manual for Social Funds*, Washington, DC: World Bank.
Sen, A. (1970) *Collective Choice and Social Welfare*, San Francisco: Holden-Day.
Sen, A. (1982) "Liberty as Control: An Appraisal," *Midwest Studies in Philosophy* 7: 207–221.
Sen, A. (1983) "Liberty and Social Choice," *Journal of Philosophy* 80 (1): 5–28.
Sen, A. (1985) *Commodities and Capabilities*. Amsterdam: Elsevier Science.
Sen, A. (1987) *On Ethics and Economics*, Oxford: Blackwell.
Sen, A. (1992) *Inequality Reexamined*, Oxford: Clarendon Press.
Sen, A. (1993) "Capability and Well-being," in Amartya Sen and Martha Nussbaum (eds) *The Quality of Life*. Oxford: Clarendon Press: 30–53.
Sen, A. (1999a) "Democracy as a Universal Value," *Journal of Democracy* 10 (3): 3.
Sen, A. (1999b) *Development as Freedom*, New York: Knopf.
Sen, A. (1999c) "The Possibility of Social Choice," *American Economic Review* 89 (3): 349–378.
Sen, A. (2002a) "Consequential Evaluation and Practical Reason," *Journal of Philosophy* 97 (9): 477.
Sen, A. (2002b) *Rationality and Freedom*, Cambridge, MA: Harvard University Press.
Stiefel, M. and Wolfe, M. (1994) *A Voice for the Excluded: Popular Participation in Development: Utopia or Necessity?*, London: Zed Books.
Streeten, P. (1984) "Basic Needs: Some Unsettled Questions," *World Development* 12 (9): 973–978.
Sunstein, C. (2001) *Designing Democracy: What Constitutions Do*, Oxford: Oxford University Press.
Sunstein, C. (2003) *Why Societies Need Dissent*, Cambridge, MA: Harvard University Press.
Uphoff, Norman (1998) "Learning about and for Participation: From Theoretical and Empirical Studies to Practical Experience, and Back to Theory," *Canadian Journal of Development Studies* 19 (3): 439–460.
Vivian, J. M. (1994) "NGOs and Sustainable Development in Zimbabwe: No Magic Bullets," *Development and Change* 25 (1): 167–193.
Vivian, J. M. and Maseko, G. (1994) *NGOs, Participation and Rural Development: Testing the Assumptions with Evidence from Zimbabwe*, Geneva: United Nations Research Institute for Social Development.
Wade, R. (1988) "Village Republics: Economic Conditions for Collective Action in South India," *Cambridge South Asian Studies* 40.
World Bank (1996) *The World Bank Participation Sourcebook*, Washington, DC: World Bank.
Young, I. M. (2000) *Inclusion and Democracy*, Oxford: Oxford University Press.

8 Sen and deliberative democracy

David A. Crocker

In this chapter I argue for two claims. First, I contend that Sen's capability approach to social ethics and international development requires democracy conceived as public discussion as well as fair and free elections. Specifically, I argue that Sen's normative assumptions – especially the way he understands and employs the concepts of agency, capability, and functionings – enable him to argue for democracy's threefold importance and that, in turn, democratic discussion and decision making are not only permitted but also required by his normative vision. Second, I make a case that Sen's conception of democracy would be fruitfully enriched and specified by explicitly drawing on some features of the theory and practice of what is called "deliberative democracy." I discuss and evaluate recent work on the nature, merits, challenges, and limits of deliberative democracy and argue that this perspective is an important resource for the capability approach in its efforts to deepen democracy, design participatory institutions, and make democracy central to development challenges of our times.

Sen's capability approach and democracy

In this chapter I argue for two claims. First, I contend that Sen's capability approach to social ethics and international development permits or, better, requires democracy conceived as public deliberation. Second, I make a case that Sen's conception of democracy, which he adumbrates in his recent work, would be fruitfully enriched and specified by the theory and practice of what is called "deliberative democracy." It is especially in *Development as Freedom* (1999b), "Democracy as a Universal Value" (1999a), and the second edition of *India: Development and Participation* (Drèze and Sen 2002) that Sen makes clear his commitment to democracy conceived as public discussion and democratic decision making.

In the chapter's first part I argue that Sen's normative assumptions enable him to argue for democracy's threefold importance and that, in turn, democratic discussion and decision making are not only permitted but also required by his normative vision. In the second part I discuss the theory and practice of deliberative democracy and argue that this perspective is an important resource for the capability approach in its efforts to deepen democracy, design participatory institutions, and make democracy central to development. In particular, recent work on the nature, merits, challenges, and limits of deliberative democracy has much to offer the capability approach as it seeks to meet the democratic and development challenges of our times.

Agency and well-being, freedom and achievement

In other places (Crocker 1992, 1995, forthcoming). I offer a detailed interpretation of the normative "foundation" of Sen's social ethic, namely, his cross-cutting distinctions of agency and well-being, on the one hand, and achievement and freedom, on the other. Here, with the help of the following diagram, I summarize the basic ideas:

	Agency	*Well-being*
Achievement	Agency achievement	Well-being achievements (functionings)
Freedom	Agency freedom	Well-being freedoms (capabilities)

Sen conceives of *agency* and *well-being* as two distinguishable but linked aspects of human life, each of which calls for respect (aid, protection) on the part of institutions and individuals. In turn, both agency and well-being have two dimensions, namely, actual *achievements* in the world and the *freedom* for those achievements. "Functioning" and "capability" are terms that Sen frequently employs, especially in his more technical writing, to connote well-being achievement and well-being freedom, respectively.

Although the concept of capability is important in Sen's social ethic, it is nevertheless regrettable that his approach is typically called the "capability approach." In some contexts, functionings are, for Sen, more important than capabilities. Moreover, since both well-being freedom and agency freedom are normatively important, he is right to refer to his overall perspective as a "freedom-centered" approach. Finally, since the exercise of and freedom for agency are not only morally crucial but often neglected in political thought and practice, there is good reason to call his outlook the "agent-oriented view" (Sen 1999b: 11). Let us examine each of these four dimensions in more detail.

Humans can and should be agents in the sense that they can decide and act to realize their aims, often making a difference to the world. Regardless of whether a person's goals are altruistic or self-regarding, her "agency achievement refers to the realization of goals and values she has reasons to pursue" (Sen 1992: 56). For Sen, if one is acted on by outside persons or other forces or happens to act on a whim or impulse but for no reason, one is not an agent (in charge of herself) but a "patient," a passive object, acted on by external or internal forces over which one has no control. A person as agent is "someone who acts and brings about change, and whose achievements can be judged in terms of her own values and objectives, whether or not we assess them in terms of some external criteria as well" (Sen 1999b: 19; see also Sen 1985: 203–241; 1999b: 4, 11, 17–18, 53, 190–191, 281, 287–288; Alkire 2002: 6 n. 18; 9).

Humans not only exhibit more or less agency, but they are often able or free to do so. One's agency freedom is "one's freedom to bring about the achievements one values and which one attempts to produce" (Sen 1992: 56). I might be an agent, but because of external coercion or internal compulsion at present I am not now free to choose or to achieve what I choose. Moreover, a person even might get what he or she wants and thereby realize a capability, but if that person "is being forced to do exactly what she would have chosen to do anyway," he or she lacks agency freedom. Increasingly Sen calls this aspect the "process aspect of freedom" in contrast to the "opportunity aspect of freedom" (2002: 331). One reason that development, conceived as good social change, is important for Sen is that it provides a variety of social arrangements in which human beings express their agency, or become freer to do so. The ethically sensitive analyst evaluates development policies and practices in the light of the extent to which they promote, protect, and restore human agency rather than merely the good or bad things that happen to people:

> Social arrangements, involving many institutions (the state, the market, the legal system, political parties, the media, public interest groups, and public discussion forums, among others) are investigated in terms of their contribution to enhancing and guaranteeing the substantive freedoms of individuals, seen as active agents of change, rather than passive recipients of dispensed benefits.
>
> (Sen 1999b: xii–xiii)

> In terms of the medieval distinction between "the patient" and "the agent," this freedom-centered understanding of economics and of the process of development is very much an agent-oriented view. With adequate social opportunities, individuals can effectively shape their own destiny and help each other. They need not be seen primarily as passive recipients of the benefits of cunning development programs. There is indeed a strong rationale for recognizing the positive role of free and sustainable agency – and even of constructive impatience.
>
> (Sen 1999b: 11)

One challenge for Sen and for deliberative democratic theorists is to give an account of how public deliberation provides devices for *collective* agency, a process for combining the decisions and agency freedoms of many agents. For Sen, groups as well as individual persons can and should be authors of their own lives.

It should not be thought, however, that Sen's emphasis on agency entails that an agent's freedom must mean that the agent him- or herself always exercises or controls the "levers" of change.[1] Even if I do not choose to vote, so long as I am not prohibited or restrained from voting I have agency freedom to vote. For Sen, my agency freedom is enhanced when something I value occurs even when I had nothing to do with its occurrence but would have chosen it had I *had* the chance. If someone else eliminates the famine that besets me, not only is my well-being improved, but my agency freedom is enhanced, since had I been able, I would have chosen to end the famine and contributed to its end. Tyrants are restrained not only by their "subjects'" agency freedom as active doing (what Sen calls "control"), but also by their knowledge that their "subjects" have the freedom of agency (even though they do not choose to use it right now) (see Pettit 1997). Even though my senator – and not me – casts a vote to disconfirm the president's nomination for attorney general, my agency freedom has been expanded despite the fact that I did not cast a vote – and was not able to do so – for or against the nomination. I voted for my senator but did not cast *this* vote. However, I would have voted the way my senator did, had I had the chance.

My agency freedom is realized, then, if someone else brings about what I value and would myself have chosen to bring about. This realization of agency freedom must be sharply contrasted with the violation of agency freedom (or "the process aspect" of freedom) that would occur if a tyrant forced me to do what I would have chosen to do on my own. Agency or "the process aspect of freedom" has to do with "the fairness or equity of the processes involved, or about the freedom of citizens to invoke and utilize procedures that are equitable" (Sen 2004: 336).

In addition to the norm of agency – both agency achievement and agency freedom – Sen proposes the norm of human well-being. Sometimes humans as agents choose to benefit themselves or gain "personal advantage," and sometimes their goals or adopted causes reach beyond themselves and even require that they sacrifice themselves. For Sen,

> the well-being achievement of a person can be seen as an evaluation of the "wellness" of a person's state of being (rather than, say, the goodness of her contribution to the country, or her success in achieving her overall goals).
>
> (1993: 36)

Of course, if a person decides that his own personal welfare or advantage is his exclusive life goal, then he has exercised his agency exclusively in the service of his well-being. Most people, however, have commitments to others and to goals beyond their own well-being. If my agency is the only source of my life's going well or ill, then my well- or ill-being owes nothing to outside causes or internal compulsions.

Sen conceives well-being not just as happiness or preference satisfaction, although such may be involved, but as a plurality of subjective and objective states of being and a variety of doings, which he calls "functionings." One exercise that individuals and groups engage in is that of evaluating which functionings they have reason to value. Unlike Nussbaum's list of those functionings, which she claims we need into order to be "fully human" (Nussbaum 2000: 87) or to flourish, Sen adamantly refuses to prescribe a list. However, to illustrate the kind of well-being achievement or functionings that may be valued, he typically gives examples of functions that people judge valuable. Moreover, to illustrate what evaluators take to be minimally acceptable levels of the most valuable or basic functionings – and thereby define poverty as the deprivation of these functionings – he frequently offers the following as a typical result of valuation:

> The functionings relevant to this analysis [of poverty] vary from such elementary physical ones as being well-nourished, being adequately clothed and sheltered, avoiding preventable morbidity, etc., to more complex social achievements such as taking part in the life of the community, being able to appear in public without shame, and so on. These are rather "general" functionings, but … the specific form that their fulfillments may take would tend to vary from society to society.
> (Sen 1992: 110)

Like agency, well-being has a freedom dimension as well as an achievement dimension. My life goes well not only when I am adequately nourished (and have other functionings that I have reason to value), but also when I am free to continue to be so or am free to be so again. Because I am on a hunger strike to protest a military invasion, I may be very deficient with respect to numerous functionings that I value, but – unlike the starving person – I have the capability (given my income and opportunities) or freedom to escape from hunger and the other deprivations. The valuable capabilities or freedoms are not part of my current well-being achievement but are *possible* achievements. *Being able* or *free* to fight off disease is as much a part of my current well-being as being healthy right now. The freedoms that enrich human life and constitute the primary end of development include not only agency freedom, just discussed, but also basic capabilities or well-being freedoms:

> The substantive freedoms include elementary capabilities like being able to avoid such deprivations as starvation, undernourishment, escapable morbidity and premature mortality, as well as the freedoms that are associated with being literate and numerate, enjoying political participation and uncensored speech and so on. In this constitutive

> perspective, development involves expansion of these and other basic freedoms.
>
> (Sen 1999b: 36)

Although sometimes Sen regrets introducing the term "capability" as a fundamental notion in his development ethics, it is a useful term so long as we note that there are other normative considerations and that capability refers to opportunities or possible functionings – related to both external enabling conditions and internal powers or other personal traits. I may have the physical and intellectual ability to cast a ballot but be unable to vote because I live in a repressive dictatorship that holds no elections. I may live in a country with fair and free elections but be incapable of voting because I am an infant or have Alzheimer's disease. To have the (actual and not potential) capability to be healthy is to have both access to health care and the internal ability to make use of it.

What is democracy?

Given the moral space of agency, both freedom and achievement, and well-being (both capabilities to function and functionings), how does Sen argue for democracy? On the level of nation-state governance, Sen argues that democratic governance is important for intrinsic, instrumental, and what he calls "constructive" reasons (see Sen 1999b: 148; 1999a: 9–11; Drèze and Sen 2002: 24–25). Let us analyze and evaluate each of these justifications and relate them to Sen's key ethical notions. Before doing so, however, it is important to grasp Sen's normative definition of democracy:

> What exactly is democracy? We must not identify democracy with majority rule. Democracy has complex demands, which certainly include voting and respect for election results, but it also requires the protection of liberties and freedoms, respect for legal entitlements, and the guaranteeing of free discussion and uncensored distribution of news and fair comment. Even elections can be deeply defective if they occur without the different sides getting an adequate opportunity to present their respective cases, or without the electorate enjoying the freedom to obtain news and to consider the views of the competing protagonists. Democracy is a demanding system, and not just a mechanical condition (like majority rule) taken in isolation.
>
> (Sen 1999a: 9–10)

This definition is normative in the sense that it sets forth what Sen calls the "ideals" of democracy, in contrast to its "institutions" and its "practice," and portrays democracy as a "demanding system" of governance. It is demanding with respect to *breadth*: for in democracy there is "widespread actual participation, including the most disadvantaged" (Drèze and Sen 2002: 24) and an "equitable distribution of power" (ibid.: 347). Democracy is also demanding with respect to *depth*, because it requires more robust modes of participation than just voting or majority rule – for example, free discussion and the give and take of opposing arguments. Finally, as we shall see in Sen's argument for its constructive importance, democracy is demanding with respect to *range* of the questions that citizens should democratically deliberate and decide.[2]

Democracy's intrinsic value

First, Sen argues that democracy is intrinsically good because it enables citizens to participate politically, and this freedom is something people have reason to value as intrinsically valuable. Democracy and political and civil rights have, says Sen, "*direct* importance in human living associated with basic capabilities (including that of political and social participation)" (1999b: 148); "[p]olitical and social participation has *intrinsic value* for human life and well-being" (1999a: 10). Opportunities for political participation as well as actual participation help make our lives go well, and "to be prevented from participation in the political life of the community is a major deprivation" (1999a: 10).

Sen might be criticized here for smuggling into his liberalism a conception that the good life and even the best life is one of political engagement. That objection, however, would assume that Sen identifies well-being and human flourishing, which he does not. Sen's concept of well-being refers to personal advantage, one's life going well, and not to a life of realizing one's "highest" potentials. Another objection might be that, far from contributing to personal advantage, political activity is for many either boring or burdensome (or both). Sen's point, however, is not about the joys of political activity so much as the loss that comes from being excluded from participation.

Let us push further. One reason that being prevented from political involvement is bad is that it means that someone makes decisions for me, someone else runs my life. Yet surprisingly Sen does not make this move. He does not say that democracy is intrinsically important because in democracy citizens exercise their agency as well as have the freedom to do so. As an agent I decide and act rather than being the recipient of someone else's decision and action. Sen can and, I believe, should say that democracy is intrinsically valuable because democracy provides each citizen with agency freedom and, often, agency achievement insofar as democracy provides its citizens with opportunities to select their leaders and their policies. Good development provides social arrangements, including democratic processes, in which human beings are free to express their agency, "shape their own destiny" (Sen 1999b: 11), and "be in charge of their own well-being" (ibib.: 288):

> Social arrangements, involving many institutions (the state, the market, the legal system, political parties, the media, public interest groups, and public discussion forums, among others) are investigated in terms of their contribution to enhancing and guaranteeing the substantive freedoms of individuals, seen as active agents of change, rather than passive recipients of dispensed benefits.
>
> (ibid.: xii–xiii)

Although he does not explicitly justify democracy by appeal to human agency, Sen does provide the materials, then, to construct such an argument. Because an individual's agency or autonomy is one basis for his or her dignity, we can also say that implicit in Sen's outlook is the argument that democracy is important because it respects people's dignity and their right of self-determination.

In democratic self-rule, agency freedom and achievement is collective as well as individual. Consider the Huaorani, a small Indian tribe that lives in the Ecuadorian Amazon. This relatively pristine region is one undergoing rapid change due to oil exploration and extraction, environmental degradation, and new settlers seeking land and work. It is also a region with newly protected areas, politically significant alliances among Indian tribes, partnerships with the government and oil companies, and new opportunities, such as ecotourism. A long-time resident of the area remarks on the Huaoranis' right to be among the agents of their own change:

> Change is inevitable. The Huaorani cannot avoid change. The real question is, on what terms will change occur? The right the Huaorani have – a basic moral right that all people have – is to be allowed to evolve their own cultural tools for dealing with change, rather than having that change imposed upon them.
>
> (Kane 1996: 75)

Another observer of the Huaorani notes that in one of their villages (Quehueire Ono), the Huaorani have decided on a creative mixture of old and new:

> [The stack of written documents that an Huaorani association had produced in its first two years of operation] suggested that while it would be tempting to see Quehueire Ono as a return to tradition that would be inaccurate. If anything, Quehueire Ono represented a Huaorani synthesis: a traditional way of living enhanced by certain modern tools that offered access to an *abundancia* not found in the forest and on which, increasingly, they had come to depend. That is, *cowode* [non-Huaorani] abundance. And in what must be considered a rat's nest of paradox and irony, one of the most valued of these new tools was literacy.
>
> (ibid.: 137–138)

Sen, I believe, would judge the "Huaorani synthesis" less as paradoxical and more as a creative outcome of people collectively exercising their agency – their human right to decide together what parts of their traditional life to abandon, what parts to retain, and what parts to adapt, and how to supplement or modify their traditional life with new ideas. Although he employs the language of capabilities at the start of the following passage, he finally makes his normative point in the language of action or agency:

> We come back again to the perspective of capabilities: that different sections of the society (and not just the socially privileged) should be able to be active in the decisions regarding what to preserve and what to let go. There is no compulsion to preserve every departing lifestyle even at heavy cost, but there is a real need – for social justice – for people to be able to take part in these social decisions, if they so choose.
>
> (Sen 1999b: 241)[3]

In effect, we see the materials from which Sen can and should construct an argument – based on the value or dignity of agency – for the intrinsic worth of democratic processes: democracy embodies or expresses individual and collective agency; agency is intrinsically valuable (because it is one basis of human dignity); so, democracy is intrinsically valuable.

This Huaorani case also alerts us that Sen should add or make explicit a third dimension in arguing democracy's intrinsic value. That dimension is equality. We have reason to value democracy as inherently good because it assumes that all adult members of the group are equal with respect to the worth or dignity of their agency. Apart from whatever good consequences it may have, democracy is intrinsically important because it treats members of the group as having *equal* status, freedom, and agency.[4] Although Sen does not explicitly offer this egalitarian argument for democracy's intrinsic worth, it is clear that he believes that "equitable distribution of power" (Drèze and Sen 2002: 347) is among the democratic ideals. He can also appeal to the link between agency and the process aspect of freedom discussed above: democracy is justified because it provides a fair and equitable procedure for social choice. In a democracy, citizens have agency or process freedom: they are "free to invoke and utilize procedures that are equitable" (Sen 2004: 336).

In summary, implicit in Sen's work is a complex argument – appealing to human well-being, agency (dignity), the process aspect of freedom, and equality – for the intrinsic worth of democracy and the inclusion of democratization in development. Daniel Little, in a volume heavily indebted to Sen and Nussbaum, felicitously combines the three components to argue for the intrinsic value of democracy in development:

> Is democracy a morally important institution? Should we include democratization within the set of fundamental values and goals of development? Democracy is a crucial aspect of human freedom. Fundamentally, it is a good thing because it facilitates free human choice and furthers the good of political participation. Democracy is a necessary component of the individual's ability to live freely and autonomously. And democracy is a political form that pays appropriate heed to the inherent worth and dignity of the person. Thus, democracy is a central constituent of the individual's ability to live freely and autonomously as a human being.
>
> (Little 2003: 229)[5]

Democracy's instrumental value

Democracy, Sen contends, is also instrumentally good. Democracies have the good consequences of not warring against each other, and in bad times democracies are more responsive than nondemocracies to the importance of protecting human agency (voice) and well-being: "Democracy has an *instrumental* role in enhancing the hearing that people get in response to their claims to political attention (including their economic needs)" (Drèze and Sen 2002: 24). Although a benevolent dictator may listen to "his" people and respond compassionately to their needs, he is likely to insulate himself from popular demands. Although narrow democracies may exclude the voices of the poor, and thin democracies may relegate the poor to voting, distributive justice is more likely to occur in even a formal or minimal democracy than in a nondemocracy (see Halperin *et al.* 2005).

A citizen's freedom not to starve, frequently benefits from the "protective power of democracy" (Sen 1999b: 43). Democracy is especially valuable in times of crisis. A free press, for example, may identify a pressing human problem such as an imminent famine and, before it becomes a reality, "demand appropriate public action" (Sen 1999b: 150–151). Or, following a disaster, such as the tsunamis of December 26, 2004, a region is more likely to prevent or mitigate a recurrence if and when citizens have the freedom to press their demands for compensation and future security. In a democratic country, government officials have an incentive – if they want to be reelected – to pay attention to what people want and demand.[6]

Democracy's constructive value

Finally, Sen argues that democratic governance is "constructively" good insofar as it provides institutions and processes in which people can learn from each other and "construct," or decide on the values and priorities of, the society (1999b: 152–153): "Value formation is as much a democratic activity as is the use of social values in the determination of public policy and social response" (Drèze and Sen 2002: 25). In this third and most original of his three arguments for democracy, Sen identifies an aspect of the capability approach to which the theory of deliberative democracy may contribute by offering a principled account of the processes groups employ to decide certain questions and form their values. What, more precisely, are these sorts of social choices? Although Sen has never listed these choices in one place, an inspection of his writings reveals at least the following:

1 *The choice of agents and participants*. Who should be a member of the group and who or what is to make (further) choices? Should the group make its own choices and make them deliberatively, or should it choose to have some other agent or authority make them? Like most participatory and deliberative theorists, Sen assumes that people who are most affected by a decision should make the decision.
2 *The choice of the process of decision making*. Just as individuals can make their own decisions in many ways (such as by coin flipping, whim, appeal to authority, appeal to expertise, critical reflection), so groups have a choice from among several collective decision-making procedures, including some form of democratic decision making. Sen has devoted much of the work over the course of his career to the rational scrutiny of various social choice processes (see, most recently, Drèze and Sen 2002).
3 *The choice of agency versus well-being*. When the community's choice to make its *own* decisions (rather than have someone else make them) is likely to reduce the well-being of its members or vice versa, it faces a fundamental decision not only about agency but also of agency versus well-being. This choice is the social version of an individual's choice between what Sen calls the opportunity aspect of freedom, which concerns capabilities for functionings, and the process aspect of freedom, which concerns agency and process:

> A person may, in a specific case, have more direct control over the levers of operation and yet be less able to bring about what she values. When such a divergence occurs, we can go in somewhat different directions. We may, in many cases, value real opportunities to achieve certain things no matter how this is brought about ("don't leave the choice to me, you know this restaurant and my tastes, you should choose what I would like to have"). But we may also value, in many cases, the process of choice ("I know you can express my views much better than I can, but let me speak for myself").
>
> (Sen 2002: 10; see also Sen 2004)

A society also has a choice between helping its members achieve their agency goals, such as by building a statue to some citizen's hero (Sen 1992: 71), or, in contrast, by "mak[ing] sure that no one has to starve, or fail to obtain medical attention for a serious but eminently treatable ailment" (ibid.: 70–71). If there were only two options (and Sen rejects such a dichotomy), is it better to have a "nanny state" in which the state and its experts both run the show and provide for basic need satisfaction of its passive citizens, or a government in which citizens exercise political agency but achieve a lower level of well-being? Sen's own judgment is clear, but the decision of the relative weights of agency versus well-being is one that groups must often make:

> The alternative to an exclusive reliance on individual responsibility is not, as is sometimes assumed, the so-called nanny state. There is a difference between "nannying" an individuals' choices and creating more opportunity for choice and for substantive decisions for individuals who can then act responsibly on that basis.
>
> (Sen 1999b: 284)

4 *The choice between functioning and capability.* Within the "space" of well-being, a community sometimes must choose between a functioning, such as some of its members being made healthy now (through curative medicine) and as a capability, members in general being made free from ill health (through preventive medicine). Decisions concerning aid to immediate versus future victims of massive natural disasters, such as the tsunamis of December 26, 2004, often have this character.

5 *The choice between functionings (or capabilities) now and functionings (or capabilities) in the future.* A community with scant food may have to decide between present and future ill functioning, such being ill-nourished now and being ill-nourished in the future. A militant group in a repressive society may forgo public protest now in order to be free to engage in it in the future.

6 *The choice and weighting of* valuable *capabilities and functionings.* As I argue elsewhere (Crocker 1992, 1995, forthcoming), once in the "space" of capabilities and functioning, individuals and communities often must decide on those capabilities and functionings that are most valuable, those that are less valuable, those that are trivial, and those that are evil. Nussbaum conceives of the task as that of constructing – on the basis of her intuitions and through critical dialogue with others – an objective but incomplete and revisable list of valuable capabilities to be embodied in the nation's constitution (Nussbaum 2000). The role that Nussbaum gives to the philosopher and a constitution, Sen gives to the society or group itself. For Sen, a society has the freedom and responsibility to choose which capabilities and functionings are most valuable and to weight or prioritize them for diverse purposes in different contexts. This additional topic for collective choice is justified because, for Sen, we have reason to want to be free of *ex ante* priority rules, algorithmic formulas of rationality (Drèze and Sen 2002:

49), or even a "unique blueprint for 'the just society'" (Sen 1999b: 287). Such weightings would "lock" a group

> prematurely into one specific system for "weighting" some of these competitive concerns, which would severely restrict the room for democratic decision making in this crucial resolution (and more generally in "social choice," including the variety of processes that relate to participation).
>
> (ibid.: 286)

7 *The choice of* basic *capabilities and thresholds*. Not only can a society select certain capabilities as ones that it generally has more reason to value than others, but also it can – for certain purposes – designate some capabilities as *basic*. For Sen, a "basic capability" is "the ability to satisfy certain elementary and crucially important functionings up to certain levels" (1992: 46 n. 19).[7] This exercise, of course, requires that the community decide on a threshold or level, taking into account its level of prosperity and expected external assistance. It is in this context that Sen argues that a community can define what it means by the (basic) needs that social arrangements should meet: "Even the idea of 'needs' (including the understanding of 'economic needs'), which is often taken to be fixed and well-defined, can respond to public discussion and exchange of information, views and analyses" (Drèze and Sen 2002: 25; see also Sen 1999b: 153–154).
8 *The choice between* basic *capabilities and expansion of* all *valuable capabilities*. Alkire correctly identifies a further choice that is only implicit in Sen's writings but one that communities sometimes face, namely between the promotion of basic capabilities and the expansion of all valuable capabilities or freedoms. Alkire remarks, "[This choice] allows commendation of activities that may be expected to meet basic needs. But it also allows a community to choose to leave some basic needs unmet" (2002: 195). This discretionary power is exactly the sort of thing that Nussbaum's constitutionalism, which I criticize in Crocker (forthcoming), intends to avoid.
9 *The choice to specify general capabilities and functionings*. Supposing that a group selects certain capabilities and functionings as valuable and even basic, it is still free to *specify* its selections in certain ways. It can, as both Nussbaum (2000: 77) and Henry Richardson (2002: 104, 154, 214, 246) argue, reason collectively about ends by specifying these capabilities and functionings, making them more precise. The capability to appear in public without shame can be specified differently in the Costa Rican rainforest than in the Norwegian tundra.
10 *The choice of distributive and other values*. Communities also can and should choose distributive and other values, how to interpret them, and how to prioritize them. Among the values open for a community

> to decide is that of just or fair distribution (strict equality, proportionate shortfall from one's potential, capability to be above a threshold, nondominance). But, while important, justice once decided, contends Sen, is not everything, and a community has the freedom to decide to value and sometimes prioritize other values such as efficiency (the maximizing of the sum of individual advantage no matter how distributed; Sen 1992: 146–147), social cohesion, social stability, social tranquility (freedom from anxiety-producing choices), and compensation for bad luck (Alkire 2002: 92).

Sen makes the same fundamental point for each of these ten kinds of choice. Each of these types of choice – including the choices of who should make the choices and how they should do so – confronts groups, from the local to the global level. It is clear, as we have seen, that for Sen "public scrutiny and criticism" (Sen 1999b: 30) have a role to play in these valuational debates, and that such debate "is a crucial part of the exercise of democracy and responsible social choice" (ibid.: 110). Rather than authorizing rule by philosophers, other experts, or a mere aggregation of citizen preferences, Sen endorses public discussion and democracy.

Sen contends that "the struggle for democracy around the world ... is the most profound challenge of our times" (2003: 28) but that the conception of democracy is often excessively narrow. In addition to balloting, which can be an enormous achievement, Sen maintains that democracy should be understood, following John Rawls, as "the exercise of public reason" (ibid.: 29). Sen continues that "this more capacious concept [of democracy] includes the opportunity for citizens to participate in political discussions and so to be in a position to influence public choice" (ibid.: 29).

But what does Sen mean by public scrutiny and public reason? How does he conceive of the process of public valuational and policy discussion? What, more precisely, are his views on democratic decision making as a kind of "responsible social choice"? Who should engage in this process, in what venues, and how should they do so – in ways consistent with Sen's basic value commitments?

Although he gives us hints, it is precisely at this point that Sen needs to go further. Alkire correctly identifies what is missing:

> The problem is that, although Sen regularly refers to the need for explicit scrutiny of individual and social goals, for reflectiveness, value judgment, practical reason, and democratic social choice, he chooses not to specify the possible range of procedures by which valuational issues are to be resolved or by which information on valuations is to be obtained.
>
> (Alkire 2002: 13)

Sen himself recognizes that the literature on deliberative democracy provides a resource for addressing these questions of democratic procedures and principles. When discussing the "practice of democracy" in both democratic and nondemocratic regimes, Sen observes that people must seize the participatory opportunities that exist. Then he adds that whether or not people take advantage of these opportunities "depends on a variety of factors." In a formal democracy these factors would include "the vigor of multiparty politics," while in a nondemocracy or predemocracy the role of opposition parties may be important. Another, and related, factor, presumably in all societies, would be "the dynamism of moral arguments and value formation" (Sen 1999b: 155–156). Then, in a footnote, Sen interestingly continues: "An important factor [in people seizing democratic opportunities] is the reach of deliberative politics and of the utilization of moral arguments in public debates" (ibid.: 329 n 9). Sen proceeds to cite leading examples of the then current (1999) works on deliberative democracy.[8] However, although Sen opens the door to an explicit engagement between the capability approach and deliberative democracy, he has only begun to venture through it.

Sen's strong endorsement of democratic "practice," and his distinguishing it from democratic ideals and institutions, is part of his claim that the latter do "not serve as an automatic remedy of ailments as quinine works to remedy malaria" (1999b: 155). Democracy is not, as the first Mayor Daley allegedly said about another matter, a "pancreas." In addition to the important role of democratic values and institutions, democratic citizens must "make democracy work" by committing themselves to and engaging in the "practice" of democracy. Yet, we must add, although it is true that deliberative politics has an important role in the "practice" of democracy, the *theory* of deliberative democracy can enrich the ideals of democracy, shape new institutional devices, and guide citizens in the practice of democratic deliberation. Or so I shall argue.

Deliberative democracy

In this second part of the chapter, I argue that there are several ways in which Sen's capability approach can benefit from recent work on deliberative democracy. As a working – but not uncontroversial – definition of deliberative democracy, I follow John Rawls:

> The definitive idea for deliberative democracy is the idea of deliberation itself. When citizens deliberate, they exchange views and debate their supporting reasons concerning public political questions. They suppose that their political opinions may be revised by discussion with other citizens; and therefore these opinions are not simply a fixed outcome of their existing private or nonpolitical interests. It is at this point that public reason is crucial, for it characterizes such citizens'

reasoning concerning constitutional essentials and matters of basic justice.

(Rawls 1999: 138–139)[9]

By considering the way certain deliberative democracy theorists pose and answer questions concerning the purpose, conditions, process, outcomes, and limits of deliberation, we (and Sen) may find resources to enrich his democratic turn in social and development ethics. Moreover, at least one deliberative democracy theorist, James Bohman, has adapted some of Sen's ideas to solve problems within deliberative democracy (Bohman 1996). It may be, then, that engaging Sen and deliberative democracy will prove beneficial in both directions.

The deliberative democracy literature – both for and against – has in recent years become a cottage industry. It is a heterogeneous literature that sports both different versions and diverse criticisms of deliberative democracy, and some of the former have been formulated to meet some of the latter. In the present chapter I have insufficient space to analyze in a systematic way the merits and weaknesses of the various versions or criticisms, although occasionally I will take sides in particular controversies. Rather, my aim here is to identify several key ideas in the deliberative democracy movement that would enable Sen and others to develop an explicitly deliberative-democratic version of the capability approach.

First, I take up the question of the purpose of deliberation, and then, second, explain three ideals that seem to me to be especially important, namely, reciprocity, publicity, and accountability. Third, drawing on these ideals, I explore answers to the question "Who deliberates?" Fourth, I address the question of background conditions that enable group members to deliberate. Fifth, I follow Richardson's reconstruction of the process of deliberation to emphasize that a deliberative group reasons together about what ought to be done by, among other things, forming joint intentions. Finally, I consider the personal capacities and virtues of deliberators.

Deliberative aims

A popular conception of both actual and ideal democracy is that democracy is having a government that holds regular, competitive elections in which the candidate or issue with the most votes wins (Przeworski 1999; Schumpeter 1942). A somewhat more robust, but still rather minimalist, definition conceives democratic politics as entailing "a rule of law, promotion of civil and political liberties, free and fair election of lawmakers" (Young 2000: 5; cf. Diamond 1999: 1–19). The general task of deliberative democrats is to start with the idea that democracy is rule by the people and then deepen and broaden the conception of "rule" by stressing a kind of inclusive and public discussion and by extending popular rule to at least some nongovernmental associations.

If such is the goal of deliberative democrats, then how do they understand the aims of deliberative discussion and decision making? Two aims stand out. First, deliberation aims to solve *concrete* problems or to devise general policies for solving specific problems; second, deliberation's goal is to provide a fair way in which free and equal members of a group can overcome their differences and reach agreement about action and policy.

In introducing *Deepening Democracy: Institutional Innovations in Empowered Participatory Governance*, a volume that presents and evaluates four case studies in deliberative democracy, editors Archon Fung and Erick Olin Wright nicely capture the practical or problem-solving orientation of deliberative democracy:

> The first distinctive characteristic of the cases … is that they all develop governance structures geared to quite concrete concerns. These experiments, though often linked to social movements and political parties, differ from both in that they focus on practical problems, such as providing public safety, training workers, caring for habitats, or constructing sensible municipal budgets. If these experiments make headway on these issues, then they offer a potential retort to widespread doubts about the efficacy of state action. More importantly, they would deliver goods to sectors of society that are often most grievously denied them.
>
> (Fung and Wright 2003: 16)

Although Sen so far has emphasized that public discussion enables group members to collectively scrutinize and improve their individual and shared values, Fung and Wright stress that "empowered participatory governance" "extends the application of deliberation from abstract questions over value conflicts and principles of justice to very concrete matters such as street paving, school improvement, and habitat management" (2003: 15). One advantage of this Deweyan "problem-solving" approach, so far not evident in Sen's work, is that it enables scholars to evaluate institutional experiments in deliberative decision making and "explore strategies to improve its quality" (ibid.: 15). Another advantage is that the practical orientation of deliberative democracy offers a way to achieve deliberative democracy's second goal of fairly reducing disagreement among group members: "This practical focus also creates situations in which actors accustomed to competing with one another for power or resources might begin to cooperate and build more congenial relations" (ibid.: 16). Emphasizing deliberative democracy as a problem-solving method does not rule out Sen's focus on value formation, for sometimes groups need to go beyond immediate problems to broader and less specific issues. Exclusive focus on, say, street paving might weaken the deliberative character of the group once the streets are paved. And solving the problem of potholes may not occur unless the group resolves the deeper problems of redistributive taxation. Yet as we shall see presently, Fung and Wright's stress on public deliberation as practical problem solving cautions group members to avoid ascending to value commitments when such ascent polarizes the group or jeopardizes practical agreements.

Deliberative democracy is a collective device not only to solve concrete problems, but also to make fair decisions. Here, fairness means that *each* member is treated with respect in that each member has the right to make his or her voice heard and to contribute to the final decision.

A group informed by this second deliberative aim contrasts with a group in which many – the poor or ethnic majorities or minorities – are excluded from the decision-making process. A deliberatively democratic group also contrasts with a group that practices a democratic procedure that is merely aggregative. In aggregative democracy, preferences or interests are formed in private and then expressed and added together in public. The aim of aggregative democracy is to elicit these private and unscrutinized preferences and additively combine them. If all the members prefer the same policy or objective, everyone gets what they want. In the usual cases where group members differ – sometimes radically – in their preferences, mere aggregation means either that the majority (or option with the most votes) wins or that there is no nonarbitrary winner, owing to voting "cycles."[10] In the former case, minority views lose out altogether and a danger of majority tyranny over the minority exists. In the latter case the lack of a nonarbitrary winner seems to doom democracy and lead to some kind of authoritarianism. Aggregative social choice, as Sen himself sees it, seems to be "inevitably arbitrary or irremediably despotic" (Sen 2002: 69).

In the version of deliberative democracy that I favor, the focus of collective choice is not on preferences (what members want to do) or beliefs (what members believe about the world), but on joint and shared intentions to strive for certain goals and enact certain policies (see Richardson 1997: 349–382; 2002: 162–176). The point of deliberation is to provide a fair way for roughly equal group members to cooperate together and forge – through the give-and-take of proposals, reasons, and criticisms – a reasoned agreement about their goals, values, policies, and actions. As a result, deliberative democracy publicly "transforms" (Young 2000: 26) rather than merely aggregates preferences. Or, more accurately, in order to solve a common and practical problem, group members together make and rationally scrutinize competing proposals for policies and respectfully hammer out mutually acceptable intentions for action.

Rather than presupposing a preexisting agreement, deliberative democracy assumes that citizens disagree – sometimes deeply and bitterly – about what is to be done. It offers public deliberation as the process by which citizens – who initially disagree and may continue to do so – may generate a social choice. As Gutmann and Thompson put it, "recognizing that politics cannot be purged of moral conflict, it [deliberative democracy] seeks a common view on how citizens should publicly deliberate when they fundamentally disagree" (1996: 93). Without clarifying his views of public reason or explaining the process of public discussion, Sen also recognizes that such discussion begins in a context of disagreement:

> The ideal of public reasoning is closely linked with two particular social practices that deserve specific attention: the tolerance of different points of view (along with the acceptability of agreeing to disagree) and the encouragement of public discussion (along with endorsing the value of learning from others).
>
> (Sen 2003: 31)

Deliberative ideals

A further contribution of deliberative democracy – especially Gutmann and Thompson's version – to Sen's capability approach consists of clarifying and defending three principles that should regulate collectively reasoned agreements: reciprocity, publicity, and accountability. The ideal of reciprocity prescribes that each group member makes proposals and offers justification in terms that others can understand and could accept: "Deliberative democracy asks citizens to justify public policy by giving reasons that can be accepted by those who are bound by it" (Gutmann and Thompson 1996: 52). Each would do so knowing that the others will do likewise. Reciprocity is an apt term, for it suggests that each make an appropriate response to a good received:[11] "The 'good received' is that you make your claims on terms that I can accept in principle. The 'proportionate return' is that I make my claims on terms that you can accept in principle" (ibid.: 55).

The aim, presupposing that the group involves cooperation among equal and free members, is to form an agreement that is mutually acceptable. Ideal deliberators build on whatever common commitments they share or come to share in order to reduce their disagreements. In such reciprocity, each does more than put up with or grudgingly forbear the – perhaps despised – views of others, for each critically engages with the others, making accommodations and sometimes deep compromises in order to fashion something all or most can endorse.

The ideal of publicity likewise is important, and Gutmann and Thompson's ideal helps us flesh out Sen's reference to "public" discussion and the importance of "rich" information for rational choice. Publicity demands, among other things, that each member is free to engage (directly or by representation) in the deliberative process, that the process is transparent to all (rather than being done, as Habermas would say, "behind their backs"), and that each knows that to which he or she is agreeing or disagreeing. Sometimes, of course, publicity must be set aside in favor of secrecy, but publicity should be the presumption, and any general limits to publicity should issue from public deliberation.

A third ideal for deliberation is that of accountability. Each group member is accountable to all (and not to him- or herself alone) in the sense of giving acceptable reasons to the others. It should not be thought that deliberative democracy concerns only face-to-face groups in which all are directly present in the give-and-take of reasons. In larger-scale deliberative forums, representatives, officials, or leaders "who make decisions on behalf of other people, whether or not they are electoral constituents, should be accountable to those people" (Gutmann and Thompson 2000: 169). Although a representative's constituents do not directly participate in the course of parliamentary deliberation, constituents rightly hold accountable those who represent them, and the former thereby indirectly participate in the deliberative process of forming joint intentions. Moreover, owing to publicity, constituents can monitor both the course of deliberation and the group's eventual decision, and through their representatives intervene in the former and challenge the latter.

Accountability extends, then, not only to one's fellow group members and their subgroups and not only to those one represents, but also to those in other groups who are bound by the group's decisions or affected by its actions. Deliberative democrats differ over whether these persons – affected by the group but not members of it – deserve an accounting or even should have a voice or some other role in the decisions that affect them. At least each of two contiguous groups may gain voice in the deliberations of the other by scaling up to form a more inclusive group or by forming a new higher-level and overlapping representative group to address mutual problems (for instance, a joint committee of the US House and the Senate, or an inter-county committee for two adjacent counties).

Who should deliberate?

This last point about voice enables us to identify a third contribution that deliberative democracy can make to Sen's version of the capability approach. If we are to emphasize deliberation and some conception of the ideals that might guide the process of deliberation, then we must answer two related questions: which groups should practice deliberative democracy and, within the deliberating groups, which members (and perhaps nonmembers) should deliberate and decide? These are large and important questions, and all I can hope to do in this chapter is identify them, urge defenders of the capability approach to take them up, and encourage proponents of deliberative democracy to contribute to their resolution.

I first address the question of the scope or reach of deliberative democracy. The most radical answers would be monistic, for they would either affirm or deny that deliberative democracy should be the ideal for every governmental and nongovernmental group at levels from the local to the global. John Dewey, for example, distinguishes between "democracy as a social ideal and political democracy as a system of government." As an ideal, democracy for Dewey would be "barren and empty save as it is incarnated" in all types of "human relationships":

> The idea of democracy is a wider and fuller idea than can be exemplified in the state even at its best. To be realized it must affect all modes of human association, the family, the school, industry, religion. And even as far as political arrangements are concerned, governmental institutions are but a mechanism for securing to an idea channels of effective operation.
>
> (1927: 143).

For a radical deliberative democrat, all groups that currently operate on nondemocratic or antidemocratic principles should be targets for internally adopted or externally promoted deliberative democracy. This list would include families, including patriarchical ones; small-scale income-generation projects in Afghanistan; associations, such as the Augusta National Golf Association; governments (at all levels), such as that of Iran; international institutions, such as the World Bank; and global institutions, such as the Roman Catholic Church. The trouble with this perspective is that it fails to respect what William Galston (2002) calls "the expressive liberty" of groups to conduct their affairs according to, if they so choose, nondeliberative and nondemocratic principles and practices.

A less radical alternative would be to affirm that democracy, in general, and deliberative democracy, in particular, has limits, for example, in scientific inquiry, judicial review, sports teams, traditional religious communities, or private golf clubs. Democratic deliberation, however, is relevant for, on the one hand, democratic politics and such governing institutions as legislative bodies, administrative agencies, and, on the other hand, nongovernmental groups whose members view themselves as free and equal and engaged in a cooperative enterprise. Even this less radical first-level position that affirms the limits of public deliberation might appeal to democratic deliberation on a second or meta-level. On this second-level approach, the clashes between groups – whether democratic or nondemocratic – as well as the scope and limits of deliberative democracy should themselves be settled by democratic deliberation. Democratic deliberation would, like the turtles mythically alleged to support the universe, "go all the way down." Are there any nondeliberative bases for challenging the results of deliberation?

Although we might agree that deliberation is one intrinsic good, because it enables people to exercise their agency, we decide when to employ deliberation on the basis of some other principle. Some evidence exists, for example, that a manipulative elite sometimes uses deliberation as a means of dominating others. If so, a group might choose deliberation or a theorist might propose it only if deliberation did not result in domination (see Shapiro 2003: chs. 1 and 2). Understanding both deliberation and nondomination as sometimes coincident and sometimes competing intrinsic values seems to be entirely compatible with Sen's value pluralism. It does not respond fully to Galston's challenge of whether respect for "expressive liberty" requires noninterference with and respect for a hierarchical group based on relations of obedience to authority.

Who has the best answer to the question of the limits and applicability of deliberative democracy (and to the second-level question of who should decide)?[12] It is not yet clear, but capability proponents should take up these issues and the various proposals. Which groups should be deliberatively democratic and who should decide this question (and how) regarding the scope of democratic deliberation? These questions raise such further questions as: which members of groups should engage in deliberation?

Some deliberative groups have formed already, some are in the process of formation, and sometimes unaffiliated individuals decide to form a deliberative group. Who in the group – or outside it – should have an (equal) opportunity to deliberate and vote? Should there be a minimum threshold of cognitive ability, perhaps with age as a proxy? Can one forfeit one's right to participate by committing a felony (see Broder 2003: 27)? Should legal or illegal immigrants havc a voicc but not thc right to votc, or should the right to vote be extended only to citizens? Should different levels of citizenship exist? More generally, should those outside the group have a voice in deliberations and a right to vote? What, if anything, should qualify someone to join a citizen's forum whose task is to address a contentious issue such as damming a pristine river or preventing snowmobilers from entering a wilderness used by cross-country skiers? Can anyone interested join the group? Is it first come, first served? What if more skiers than snowmobilers attend? How small should the decision-making group be kept and who should decide?

One answer to these kinds of questions is to give responsibility to the deliberative body itself and to allow it to debate and decide who should be a member. That answer, however, is not completely satisfying, for it already, perhaps arbitrarily, excludes people from deliberation. Alternatively, one might say that anyone *affected* by the group should have a role in its deliberations and decisions, but that might give someone halfway around the world the same deliberative and decision-making status as those in the group. Perhaps these outsiders should be consulted for their view, but should they be treated as equal members with the right to decide? Are Gutmann and Thompson right when they say that "if representatives are accountable to their moral constituents as well as their electoral constituents, deliberative democracy should create forums in which citizens of foreign countries could present their claims and respond to the counterclaims of our legislators" (1999: 273)? Should protesters in

Washington, DC not only be listened to or consulted, but also be given a vote in the World Bank proceedings about debt forgiveness? Just because a rose cultivation project in Pakistan affects neighbors (some neighbors were envious of the rose cultivators' success), it does not seem to entail that the neighbors should be included in the group's discussions and decisions (see Alkire 2002: 271–277). Again, on a second-order level, should group membership be decided democratically or in some other way and, if the latter, does this option undermine democracy? Shapiro and Hacker-Cordón call this "a chicken-and-egg problem that lurks at democracy's core" (1999a: 1), and Shapiro more recently observes, "Questions relating to boundaries and membership seem in an important sense prior to democratic decision making, yet paradoxically they cry out for democratic resolution" (2003: 52). Once more, these are pressing questions being debated by deliberative and other democratic theorists. Sen could benefit from the controversy and perhaps contribute to its resolution.

Enabling conditions

A fourth way in which deliberative democracy can contribute to the capability approach is to help identify background and institutional conditions that are presupposed by – or, better, conducive to – a group's democratic deliberation. These conditions coincide with and reinforce institutional arrangements that Sen himself advocates. That they are conducive to democratic deliberation only provides additional justification for their instrumental importance. Richardson has helpfully identified what he calls "institutions needed to preserve the background justice of democratic deliberation" (2002: 88), especially with respect to the normative equality (to be discussed presently) of deliberators within or between groups. Where these conditions do not exist – because the potential deliberators live in dictatorships, in racist and anti-poor oligopolies, or in failed states beset by civil war – democratic deliberation may exist in underground venues but be exceedingly vulnerable. What, then, are the conditions that contribute to democratic deliberation?

Equal political liberty

Equal political freedoms, contends Richardson, means among other things that "each citizen is to enjoy the same freedoms of speech, assembly, and political participation" (2002: 88). These freedoms contribute to deliberator equality and deliberative democracy in local, national, and global venues. These liberties or civil and political rights must be protected and not merely be part of the legal code. Sen concurs: "one of the strongest arguments in favor of political freedom lies precisely in the opportunity it gives citizens to discuss and debate – and to participate in the selection of – values in the choice of priorities" (1999b: 30).

Equality before the law

Equality before the law affords the same fundamental constitutional rights to each citizen, regardless of ethnicity, religion, class, education, or sexual preference. More generally, this background condition means that no one is justified in claiming to be above the law and no one is beneath the protection of the law. This condition has been and continues to be especially important in the practice of religious freedom and toleration.

Economic justice

Economic poverty, inequality, and concentration of wealth can impede if not doom people's freedoms and deliberative participation. Hence, it is important to create just conditions and protect social and economic rights that enable people *individually* and *collectively* to choose the lives they want to lead. As Jean Drèze and Amartya Sen argue:

> Large sections of the population have very limited opportunities to speak for themselves. The daily struggle for survival leaves them with little leisure to engage in political activity, and efforts to do so sometimes invite physical repression. Lack of formal education and access to information restricts their ability to intervene in public discussions and electoral debates, or to make effective use of the media, the courts, and other democratic institutions. Lack of adequate organizations further enhances this political marginalization.
>
> (2002: 29; cf. Richardson 2002: 89)

Procedural fairness

Richardson's final background condition for equality among deliberators and deliberative democracy is that "the process of democratic debate and decision must itself be structured so as to allow each person a fair chance to participate and to counteract to a degree the potential influence of disparities in economic and political power" (2002: 88). Different measures – to provide fair chances and reduce the threat of elite capture – will be appropriate in different contexts. Campaign finance reform, abolition of the US Electoral College, and reform of registration and voting procedures would lessen inequality in US national elections. Requiring that one-third of members of Afghanistan's legislature be women is an egalitarian institutional device; enforced limits on deliberator speaking time is yet another.

The objection might be made to the deliberative democrat's appeal to these background conditions. First, it looks as though the society in which deliberative democracy exists must already be just (have equal political power and economic opportunity) if deliberative democracy is to "work" and promote justice. If such demanding conditions must be in place *before* deliberative democracy is possible, then deliberative democracy is unreasonably utopian, for the conditions are either impossible or unlikely to obtain (see Denuelin 2005).

How should we respond to this charge of unrealistic utopianism? I respond in four steps. First, it is important to concede that deep economic and other inequalities exist in actually existing democracies. For example, an overriding concern of the United Nations Development Programme's 2004 report on Latin American democracies is that although most of the region's nations have abandoned authoritarianism in favor of democracy, the regions exhibit worsening poverty and inequality. In unjust conditions, economic and political elites often capture democratic institutions and procedures and use them to protect and even to intensify their social dominance. The result is frequently disillusionment with democracy.

Second, although formal or minimalist democracies often do badly in reducing poverty and inequality, autocracies at the same economic levels do as badly as, and often worse than, their democratic counterparts. Employing a fairly minimalist definition of democracy,[13] Halperin *et al.* present impressive evidence that democracies and democratizing states on average do a better job than authoritarian states in reducing poverty and inequality.

Third, as Iris Young – following Frank Cunningham and his notion of a "democratic fix" (Cunningham 1994) – argues, "in formally democratic societies with serious injustices it must be possible to promote social changes towards greater justice through democratic means" (Young 2000: 35). Halperin *et al.* explain this possibility and the "democratic advantage" on the basis of even a minimalist democracy's accountability, allocation of opportunity, openness (including access to information), stability, and ability to learn (2005: 146–151). Rather than a country first achieving certain enabling conditions for democracy and then achieving democracy, the country gradually may achieve the "enabling conditions," for instance greater political liberty and economic equality, *by means of* democracy. Sen puts it aptly: "A country does not have to be deemed fit *for* democracy; rather, it has to become fit *through* democracy" (1999a: 4).

Fourth, the potential for democracy's reducing political and economic inequality is even greater when a society – in the light of a firm grasp of democratic values – moves beyond formal or minimalist democracy to deepen and broaden its democratic institutions. The cure, then, for the deficiencies of democracy is not some nondemocratic system, but more and better democracy. John Dewey put it extremely well in 1927:

> We object to the common supposition of the foes of existing democratic government that the accusations against it touch the social and moral aspirations and ideas which underlie the political forms. The old saying that the cure for the ills of democracy is more democracy is not

> apt if it means that the evils may be remedied by introducing more machinery of the same kind as that which already exists, or by refining and perfecting that machinery. But the phrase may also indicate the need of returning to the idea itself, of clarifying and deepening our apprehension of it, and of employing our sense of its meaning to criticize and re-make its political manifestations.
>
> (1927: 144)

The theory and practice of deliberative democracy is precisely an attempt to rethink the ideal and institutions of "rule by the people." We need not assume that Richardson's background conditions must be fully attainable or completely in place before roughly free and equal group members can engage in injustice-reducing deliberation. In spite of political and economic inequalities, with the help of what Fung and Wright call "self-conscious intentional design efforts" (2003: 23), such as training in public speaking and reason giving, people *in and through* the deliberative process itself may reduce their differences and promote justice as they together forge answers to practical problems. In deliberative venues as "schools of democracy," they may learn (to deliberate and promote justice) by doing (deliberating justly) (cf. Fung and Wright 2003: 28, 32; Baiocchi 2003: 56–58; Drèze and Sen 2002: 362–363). Gianpaolo Baiocchi submits evidence that one of the important experiments in deliberative democracy, that of participatory budgeting in Porto Alegre, Brazil, has had the outcome of reducing member inequalities and the occurrence of domination:

> Despite significant inequalities among citizens, the didactic features of the [Porto Alegre] experiment have succeeded in large part in offsetting these potentials for domination. This confirms the expectations of democratic theorists who, while assuming that persons may come to deliberative settings with certain inequalities, expect that over time participation will offset them.
>
> (2003: 52)

The Porto Alegre experiment also shows that the participatory budgetary exercise itself has been "highly redistributive" (Baiocchi 2003: 67), contributing to the conditions that in turn help enable deliberative democracy. Deliberative democracy often results in the bringing about of conditions that in turn contribute to more egalitarian distribution and deliberation. This point reinforces and gives empirical support to Drèze and Sen's point that there is a "virtuous circle" of "achieving greater equity," on the one hand, and citizen participation or "democratic practice," on the other: "A reduction of inequality both contributes to democratic practice and is strengthened by successful practice of democratic freedoms" (Drèze and Sen 2002: 357). The conditions for deliberative democracy can be built through the practice of such democracy.

The process of deliberative democracy

A fifth contribution that deliberative democracy can make to the capabilities approach is to enrich – by making more concrete and detailed – the capability account of the process of public discussion and decision making. It is at this point that the recent work of Henry Richardson becomes particularly relevant. One of Richardson's innovative contributions to deliberative democracy is to recast the understanding of the deliberative democratic process from a focus on preferences – regardless of whether simply aggregated or transformed through discussion – to a focus on partially joint intentions and shared ends for concrete action (see Richardson 1997; 2002: ch. 10). One advantage of the intention/action perspective is that it enables us to see deliberation as a kind of practical reasoning in the sense that deliberators reason together about what the group (and they as individuals) ought to do. The aim is to agree on, or fashion together, not beliefs about the world or ultimate values, but a plan or policy (end plus means) to which all can agree and act to realize.

I turn now to Richardson's modeling – in terms of reasoning about and deciding on partially joint intentions – of "collective, political deliberation by individual reasoners with potentially distinct views" (Richardson 2002: 162). For Richardson, joint intentions are the outcome of a four-stage process of "formulating proposals; discussing their merits; coming to an informal agreement; and converting informal agreement into official decision" (ibid.: 164). It is appropriate that Richardson designates each stage with a gerund, for public deliberation is a practice or complex action, structured by norms, whose outcome is a joint intention to act (or an agreement to disagree).

Stage 1: formulating proposals

If, instead of deliberation, social choice were merely the aggregation of private preferences, we might just consult preferences in a relevant focus group. Or we might collect our preferences and those of others, ask about willingness to pay for a benefit, and accept compensation for a burden. Or we might forsake mere aggregation and either defer to some wise man or expert or obey a dictator or religious leader with respect to what the group should do. If we had nothing but a fair procedure, each of us might try to outdo other group members by influencing them more than they influence us. Finally, a group might try to eliminate deliberation by uncritically appealing to the nation's constitution or its judicial interpreters.

Richardson, however, reframes our group task as that of reasoning together to fashion an answer to what we collectively ought to do. We begin when one (or a subgroup) among us makes a proposal to the rest. Even prior to that initial proposal, a point that Richardson neglects, it may be useful for the group to brainstorm about the nature of the problem it faces and some possible solutions (Fung 2003: 118). When a proposed solution is made, it is an individual – and not some big collective deliberator or general will – that makes it. Although the proposal may (or may not) also express private preferences or desires, the act of proposing what *we* ought to do is a *public* act, the performance of which the others are aware of and the content of which others can grasp. Each and every group member is free to make proposals, for each has equal status as a source of claims and as a group member. I face other group members not (merely) as enemies to be hated, or persons to be disapproved of, or rivals to be bested, but (also) as fellow citizens in a cooperative scheme. In spite of our differences, the ideal of reciprocity, as well as my respect for each member's dignity and autonomy, demands that what I propose to others is something that they understand (no foreign languages in the absence of translators) and either do or could accept (given appropriate reasons). I also would require the same from them.

Finally, although my proposal is about what we should do together, to make the proposal honestly is also to indicate my willingness to do my part in carrying out the plan and my promise to do so if my proposal gains acceptance. The making of such a promise, of course, would be contingent, negatively, on encountering no unforeseen obstacles as well as, positively, on others (who accept the proposal) freely agreeing to do their parts. The making of one proposal often results in the making of additional proposals, whether they are modifications of the first or rivals to it. This brings us to stage 2.

Stage 2: arguing the proposals' merits

In deliberative democracy, those who make proposals give reasons for the actions or policies they favor, and the members engage in a deliberative give-and-take to identify the strengths and weaknesses of the proposal. Here it is important to connect the notion of a proposal with the concept of intention as a sort of means–end package.

In making a proposal I offer reasons for its acceptance (and perhaps reasons for my reasons). Other group members do not just listen to or record my proposals (as vote counters might register my vote, as interviewers might record my expression of willingness to pay, or as focus-group members might acknowledge my opinion). Rather, each member has the opportunity to scrutinize rationally both means and ends. Others may defend my proposed action, but as a means to additional or alternative ends. Or they may reject my proposal in favor of what they take to be a better means; they may reject my intention altogether and propose different actions and ends. Agreeing with Jürgen Habermas, Richardson criticizes exclusive reliance on instrumental thinking that takes ends as given and reasons only about the most efficient or effective means. Practical reasoning should assess ends, for we often differ on and decide about not only "know-how" but also on "know-whether." Going beyond Habermas, Richardson gives an account in stage 3 of how, more specifically, we can reason about ends.

Such assessment of ends often leads back to what Richardson (2002: 12) calls "final ends" – ends that are valued in themselves (whether or not they are also valued instrumentally). One way to interpret these final ends is as different interpretations of a public good, not as something independent waiting to be discovered but as something to be hammered out or agreed to through discussion. Democratic deliberation, however, need not and often should not push back (or down) to one's *ultimate* ends in the sense of those highest goals in one's goal hierarchy. The principle of reciprocity requires that I offer only reasons that my fellow deliberators can understand and accept, and ascending to ultimate ends or reasons often prevents the group from forming an intention to act.

Here Richardson departs from Rawls's as well as Gutmann and Thompson's notion of "public reason," however; for, unlike them, Richardson (2002: 82) permits deliberators to *supplement* (not *replace*) their publicly accessible reasons and values with a public profession of their ultimate values – for instance, religious values – presumably when these ultimate values may help other members understand where a person is "coming from."

Richardson's view is a promising third way between (i) Habermas's view (1995) that there should be *no* restrictions on the content of what is offered in public deliberation, and (ii) Rawls's contention (1999: 140–148) that the idea of "public reason" should filter out whatever other citizens are unable to accept.[14] To respect my fellow citizen I should welcome his (or her) attempt to *clarify or explain* (not justify) his proposal (and its reasons), even if that means he does so by appealing to matters he knows I cannot accept. To respect and tolerate me, he may profess his belief in God's will as a way of helping me understand his proposal, but if he knows I am a nonreligious person, he should not offer this profession as a way to *justify* his proposal. To do so would be to disrespect me as one he knows to be nonreligious. If I argue that a particular action (if not "everything") is permitted because God does not exist, not only does my conclusion not follow from my premise, but also my premise is one with no chance of being accepted by the theist and, in fact, disrespects him or her.

Stage 3: coming to an informal agreement

In Richardson's account of deliberation, the first two stages give the deliberators an abundance of riches. Group members may offer competing proposals about what to do, but the proposed actions and reasons (ends and values) submitted may be significantly, even radically, different. How does Richardson's version of deliberative democracy deal with these differences? How can the many, especially when heterogeneous, be reduced to a one that yields unitary collective action? Here is one place that deliberative democracy advances beyond balloting and majoritarian democracy, because, in stage 3, deliberation includes several ways in which (most) group members (both majority and minorities) respectfully and tolerantly cooperate together to forge a joint intention.

One way to form a joint intention, contends Richardson, is to agree on the same action and policy and yet agree to disagree on its justifications: "We may all agree on what ought to be done but each have quite different reasons for coming to this conclusion" (2002: 173). Cass Sunstein terms an agreement of this sort an "incompletely theorized agreement on particular outcomes" (2001: 57). It is, I believe, a particularly effective way to practice tolerant deliberation in the face of deep valuational disagreement.

Alternatively, we may seek out intermediate final ends that lead to the same policy but do not rank high in our hierarchy of ends, and in any case we refuse to advance together to the realm of potentially divisive or "hot-button" higher-order final or ultimate ends.[15] Or we may deliberate about two competing final ends, at least one of us showing the other that there is good reason to be guided by the hitherto neglected end. We may agree on a final end, disagree on its specification, and through give-and-take come to agree on one of the competing specifications or together invent a new and more comprehensive specification that does justice to both sides. Furthermore, deliberators may creatively and collectively fashion a new and higher-order end that can be specified in two complementary lower-order ends. Finally, and most radically, through what Richardson calls "deep compromise," ends can be refashioned rather than held as fixed:

> Deep compromise, by contrast [with "bare compromise," which is only a change in means] is a change in one's support of policies or implementing means that is accompanied and explained or supported by a change in one's ends that itself counts as a compromise.
>
> (2002: 147)

The joint intention (action, whether or not combined with justifying reasons) that is agreed to is not just a set of individual intentions to perform a similar action. Rather, it is an agreement to do something together, and this "togetherness" means that:

> (1) each of the parties intends to do his or her part as required by the joint plan; (2) each of the parties believes that the joint action can be carried out if enough do their parts; and (3) these intentions and beliefs are common knowledge.
>
> (Richardson 2002: 165)

Why would fellow deliberators want to adopt one of these ways to handle disagreement about ends, especially that of deep compromise?

Richardson offers two plausible motivations. First, through increased information that discussion brings to light, one or more members may become convinced that the limited available means require a change of ends or that past attempts to realize a given end resulted in unintended and unanticipated effects that now should be avoided (see Sen 1999b: 256–261). Richer information about facts leads to refashioning of values. Second, deliberators, as free and equal partners informed by the ideals of reciprocity and toleration in a fair cooperative enterprise, are obliged to be responsive to and – within limits – to accommodate each other's ends (Richardson 2002: 172). More work is needed on the limits of toleration, especially in relation to dogmatically held or intolerable – for instance, racist or sexist – ultimate beliefs.[16]

Does, asks Richardson, this affirmation of an obligation based on a debt of gratitude "pull a normative rabbit out of a positive hat?" (2002: 172). Not if we accept the principle of reciprocity and the notion that "I, in turn, owe you" is a fitting response when you assume a burden or bestow on me a benefit. A balance obtains between self-interest and obligation.

Stage 4: converting informal agreement into official decision

Majoritarian democracy emphasizes majority vote and downplays or neglects public discussion leading up to the vote. In contrast, deliberative democracy emphasizes the first three stages of the deliberative process and views majority vote as one means to obtain official conversion (stage 4) of the informal mutual agreement already achieved (stage 3). Rather than being an aggregator of preferences, voting in deliberative democracy is a "closure device" (Richardson 2002: 204) that expresses or acknowledges acceptance of a proposal and commitment to a joint intention, including one's role in executing it. Sometimes in face-to-face groups voting is a mere formality, for it is readily apparent that most if not all members have already agreed to a joint intention. The informal agreement is acknowledged and in a sense ratified, for example, when a Quaker-style moderator formulates what he or she takes to be "the sense of the meeting" and no one objects. At other times, especially in large and even nationwide groups, a vote indicates that more members are for than against a proposal (or more are for one proposal rather than another). Those in the majority will have tried but failed to accommodate sufficiently the minority to the joint intention, making it partially rather than completely joint. There are deliberative disagreements as well as deliberative agreements. Minorities, however, can often accept the results insofar as the process was fair – they had their say – and the majority tried to accommodate (and perhaps partially succeeded in accommodating) what turned out to be minority views. The result is a *partially* joint intention that gains legitimacy from a fair substantive process – even though not everyone voted for it or some voted against it.

It is astonishing the extent to which Dewey anticipated this view of the relation of deliberation to the majority vote:

> The man who wears the shoe knows best that it pinches and where it pinches, even if the expert shoemaker is the best judge of how the trouble is to be remedied. ... A class of experts is inevitably so removed from common interests as to become a class with private interests and private knowledge, which in social matters is not knowledge at all. The ballot is, as often said, a substitute for bullets. But what is more significant is that counting of heads compels prior recourse to methods of discussion, consultation and persuasion, while the essence of appeal to force is to cut short resort to such methods. Majority rule, just as majority rule, is as foolish as its critics charge it with being. But it never is *merely* majority rule. As a practical politician, Samuel L. Tilden, said a long time ago: "The means by which a majority comes to be a majority is the more important thing": antecedent debates, modification of views to meet the opinions of minorities, the relative satisfaction given the latter by the fact that it has had a chance and that the next time it may be successful in becoming a majority. ... The essential need, in other words, is the improvement of the methods and conditions of debate, discussion and persuasion.
>
> (Dewey 1927: 207–208)

Radical participatory democracy rejects voting because it allegedly violates the rights of the losing side(s) and sets people – as competitors – at odds with each other. Instead, radical democrats urge that deliberation continue until there is absolute consensus or complete unanimity. Then everyone in fact would get what they want, people would not be set at odds with each other, and a majority would not tyrannize a minority. In fact, rule by consensus can be more tyrannical than majority voting, for one or a small number of dissenters can block a decision to make changes. As Richardson points out, the consequence of rule by consensus is that the status quo, no matter how unjust, is "unduly privileg[ed]" (2002: 205). Furthermore, as Gutmann and Thompson (1996: 32–33) observe, a decision on when to use majority rule and other decision rules, such as the unanimity rule in juries, executive action, or parental authority, should itself be a matter of public deliberation rather than being imposed by the individual or faction that controls the agenda.

Several reasons converge to make Richardson's four-stage process both morally attractive and an appropriate specification or consistent development of some of Sen's commitments. First, the positive valuation of the *outcome* of the deliberative process – a partially joint intention – is coupled with the positive evaluation of the *process* itself. Just as a soccer team committed to fair play wants not only to win, but to win fairly, so a deliberatively democratic community values not only a joint intention, but also the fair process by which group members generate that intention. Richardson's stages are a nice illustration of Sen's notion of a "'comprehensive outcome' that incorporates inter alia the process through which the 'culmination outcome' [the joint intention] comes about" (1999b: 27). Second, the so-called impossibility or arbitrariness of combining individual preferences into a social function may be able to be avoided if deliberators are conceived as fashioning – in and through the giving and sifting of proposals and reasons – (partially) joint intentions and (sometimes) shared ends.

Third, Richardson's focus on joint intentions enables us to avoid the equally unpalatable extremes of, on the one hand, collapsing individual deliberators into one organic deliberator or, on the other hand, elevating individual intentions to the detriment of joint intentions. Richardson's insight is that joint intentions grow out "of what each of us, as distinct individuals, think ought to be done" (2002: 164) but also enable us to act in concert, with each of us having responsibilities to do our own share. Another way of making the point is to say that Richardson has found a "way of conceiving of public decision-making that is at once sufficiently cognitive to make it truly deliberative and also sufficiently responsive to the positions of individual citizens to count as democratic" (Richardson 1997: 359). Finally, Richardson's account of the course of practical reasoning enables him to do justice to the way in which deliberation usually builds on present commitments but also – through deep compromise and innovation – may creatively forge novel purposes that at least a majority of participants can endorse.

Deliberator capacities and virtues

So far, I have explored the resources of deliberative democracy for understanding the aims, ideals, groups and group membership, background conditions, and the process of deliberation. But I have said little about the kinds of persons who would make competent and virtuous deliberators. What sorts of skills and virtues should deliberators have and how might they be acquired?

Bohman has offered an answer to the question of deliberator skills in the context of his adapting some of Sen's ideas about well-being to generate an ideal of political – in contrast to moral – equality. For Bohman, citizens in a democratic society should be politically equal in the sense that they at least cross a threshold of minimal "political functioning" and "effective social freedom" (1996, 1997). Just as Sen stresses that economic equality should be defined in the metric of basic functionings such as adequate nutritional well-being and health and the capacities for such functionings, so Bohman urges deliberative democrats to view qualitative political equality as a certain level of political functioning and capacities.

A person would be politically poor if he or she were not able to function above the minimal threshold.

Faithful to the spirit of Sen's approach, Bohman conceives political participation as one way in which our lives go well (or function in a way that we have reason to value). But Bohman also advances beyond Sen in two ways. First, he provides a detailed description of specific capacities or skills that contribute to political functioning. Second, he argues that in opposition to equality of resources, equal access to resources, or equality of opportunity, "only equality of political capacities makes deliberation fully democratic" (1996: 109). In this context I am interested in Bohman's first adaptation, supplemented by some of Richardson's and my own ideas.

Space permits me to do little more than list the sorts of skills that good deliberators would have for minimally adequate "political functioning" (Bohman 1996: 124, 12) These include (i) the skill of initiating public dialogue or making proposals about an issue such that one's reasons "receive deliberative uptake" (ibid.: 110);[17] (ii) the ability to engage in argument and counterargument – what Richardson terms "sift[ing] reasons and arguments" – in order "to figure out what really ought to be done" (Richardson 2002: 76); (iii) skills in framing and reframing a debate, showing that some dichotomies are neither exclusive nor exhaustive, and finding ways to harmonize proposals and compromise values; (iv) an ability for persuasive but not manipulative rhetoric (ibid.: 90). A further topic to be addressed would be the merit of different ways that citizens most effectively acquire these skills – for instance, formal and informal education, "learning by doing" (participation in deliberative processes), and civic empowerment movements (ibid.: 92; see also Stromquist 2003).

It is clear that group members differ significantly with respect to these deliberative capacities – just as they may differ with respect to economic power and social status. It is also apparent that it is difficult, if not impossible, to formulate a quantitative measure of when someone has crossed a minimal threshold of being able to make proposals and so forth. This difficulty, however, should not – as it is in danger of doing – lead Richardson to revert to a realism about extant differences that rejects "direct approaches" (2002: 89) to promoting the social ideal of equal (basic) political capacities. He rightly insists that "the basic institutions of society should be arranged so as to support the capability of each citizen to engage meaningfully in democratic deliberation" (ibid.: 89). But his list of these institutions surprisingly does not include both formal and informal educational institutions and capacity-building initiatives, which may play a direct role in nurturing and improving citizens' deliberative capacities. The experiments in Empowered Participatory Governance function as "schools of democracy" for group members to acquire or improve the skills important to democratic citizenship and deliberation (Fung and Wright 2003: 23, 56, 119–128).

In addition to capacities that contribute to an individual's political functioning in democratic forums, the practice of democratic deliberation requires that group members exhibit and are motivated by certain excellences of character or civic virtues. Gutmann and Thompson have made the most significant contribution to this topic. They propose three deliberative virtues of democratic citizens: (mutual) respect, civic integrity, and civic magnanimity. Although the development of the point is beyond the scope of the present chapter, to Gutmann and Thompson's list I would add the virtue of tolerance and suggest that deliberative tolerance combines aspects of the other three virtues. This sort of tolerance has an important role to play when citizens strongly disapprove of each other's opinions, beliefs, or way of life (see Crocker 2004; Oberdiek 2001).

A virtuous deliberator respects other group members in the sense that – though she (or he) might not like the others and have profound disagreements with them – she has "a favorable attitude toward, and constructive interaction with, the persons with whom one [she] disagrees" (Gutmann and Thompson 1996: 79). The virtuous citizen respects her fellow citizens (and fellow human beings) by trying to understand and honestly evaluate their proposals and their evaluations of her own proposals. Informed by the principle of reciprocity, the admirable deliberator respects others by making proposals and offering reasons for them that fellow citizens understand and can in principle accept.

In addition to respect for fellow citizens, virtuous deliberators demonstrate civic integrity. Virtuous deliberators express civic integrity when they are sincere and honest, putting forward the proposals and reasons they do because they believe them and not (merely) for strategic reasons. Civic integrity also means that deliberators practice what they preach and accept the practical implications of their moral principles. Finally, civic integrity does *not* mean that one has to hold dogmatically to the core of one's values or ends, for – through the deliberative process itself – one can freely fashion new values (and a new personal identity).[18] This creative refashioning occurs when constructive engagement with the other expresses a third virtue, namely, civic magnanimity.

Deliberators demonstrate civic magnanimity by the attitudes they have toward the proposals, reasons, or ends of those they disagree with or disapprove of. First, deliberators treat each other's proposals and positions as expressing their sincerely held moral views rather than as a cover for a political strategy or economic interest. Virtuous deliberators assess the merits of each other's *arguments* rather than – as is typical of many US talk shows – engage in attacks *ad hominem*. Second, civic magnanimity requires the virtue of open-mindedness, for the person with whom I initially disagree may turn out – on further reflection – to have a better idea or something surprising to contribute to a partially joint intention. And "willingness to search for deep compromise is a particularly important form of open-mindedness" (Richardson 2002: 187). This virtue also demands, as we have seen, that we focus on deliberative solutions to the problem at hand rather than offering foundational principles sure to be rejected by our fellow deliberators. The magnanimous deliberator also hears out others when they *explain* themselves by referring to beliefs inaccessible or unacceptable to some of their interlocuters. Put positively, citizens are magnanimous when they "try to minimize the range of their public disagreement by promoting policies on which their principles converge" (Gutmann and Thompson 1996: 89) – even though those principles are well short of their high-ranking or ultimate principles. Civic magnanimity contributes to a deliberative reconstruction of tolerance by enjoining the tolerant deliberator to be open to the possibility that his or her initial preferences might be transformed in and through the deliberative process itself.

Many are the personal and social factors that make these deliberative virtues difficult to acquire, maintain, and exhibit. However, although I cannot argue it here, I would contend that civic education, exemplary persons, and initiation in deliberative processes themselves all have a role in overcoming these obstacles and promoting these civic virtues.

Without participants with the "right stuff," the deliberative approach to democracy might not manifest respect for persons, result in mutually acceptable decisions, or promote justice. As Jean Drèze and Amartya Sen remark, in addition to importance of the democratic ideals and institutions of (deliberative) democracy, democracy requires that citizens must "make democracy work" (2002: 347–352). If deliberative democracy is to be put into practice, it requires group members with certain sorts of skills and virtues. Deliberative democrats Bohman, Gutmann, and Thompson offer proposals for the nature of those skills and virtues that flesh out the defense of deliberative democracy and supplement Sen's suggestive but brief discussion of "individual freedom as a social commitment" (Sen 1999b: 282).

Concluding remarks

Amartya Sen's capability approach, I have argued, requires democracy conceived as "open public reasoning" (Sen 2003: 33) about matters of social concern. Sen himself urges that this deliberative ideal of democracy be built into our conception of the ends as well as the means of development, whether in "developed" or "developing" countries:

> Such processes as participation in political decisions and social choice cannot be seen as being – at best – among the *means* to development (through, say, their contribution to economic growth), but have to be understood as constitutive parts of the ends of development in themselves.
>
> (1999b: 291).

Not only should this emphasis on public reason change how we engage in the theory and practice of "development," but it should also change how we think about equality and justice. Sen's own answer to his famous question "Equality of what?" (Sen 1980) is not only an equality of democratically decided basic capabilities, but also, and more importantly, equality of agency or process freedoms. As a result, rather than offering one theory designed to best the others or to yield a definitive blueprint of "the just society," Sen takes the ball away from philosophical theory and throws it to an agency-oriented conception of democratic decision making. In an important passage, already quoted in part, Sen states:

> At the level of the pure theory of justice, it would be a mistake to lock prematurely into one specific system of "weighting" some of these competitive concerns [such as "weights" to be given to various capabilities or to aggregative versus distributive concerns], which would severely restrict the room for democratic decision making in this crucial resolution (and more generally in "social choice," including the variety of processes that relate to participation). Foundational ideas of justice can separate out some basic issues as being inescapably relevant, but they cannot plausibly end up, I have argued, with an exclusive choice of some highly delineated formula of relative weights as being the unique blueprint for "the just society."
>
> (1999b: 286–287)

Sen also contends both that "the value of public reasoning applies to reasoning about democracy itself hair" and, following Dewey, that "the defects of democracy demand more democracy not less" (Sen 2003: 34). I have also argued that the academic theory and institutional practice of deliberative democracy have much to contribute to Sen's own capability approach and to the public discussion about the ideals, institutions, and practice of democracy. Deliberative theorists and scholars of deliberative experiments have enriched public discussion with respect to the aims, norms, enabling conditions, process, and limits of deliberative democracy as well as the capacities and virtues of deliberative citizens. As Sen and others informed by the capability approach contribute to the public debate about democracy, they will benefit much from the challenges, concerns, insights, and limitations of deliberative democrats. The resultant public debate about the ends and means of democracy and democratization will, one hopes, also contribute to meeting our greatest national and global challenge: developing deeper, more inclusive, and more resilient democratic institutions and ways of life.

Notes

For helpful comments – not all of which are yet addressed adequately – on an earlier drafts, I thank Sabina Alkire,Verna Gehring, Douglas Grob, Laura Antkowiak Hussey, Judith Lichtenberg, Christopher Morris, Joe Oppenheimer, Henry Richardson, and students in the Pro Seminar of the Committee on Politics,

Philosophy, and Public Policy at the University of Maryland. An early version of the chapter contributed to a World Bank project, which I co-directed with Sabina Alkire, entitled "Responding to the Values of the Poor: Participation and Aspiration," February 2002–December 2003. I gave presentations based on the chapter at the Philadelphia Area Philosophy Consortium, St. Joseph's University; Fundación Nueva Generación Argentina y Centro de Investigacciones Filosóficas, Bajo Belgrano, Argentina; Department of Philosophy, Michigan State University; Workshop on "Deliberative Democracy: Principles and Cases," University of Maryland, May 12–13, 2003. This chapter will form a part of the final chapter in my forthcoming book *Deliberating Global Development: Ethics, Capability, and Democracy*.

1 G. A. Cohen makes this mistake when he charges Sen with "athleticism." (1993: 25–26)
2 I borrow the terms "breadth," "depth," and "range" from Carl Cohen (1971). See also Stojanović (1973) and Crocker (1983: 293, 299–300).
3 See also Sen (1999b: 241; 2004: 335–336).
4 Daniel Little (2003: 222) usefully clarifies two of the "tenets of normative democratic theory": "the universal citizenship principle" and "the liberty principle and the equality principle." The former holds that "All adult members of the collectivity ought to have the status of citizens (that is, there should be no restriction in political rights for different groups of people within the polity)." The latter affirms that "All citizens ought to have the broadest set of political rights and liberties possible, compatible with the extension of equal rights to all."
5 Another question with respect to the Huaorani in the context of Ecuador and the Amazon, of course, is how the Huaoroni and other Amazonian tribes but also other affected groups – including the Ecuadorian, other national governments and the transnational oil companies – can and should decide collectively and fairly the fate of the region as well as reap the instrumental benefits of democracy. Needed are principles for deciding who comes to the table, sets the agenda, and deliberates about the ends and means of policy.
6 For arguments for and against the claim that democracy promotes justice, equality, efficiency, and freedom, see Shapiro and Hacker-Cordón (1999a). Fareed Zakaria (2003) argues that (illiberal) democracy often diminishes liberty. Robert Kagan (2003: 27–37) critically reviews Zakaria's volume. For a massive and rigorous study on what the evidence shows (and does not show) with respect to democracy's effects on economic growth and human development, see Siegel 2001. See also Halperin *et al.* (2005).
7 This passage is evidence that Nussbaum is mistaken when she says, "Sen nowhere uses the idea of a threshold" (2002: 12).
8 These include the following: Habermas (1994), Benhabib (1994), Bohman and Rehg (1997), Fishkin (1971), Dahrendorf (1988), Hamlin and Pettit (1989), Sunstein (1993), and Gutmann and Thompson (1996). Among the most important volumes defending or evaluating deliberative democracy that Sen does not cite (many of which were published after 1999) are, in the order they appeared, Bohman (1996), Cohen (1989, 1996), Elster (1998), Macedo (1999), Shapiro and Hacker-Cordón (1999a, b), Paul *at el.* (2000), Young (2000), Sunstein (2001), Richardson (2002), Fung and Wright (2003), Shapiro (2003), Ackerman and Fishkin (2004), Fung (2004), Gutmann and Thompson (2004), and Leib (2004). In his 2004 essay "Elements of a Theory of Human Rights" (2004b: 349 n. 57 and n. 58), Sen cites Cohen (1996) and Gutmann and Thompson (1996) in relation to deliberative democracy and public reasoning, respectively.
9 Joshua Cohen, in an essay that helped initiate the recent deliberative democracy movement, says, "By a deliberative democracy, I shall mean, roughly, an association whose affairs are governed by the public deliberation of its

members" (1989: 17). Cf. Amy Gutmann and Dennis Thompson's definition: "Deliberative democracy is a conception of democratic politics in which decisions and policies are justified in a process of discussion among free and equal citizens or their accountable representatives" (2000: 161).

10 "Cycling" refers to the way in which, as Sen puts it, "majority rule can be thoroughly inconsistent, with A defeating B by a majority, B defeating C also by a majority, and C in turn defeating A, by a majority as well" (Drèze and Sen 2002: 68). See also Mackie (2003).

11 Gutmann and Thompson rely on Lawrence Becker's concept of reciprocity as "making a proportionate return for good received"; see Becker (1986: 73–144). The principle, however, may plausibly be pitched on a more abstract level to include proportionate responses to bads as well as goods received; see J. L. Crocker (1992: 1059).

12 Gutmann and Thompson discuss these issues (2004: 116–138).

13 Halperin *et al.* define democracies as "those countries that have met the relatively high standards of having instituted genuine checks and balances on executive power and created mechanisms for popular participation in the political process" (2005: 66).

14 For an analysis of these two options and an argument for the second, see Guariglia (2001: 147–155).

15 Cf. Sen: "A consensus on public decisions may flourish so long as the exact grounds for that accord are not very precisely articulated" (Sen 2002: 558, quoted by Alkire 2002: 92–93). See also Sunstein (2001: 56–58; 1999: 123–150).

16 I explore these issues in Crocker (2004).

17 Bohman, borrowing from Austin (1955), defines "'deliberative uptake' among all the participants in deliberation" as "deliberation on reasons addressed to others, who are expected to respond to them in dialogue. This uptake is directly expressed in the interaction of dialogue, in give and take of various sorts" (Bohman 1996: 59).

18 Sen (1998, 2000) has rejected convincingly identity determinism and essentialism and argued for our human ability to shape and transcend our (multiple) identities and freely create complex identities. Cf. Young (1997).

References

Ackerman, B. and Fishkin, J. S. (2004) *Deliberation Day*, New Haven, CT: Yale University Press.

Alkire, S. (2002) *Valuing Freedoms: Sen's Capability Approach and Poverty Reduction*, Oxford: Oxford University Press.

Austin, J. L. (1955) *How to Do Things with Words*, Oxford: Oxford University Press.

Baiocchi, G. (2003) "Participation, Activism and Politics: The Porto Alegre Experiment," in A. Fung and E. O. Wright (eds) *Deepening Democracy: Institutional Innovations in Empowered Participatory Governance*, London: Verso.

Becker, L. C. (1986) *Reciprocity*, London: Routledge and Kegan Paul.

Benhabib, S. (1994) "Deliberative Rationality and Models of Democratic Legitimacy," *Constellations* 1 (1): 41–45.

Benhabib, S. (1996) (ed.) *Democracy and Difference: Contesting the Boundaries of the Political*, Princeton: Princeton University Press.

Bohman, J. (1996) *Public Deliberation: Pluralism, Complexity and Democracy*, Cambridge, MA: MIT Press.

Bohman, J. (1997) "Deliberative Democracy and Effective Social Freedom: Capabilities, Resources, and Opportunities," in J. Bohman and W. Rehg (eds) *Deliberative Democracy*, Cambridge, MA: MIT Press.

Bohman, J. and Rehg, W. (eds) (1997) *Deliberative Democracy*, Cambridge, MA: MIT Press.

Broder, D. (2003) "Endangered Suffrage," *Washington Post* (September 17): 27.

Cohen, C. (1971) *Democracy*, Athens: University of Georgia Press.

Cohen, G. A. (1993) "Equality of What? On Welfare, Goods, and Capabilities," in M. Nussbaum and A. Sen (eds.) *The Quality of Life*, Oxford: Clarendon Press.

Cohen, J. (1989) "Deliberation and Democratic Legitimacy," in A. Hamlin and P. Pettit (eds) *The Good Polity*, Oxford: Blackwell.

Cohen, J. (1996) "Procedure and Substance in Deliberative Democracy," in S. Benhabib (ed.) *Democracy and Difference: Contesting the Boundaries of the Political*, Princeton, NJ: Princeton University Press.

Crocker, D. A. (1983) *Praxis and Democratic Socialism: The Critical Social Theory of Marković and Stojanović*, Atlantic Highlands, NJ: Humanities Press; Brighton, UK Harvester Press.

Crocker, D. A. (1992) "Functioning and Capability: The Foundation of Sen's and Nussbaum's Development Ethic," *Political Theory* 20 (4): 584–612.

Crocker, D. A. (1995) "Functioning and Capability: The Foundation of Sen's and Nussbaum's Development Ethic, Part 2," in M. Nussbaum and J. Glover (eds) *Woman, Culture and Development*, Oxford: Clarendon Press.

Crocker, D. A. (2004) "Tolerance and Deliberative Democracy," paper given at the Fourth Conference of the Human Development and Capability Association, Pavia, Italy, September 5–7.

Crocker, D. A. (forthcoming) *Deliberating Global Development: Ethics, Capability, and Democracy*.

Crocker, J. L. (1992) "The Upper Limits of Just Punishment," *Emory Law Journal* 42: 1059–1110.

Cunningham, F. (1994) *The Real World of Democracy Revisited*, Atlantic Highlands, NJ: Humanities Press.

Dahrendorf, R. (1988) *The Modern Social Contract*, New York: Weidenfeld & Nicolson.

Deneulin, S. (2005) "Promoting Human Freedom under Conditions of Inequalities: Can Development and Democratic Practice Be Reconciled?" *Journal of Human Development* 6(1): 75–92.

Dewey, J. (1927) *The Public and Its Problems*, Athens, OH: Swallow Press, Ohio University Press.

Diamond, L. (1999) *Developing Democracy*, Baltimore: Johns Hopkins University Press.

Drèze, J. and Sen, A. (2002) *India: Development and Participation*, 2nd edn., Oxford: Oxford University Press.

Elster, J. (ed.) (1998) *Deliberative Democracy*, Cambridge: Cambridge University Press.

Fishkin, J. (1971) *Democracy and Deliberation*, New Haven, CT: Yale University Press.

Fung, A. (2003) "Deliberative Democracy Chicago Style: Grass-roots Governances in Policy and Public Education" in Fung A. and Wright, E. O. (eds)

(2003) *Deepening Democracy: Institutional Innovations in Empowered Participatory Governance*, London: Verso.
Fung, A. (2004) *Empowered Participation: Reinventing Urban Democracy*, Princeton, NJ: Princeton University Press.
Fung, A., and Wright, E. O. (eds) (2003) *Deepening Democracy: Institutional Innovations in Empowered Participatory Governance*, London: Verso.
Galston, W. (2002) *Liberal Pluralism*, Cambridge: Cambridge University Press.
Guariglia, O. (2001) *Una ética para el siglo XXI. Ética y derechos humanos en un tiempo posmetafísico*, Buenos Aires: Fondo de Cultura Económica.
Gutmann, A. and Thompson, D. (1996) *Democracy and Disagreement*, Cambridge, MA: Harvard University Press.
Gutmann, A. and Thompson, D. (1999) "Democratic Disagreement," in S. Macedo (ed.) Deliberative Politics: Essays on Democracy and Disagreement, Oxford: Oxford University Press.
Gutmann, A. and Thompson, D. (2000) "Why Deliberative Democracy Is Different," in E. F. Paul, F. D. Miller Jr. and J. Paul (eds) *Democracy*, Cambridge: Cambridge University Press.
Gutmann, A. and Thompson, D. (2004) *Why Deliberative Democracy?*, Princeton, NJ: Princeton University Press.
Habermas, J. (1994) "Three Normative Models of Democracy," *Constellations* 1 (1): 1–10.
Habermas, J. (1995) "Reconciliation through the Public Use of Reason: Remarks on John Rawls's *Political Liberalism*," *Journal of Philosophy* 92: 109–131.
Halperin, M. H., Siegle, J. T., and Weinstein, M. M. (2005) *The Democracy Advantage: How Democracies Promote Prosperity and Peace*, New York: Routledge.
Hamlin, A. and Pettit, P. (eds) (1989) *The Good Polity*, Oxford: Blackwell.
Kagan, R. (2003) "The Ungreat Washed: Why Democracy Must Remain America's Goal Abroad," *The New Republic* (July 7 and 14): 27–37.
Kane, J. (1996) *Savages*, 2nd edn., New York: Vintage.
Leib, E. (2004), *Deliberative Democracy in America: A Proposal for a Popular Branch of Government*, University Park, PA: Pennsylvania State University Press.
Little, D. (2003) *The Paradoxes of Wealth and Poverty: Mapping the Ethical Dilemmas of Global Development*, Boulder, CO: Westview Press.
Macedo, S. (ed.) (1999) *Deliberative Politics: Essays on Democracy and Disagreement*, Oxford: Oxford University Press.
Mackie, G. (2003) *Democracy Defended*, Cambridge: Cambridge University Press.
McMurrin, S. (ed.) (1980) *Tanner Lectures on Human Values*, Cambridge: Cambridge University Press.
Nussbaum, M. (2002) *Women and Human Development: The Capabilities Approach*, Cambridge: Cambridge University Press.
Nussbaum, M. and Glover, J. (eds) (1995) *Women, Culture and Development*, New York: Oxford University Press/Clarendon Press.
Nussbaum, M. and Sen, A. (eds) (1993) *The Quality of Life*, Oxford: Clarendon Press.
Oberdiek, H. (2001) *Tolerance: Between Forbearance and Acceptance*, Lanham, MD: Rowman & Littlefield.
Paul, E. F., Miller, F. D. Jr., and Paul, J. (eds) (2000) *Democracy*, Cambridge: Cambridge University Press.

Pettit, P. (1997) *Republicanism*, New York: Oxford University Press.
Przeworski, A. (1999) "Minimalist Conception of Democracy: A Defense," in I. Shapiro and C. Hacker-Cordón (eds) *Democracy's Value*, Cambridge: Cambridge University Press.
Rawls, J. (1999) *The Law of Peoples with "The Idea of Public Reason Revisited,"* Cambridge, MA: Harvard University Press.
Richardson, H. (1997) "Democratic Intentions," in J. Bohman and W. Rehg (eds) *Deliberative Democracy*, Cambridge, MA: MIT Press.
Richardson, H. (2002) *Democratic Autonomy: Public Reasoning about the Ends of Policy*, Oxford: Oxford University Press.
Schumpeter, J. (1942) *Capitalism, Socialism, and Democracy*, New York: Harper.
Sen, A. (1980) "Equality of What?" in S. McMurrin (ed.) *Tanner Lectures on Human Values*, Cambridge: Cambridge University Press.
Sen, A. (1985) "Well-being, Agency and Freedom: The Dewey Lectures 1984," *Journal of Philosophy* 82 (4): 169–221.
Sen, A. (1992) *Inequality Reexamined*, Cambridge, MA: Harvard University Press.
Sen, A. (1993) "Capability and Well-being," in M. Nussbaum and A. Sen (eds) *The Quality of Life*, Oxford: Clarandon Press.
Sen, A. (1998) "Reason before Identity," Romanes Lecture, Oxford University, November 17, 1998.
Sen, A. (1999a) "Democracy as a Universal Value," *Journal of Democracy* 10 (3): 3–17.
Sen, A. (1999b) *Development as Freedom*, Oxford: Oxford University Press.
Sen, A. (2000) "Beyond Identity: Other People," *The New Republic* 223 (25): 23–30.
Sen, A. (2002) *Rationality and Freedom*, Cambridge, MA: Harvard University Press.
Sen, A. (2003) "Democracy and Its Global Roots," *The New Republic* 229 (4): 28–35.
Sen, A. (2004) "Elements of a Theory of Human Rights," *Philosophy and Public Affairs*, 32 (4): 315–356.
Shapiro, I. (2003) *The State of Democratic Theory*, Princeton, NJ: Princeton University Press.
Shapiro, I. and Hacker-Cordón, C. (eds) (1999a) *Democracy's Edges*, Cambridge: Cambridge University Press.
Shapiro, I. and Hacker-Cordón, C. (eds) (1999b) *Democracy's Value*, Cambridge: Cambridge University Press.
Siegel, J. (2001) *Democratization and Economic Growth: The Contribution of Accountability Institutions*, Ph.D. dissertation for the School of Public Affairs, University of Maryland.
Stojanovic, S. (1973) *Between Ideals and Reality: A Critique of Socialism and Its Future*, trans. G. Sher, Oxford: Oxford University Press.
Stromquist, N. P. (2003) "Gender, Education, and the Possibility of Transformational Knowledge," panel on "Women, International Justice, and Education," American Philosophical Association Eastern Divisional Meeting, December 27–30.
Sunstein, C. (1993) *The Partial Constitution*, Cambridge, MA: Harvard University Press.
Sunstein, C. (2001) *Designing Democracy: What Constitutions Do*, Oxford: Oxford University Press.

United Nations Development Programme (2004) *La democracia en América Latina: Hacia una democracia de ciudadanas y ciudadanos*, New York: United Nations Development Programme.

Young, I. M. (1997) "Difference as a Resource for Democratic Communication," in J. Bohman and W. Rehg (eds) *Deliberative Democracy*, Cambridge, MA: MIT Press.

Young, I. M. (2000) *Inclusion and Democracy*, Oxford: Oxford University Press.

Zakaria, F. (2003) *The Future of Freedom: Illiberal Democracy at Home and Abroad*, New York: W. W. Norton.

9 Attending to nature

Capabilities and the environment

Victoria Kamsler

The literature on capability theory offers a revision of the relatively impoverished measures of value in development economics. Despite its contribution to the enrichment of theories of value, it has been rather narrowly focused on capability as an account of human flourishing. But (i) there is nothing in the idea of capability that necessarily limits it to *human* flourishing, and (ii) environmental issues are a legitimate object of practical concern for development policy.

These unresolved ambiguities contribute to problems of practical indeterminacy in capability theory – that is, problems of how to specify this relatively abstract account of flourishing to a degree that makes it practically valuable in shaping and assessing development policy. Martha Nussbaum and Sabina Alkire have each presented distinctive ways of using a list as a means to specify capabilities to enhance their practical applicability, making them "operational." Capability theory, as we have it, does not lend itself very well to thinking about the environment. This chapter considers the way that capability lists enable the inclusion of environmental issues in a theory that is anthropocentric in its standard formulation. Do we add environmental issues to the list of human capabilities, or revise the basic understanding of capability to make it inclusive of other forms of flourishing? Recently, Martha Nussbaum has sought to extend the account of capabilities to the flourishing of individual nonhuman animals. I consider the significance and limitations of this approach.

Capabilities theory is a theory of human flourishing, and as such provides an alternative to market- and preference-based accounts of value. The etymology of *flourishing* and *flowering* suggests that we understand human flourishing "by analogy with similar states of other organisms, such as animals and even plants" (Hurka 1999: 44). However, capabilities theory, as we now have it, retains a focus on flourishing *human* capabilities with which, under some interpretations, the flourishing of other species and ecosystems is not consistently compatible.

Practical indeterminacy and lists

How do we overcome the practical indeterminacy of theories of capability? Much recent discussion has centered on ways of using a list to specify capabilities for practical purposes. In this chapter I will argue that, apart from their role in specifying, and thus making capabilities practically applicable or "operational," lists also play a crucial role in determining the kind of attention we pay to aspects of capability. When list theories explicitly include an environmental dimension of evaluation, they invite us to reflect upon the basic understanding of *human well-being* at the core of current capability theory.

I would like to emphasize an aspect of the role of lists in capability theory: their capacity to focus attention. I will argue that this feature of list theories of capability has crucial significance for the inclusion of environmental issues in the specification of capabilities. Capability theory has had as its aim the elaboration and practical implementation of an account of human flourishing. However, there is nothing inherent in the idea of capabilities, understood as the achievement of valuable doings and beings, that limits the idea of capability to *human* capability. Environmental goals may legitimately be considered an object of practical reasoning about development policy. Yet environmental values may be tenuously or only partially evoked in capability-oriented considerations of human well-being. What kind of attention should capability theories pay to nature?

Lists and attention

Much of this chapter will be taken up with a discussion of list theories of capability. Lists function *inter alia* as devices to focus attention, and I will be concerned to show that the way they focus attention matters a great deal for the inclusion of environmental values in theories of capability. Before we plunge into the more familiar ground of capability theory, I would like to begin with a few words about attention, and why it matters.

When our attention is consciously directed, the cognitive effects can be powerful and startling. Here is an illustration. I recently attended a workshop on risk and climate change at which Daniel Kahneman conducted an experiment … on us. Kahneman showed a film of college students engaged in a drill of passing a basketball (Simons 2003). He asked the (somewhat bemused) workshop participants to keep a running tally: to list the number of bounce passes and the number of air passes. With the academic's competitive willingness to master cognitive tasks, we applied ourselves to our lists. Speaking for myself at least, keeping count was a bit harder than I'd thought. At the end of the film, he asked us to report our counts (wildly varied). He also asked if we had noticed anything about the film. A single hand went up, and a workshop participant said, "The gorilla." This was met with amusement and incredulity, until Kahneman replayed the film, this time without asking us to count. And there it was. About halfway through the film a person in a gorilla suit wandered into the middle of the basketball drill. The "gorilla" stood precisely in the center of the game for several seconds (I later discovered that the total duration of the gorilla's appearance was exactly 9 seconds) (Carpenter 2001). The ball was passed in front, behind, and around her or him. Just how much can we ignore when our attention is directed to a task? At this point, the "gorilla" looked directly into the camera and beat its chest à la King Kong before wandering off stage left. Same film. Only one of us had seen it. A rare moment in an academic workshop: we were genuinely astonished.

The "basketball and gorilla" film records an experiment by Ulric Neisser (D. Kahneman, personal communication, 2004) in an area of cognitive psychology known as the "selective attention task." Research in this area has led to the development of a theory of "inattentional blindness," originally focused on selectivity phenomena in visual perception (Mark and Rock 1998). The domain of "inattentional blindness" studies is now being broadened to include nonvisual aspects of selective perception. What the gorilla experiment shows is that the mere presence of a stimulus in the perceptual field does not guarantee a response. If we consider the stimulus alone (film with basketball and gorilla), our cognition is not predictable on that basis. Attention matters fundamentally. Selective attention appears to be crucial to our capacity to process experience, and "gating" of perceptual attention can occur at many levels, including visual processing. Because of the way we are wired – as beings with mechanisms of selective attention that allow for certain forms of concentration – there are attentional biases in the way we perceive and evaluate. For Kahneman (2004), the broader lesson to be drawn from these and other experiments on the nature of attention is the crucial role that selective attention plays in everything from assessments of experiential utility to political agenda control. Kahneman considers that what one pays attention to forms the crux of psychological assessments of utility. This evaluative limitation is inescapable, and arises from our limited capacity to attend. Now, if it is indeed the case that "inattentional blindness" is a phenomenon that extends in these ways beyond the domain of the original studies in visual perception, it would seem that attention profoundly affects both our personal evaluations of well-being and our formulation of focused goals, such as political agendas.

With regard to environmental values, the attention question can be posed rather bluntly: is there a gorilla in the room? Any capability theory that employs a list provides a particular kind of answer because, among other functions, a list is a device to focus attention. The general formulation of capabilities as human flourishing used in current capability theories directs our attention to human capacities and achievements. In this context the question of capabilities lists matters, because the use or avoidance of lists can strongly affect what we pay attention to, and how we attend to it. The use of a list, or a menu, or any other cognitive or evaluative prompt can have powerful effects on the way we assess a situation. I will argue that focusing attention on the environment matters in capability theories, *to the extent that* the basic formulations of such theories (as theories of *human* well-being) do not *directly* prompt us to think about the environment. If capability theories are to provide the basis for evaluation of development, and if concern for the environment is a legitimate object of development policy, we need to ask how environmental issues appear through the lens of capability theory.

An important caveat is now in order. Capabilities lists are employed in a deliberative setting. Thus, these lists bear a *limited* resemblance to the perceptual tasks used in selective attention experiments. The reflective and intersubjective aspects of deliberation open our initial evaluative assessments to revision and modification *within* the procedure of assessing capabilities. By contrast, in selective attention experiments we have to step outside the task and be prompted by a new frame of reference before we can "see" what we have overlooked. Capability theory relies on the power of deliberative adjustment within the evaluative practice to correct for biases and limitations of our initial evaluative assessments. We will return to the role of deliberation in capability theory in the conclusion to this chapter.

What kind of attention do capability theories pay to nature? Part of the answer to this question is obvious enough. Capability theory provides an account of human flourishing or well-being that is meant as a corrective to the relatively impoverished measures of development found in contemporary economics. To the extent that development economics has narrowly focused attention on value understood in terms of subjective preferences and priced economic goods, capability theories retrieve the richness of broader conceptions of value by enhancing the informational and normative bases of value judgments (Holland 2004). The difference can be brought sharply into view by contrasting the idea of capabilities with standard economic techniques of attributing value to nature. So, for example, Amartya Sen describes the economic model of *contingent valuation* as

> arriving at the valuation of the "existence" of some objects (such as species of birds), not because the persons concerned have any direct use of those objects … but because they simply would like them to be there, rather than being destroyed.
>
> (2002: 536–537)

Sen describes how contingent valuation, which came into prominence in the wake of the *Exxon Valdez* disaster, may be thought of as a counterfactual market valuation based on "willingness to pay" for things not bought and sold through markets. "Willingness to pay" models, with as-if market pricing, direct our attention to subjective preferences and the way that markets can represent them. "Contingent valuation" thus allows for preferences that may be unrelated to human flourishing as capability theory understands it. As Sen's description suggests, contingent valuation can provide an *indirect* channel for the view that aspects of nature are *intrinsically valuable*. Of course, the "intrinsic value" of nature is not the direct object of contingent valuation exercises – rather, subjective preferences for certain items, species, and habitats, based on the belief that they are intrinsically valuable, are filtered through a market pricing mechanism. The difference lies in the contrast between valuing nature intrinsically, and valuing preferences for aspects of nature that (some) individuals happen to believe are intrinsically valuable. In the latter case, what ends up on the list of "intrinsically valuable" aspects of the environment is contingent and potentially arbitrary. Contingent valuation asks what people happen to prefer such that they would pay for it, not what reasons there might be for valuing and preserving nature. By contrast, capability theories offer an account of human flourishing that cannot be reduced to "willingness to pay," and which may in fact counteract certain predictable irrationalities both in the way that preferences are expressed, and in the way that markets respond to preferences. For our purposes here, we note that capability theories ask us to change the sort of things that we pay attention to when we evaluate the consequences of a policy. When capability theories have drawn attention to the environment, they have done so against the background of a primary commitment to human flourishing, understood functionally in terms of valuable human beings and doings.

Contingent valuation exercises filter the value of nature through market preferences. Capability theories have tended to filter the value of nature through the lens of human capability. In this context, Martha Nussbaum's recent discussion of capability theory as a basis for animal entitlements marks a significant departure from the initial specification of capabilities in terms of human dignity. Nussbaum acknowledges that there is a more basic intuition behind capability theory, which "wants to see each thing flourish as the sort of thing that it is" (2004: 306). In this spirit, she applies her list of the central human capabilities to an account of animals' entitlements: the kind of duties, both positive and negative, that are owed to animals in virtue of their species-specific capacity to flourish.

Nussbaum's recent contribution makes evident what should have been obvious all along about the implications of capability theory for nonhuman animals. It also makes evident that there is a choice about how to express the role of environmental values in capability theories. We might begin with a list of human capabilities and describe environmental values in relation to us. Or we might begin with a more general account of flourishing that extends (as in Nussbaum's recent argument) to animals, or perhaps even further (and on somewhat different grounds) to encompass ecosystems. We will return to Nussbaum's account of animal capabilities. But first, let us begin by examining standard approaches to human capabilities and the way they deal with environmental values.

To list or not to list

Martha Nussbaum's capability theory differs from Amartya Sen's most notably in her willingness to stipulate an explicit list of central human capabilities. Sen avoids this, arguably to preserve an emphasis on deliberative freedom in the specification of capabilities (Nussbaum 2003: 44). Recently, Sabina Alkire (2002) has proposed a third way of thinking about the question of specifying capabilities. Alkire has a practical and very specific goal of finding ways to "operationalize," or implement, capabilities assessments in local, microeconomic development projects. She seeks to enhance the evaluation of development projects by soliciting the judgments of participants, thus better informing the projects' sponsors of the dimensions of their success or failure. To do so, she endorses the use of a list of types of practical reasons (understood as types of goals of action, not as specific capabilities). These practical reasons are specified at the most general level as objectives such as life, health, and security. By framing the list in this way, she seeks to capture the advantages of a focused agenda for discussion, while allowing deliberative space for participants to educe their own sense of the shape, value, and priority of these general goals. In other words, Alkire's list is explicitly employed not as the basis of a (prospective) overlapping consensus, but as a device to focus deliberative attention. Any capabilities list will have the effect of focusing attention, but Alkire's theory makes these attentional effects central to her account of how lists are used.

Which one of the three approaches is to be preferred? I will not address foundational matters here. At the practical level I am inclined to believe that each offers specific advantages for particular purposes, in particular settings. The use of a substantive list like Nussbaum's affords certain advantages in establishing constitutional essentials and framing international legal norms. In this setting, the need to set standards for cross-country comparisons puts a premium on explicitness and uniformity. Stipulating a list of capabilities also helps to avoid the notorious problems of "adaptive preference formation" that skew deliberations away from the self-interests of the subordinate, a crucial problem for development policy regarding the status of women (Nussbaum 2000a). Sen's political emphasis on "the need to discuss the valuation of diverse capabilities in terms of priorities" without stipulating a list may perhaps suit a popular context of broadly discursive democracy, in which institutional structures do not or cannot set limits on the agenda of debate. For Sen (1999: 110), "Public participation in these valuational debates – in explicit or implicit forms – is a crucial part of the exercise of democracy and responsible social choice." (Here the difference with Nussbaum is one of emphasis, as Nussbaum emphasizes the revisability of her list through further deliberation.) And Alkire's approach seems admirably suited to the context she has in hand, namely, establishing retrospective judgments about local, participatory development programs in a context of asymmetrical information and inequality between the program's participants and its sponsors. Her emphasis on creating a list not of capabilities *per se*, but of the goals of practical reason, serves to focus discussion about capabilities while preserving the spirit of the type of deliberative freedom advanced by Sen.

In fact, Alkire (2002: 44) allows that her own approach has specific merit in overcoming certain problems of implementation at the local level, particularly in cases where the deliberative body (a women's rose-growing collective, for example) is constitutionally protected from gender-related problems of speech inequities that arise in mixed-sex groups. Where women are not silenced and intimidated in the expression of their experiences, an open-ended list of practical reasons may have special merit in encouraging their active participation, and in adding to the informational basis of decisions. The directness and immediacy of the women's evaluations might work to overcome a problem of an earlier version of Nussbaum's list theory identified by Benhabib, who writes:

> What I find lacking in the Aristotelian account of capabilities is the space, both in theory and practice, which allows one's understanding of the "human condition" in Aristotelian terms to be translated into actively generated moral insight on the part of human actors.
>
> (1995: 255, quoted by Alkire 2002: 37)

It should be noted, however, that Nussbaum's most recent formulations of her theory have moved away from the substantive Aristotelianism of her earlier views, and Nussbaum herself (2000a, b, 2003) has explored ways to keep her list open to deliberative modification.

Alkire sees herself as advancing a version of Sen's capability theory and seeks to avoid stipulating a specific list of capabilities to be implemented. Building upon John Finnis's arguments in *Natural Law and Natural Rights* (1980), she conceives of her approach not as "a normative list of things to be done" (Alkire 2002: 54), but as identifying basic reasons for human action that constitute the building blocks of normative assessment. However, for my purposes I will consider Alkire and Nussbaum together as both advancing list theories of capability, because my object is to consider the use of lists in focusing attention. Despite substantive differences, both Nussbaum's and Alkire's lists shape the capabilities agenda by focusing attention, be it on specific capabilities or on broad categories of the goals of practical action.

Both Nussbaum and Alkire explicitly mention aspects of environmental value in their lists of human capabilities and practical reasons respectively. How these authors justify that inclusion is beyond the scope of the current chapter. Here we merely observe that they both choose to focus attention on environmental value in ways that may not be immediately obvious when we consider the core association of capability theory with human well-being. Why is the connection between environmental values and human well-being not immediately obvious? Part of the answer is suggested by Stephen Jay Gould:

> We must squarely face an unpleasant historical fact. The conservation movement was born, in large part, as an elitist attempt by wealthy social leaders to preserve wilderness as a domain for patrician leisure and contemplation (against the image, so to speak, of poor immigrants traipsing in hordes through the woods with their Sunday picnic baskets). We have never entirely shaken this legacy of environmentalism as something opposed to immediate human needs, particularly of the impoverished and unfortunate. But the Third World expands and contains most of the pristine habitat that we yearn to preserve. Environmental movements cannot prevail until they convince people that clean air and water, solar power, recycling, and reforestation are best solutions (as they are) for human needs at human scales – and not for impossibly distant planetary futures.
>
> (Gould 1990: 217–218)

Clearly, there are important instrumental links between environmental and human flourishing. Yet concern for the environment may, at some points, conflict with capability theory's original focus on human well-being. A Venn diagram might be drawn to represent the areas of overlap of human and ecological flourishing, while indicating the areas where human flourishing is bought at the expense of the environment, and vice versa. In our imagined Venn diagram of the relation of human and ecological flourishing, there would be a broader area of overlap between (ecosystem and human) flourishing than there is between either (species and human) or (individual nonhuman being and human) flourishing.

Problems of biodiversity, of genetically modified organisms, and some versions of the path of climate change may cut very differently if evaluated from the standpoints of human, of individual animal, or of ecosystemic flourishing. So, for example, what if genetically modified foods diminish biodiversity but alleviate hunger? A well-considered solution to this problem turns on our ability to avoid construing this dilemma as a tragic choice. Genetically modified foods may not be the only or the best answer to alleviation of hunger. In another case, what if human beings handle a certain degree of climate change fairly well, but it causes a cascade of extinctions? Clearly, biodiversity loss is an effect of climate change, but capability theory might deal with each of them rather differently.

What counts as the best answer to these value conflicts will take into account the ability to get results without diminishing biodiversity. These considerations cannot be compassed in an extension of human capability theory to the flourishing of individual animals as species-members. Yet Nussbaum's new interest in capabilities as establishing the basis of duties to animals leads her to focus exclusively on the flourishing of individual animals according to the norms of flourishing for their species:

> It seems that here, as in the human case, the focus should be the individual creature. … As for the continuation of species, this would have little moral weight as a consideration of justice (though it might have aesthetic significance or some other sort of ethical significance) … damage to species occurs through damage to individuals, and thus individual damage should be the focus of ethical concern within the capabilities approach.
>
> (2004: 308)

The intuitive basis for Nussbaum's argument lies in an appeal to dignity and wonder: in the sense of the "dignity of living organisms" and the idea that "there is something wonderful and wonder-inspiring in all the complex forms of animal life" (Nussbaum 2004: 306). Now, unless there is some strong reason for holding that these conditions are jointly necessary, we should admit that flourishing ecosystems are at least as capable of inspiring wonder as are forms of animal life. This is in part because both individual animals and entire ecosystems rely on complex cybernetic or homeostatic processes for their integrity of function. As Simon Levin puts it,

> Biological systems rely on a dazzling array of cybernetic or homeostatic mechanisms. These are not the work of a master designer, however … they are the result of tinkering. Natural selection builds on past innovations, adopting those mutations that provide improved fitness. In this way, an endless process of change replaces one solution with another, each somewhat better suited to the ever-changing environment than were its immediate predecessors. Such evolutionary sequences are played out over and over again across space and time, each realization taking its own unique form. … For the solutions that have been shaped by natural selection, the influence of history and local variation clearly enhances variety. Thus, the solutions to biological control problems appear in stunning diversity and provide an almost inexhaustible library of spectacular complexity.
>
> (1999: 30–31)

Biodiversity may matter for human flourishing, and it may matter for the flourishing of individual animals, but then again in some cases it may not. Now if, despite best efforts, it turns out that we are in the land of non-compossible values, then conflicts, compromises, and trade-offs are close at hand. How serious is this potential conflict? Not surprisingly, the different evocations of environmental value on Nussbaum's and Alkire's lists focus our attention on different answers.

Alkire's list

For Alkire (2002: 282), the environment appears as part of the fourth item on a list of seven broad categories of the goals of practical activity. Coming after (1) life/health/security, (2) knowledge, and (3) work/play, we encounter (4) *beauty/environment*, followed by (5) self-integration/inner peace, (6) religion, and (7) empowerment. Alkire's fourth item draws a connection between environment and the aesthetic, hinting at a measure of experiential utility in the pleasure we take in the beauty of our surroundings.

One delightful feature of Alkire's narrative of the rose-growers' collective is the great pleasure the women take in their work when the scent of roses lingers on them and permeates their clothes. An economist asking about the profitablity of rose growing would never be let in on the very personal way this work enhances these women's lives. In the rose-growers' collective the environment is a source of aesthetic experience that gives delight beyond the limits of their practical goals.

The association of environment and beauty clearly works to enlarge the base of information about what the rose growers value. At the same time, Alkire's focus on environmental aesthetics is not a neutral implement to elicit views about the goals of practical activity. It creates a very specific prompt to focus evaluative attention. More specifically, the aesthetic framing of environmental issues is likely to divert attention away from the potential for conflict between environmental values and human flourishing as goals of development policy. It may also distort our sense of *which* environmental features are significant for human flourishing. When we see the environment through the lens of aesthetics, we selectively evoke those aspects of the environment that give us aesthetic pleasure. This is an inadequate basis for environmental goals such as the preservation of biodiversity, since many species are neither cute nor comely. (For an argument *endorsing* this effect of aesthetic evaluation of nature, see Russow 1981.) Gould observes:

> [E]nvironmentalists continually face the political reality that support and funding can be won for soft, cuddly, and "attractive" animals, but not for slimy, grubby, and ugly creatures (of potentially greater evolutionary interest and practical significance) or for habitats. This situation has led to the concept of "umbrella" or "indicator" species – surrogates for a larger ecological entity worthy of preservation. Thus, the giant panda (really quite a boring and ornery creature despite its good looks) raises money to save the remaining bamboo forests of China (and a plethora of other endangered species with no political clout).
>
> (1990: 215)

Ostensibly, not every significant ecosystem, or group of grubby but endangered species, will have a giant panda in its midst allowing environmental benefits to trickle down. If preservation of the environment is a legitimate goal of development policy, the reasons for their preservation should be considered directly.

Nussbaum's list

Nussbaum includes environmental issues eighth in her list of ten human capabilities. Capability number 8: "Other Species: Being able to live with concern for and in relation to animals, plants, and the world of nature" (2000b: 80; 2003: 42). I will refer to Nussbaum's eighth capability as the "ecological capability," to distinguish it from the tenth capability, which concerns political and material control over one's environment.

You don't need to be a professional pollster to surmise that the way Alkire's and Nussbaum's lists are composed is likely to affect the responses they elicit. Where Alkire's association of *environment/beauty* prompts us to think of environmental aesthetics, Nussbaum's eighth capability draws our attention to matters of environmental ethics. Nussbaum (2003, 2004) invites the interpretation and possible revision of her list, which should be viewed as provisional and subject to contextualization. In the following I hope to take her up on her offer.

Nussbaum argues that the capabilities on her list are mutually supportive in complex ways (2000b: 81). They are also related via the integrating role of two important capabilities, "*practical reason* and *affiliation* … [which] organize and suffuse all the others, making their pursuit truly human" (ibid.: 82). Breena Holland (2004) points out a significant connection between the ecological capability and other capabilities that emphasize "the importance of *connectedness* between people and between people and things." (To be consistent, we should amend this to include "between people and nonhuman beings," but the general point is well taken.) So, for example, "'Emotions' (capability number five) involve "Being able to have attachments to things and people outside ourselves" (ibid.: 12). On this view, the ecological capability is a specific instance of the broader concern with connectedness also captured in the account of emotion. As Holland puts it, "a particularized connection to people and to things partially enables people to become self determining beings" (ibid.: 13). Holland's reading of the ecological capability sets it squarely within an account of *Bildung* or human self-development. It thus helps to explain the presence of the ecological capability on Nussbaum's list of human capabilities. Seen in this light, we can understand the way that ecological value, as concerning the capacity for relatedness, forms part of "a conception of the dignity of the human being, and of a life that is worthy of that dignity" (Nussbaum 2003: 40). It now makes sense to think of environmental value as bearing some relation to a "minimum account of social justice: a society that does not guarantee these to all its citizens, at some appropriate level, falls short of being a fully just society, whatever its level of opulence" (ibid.: 40) The emphasis on connectedness would also settle the question of the relation of environmental value to human well-being, because the value of the natural world, being relational in this sense, cannot be viewed as merely instrumental to human ends.

However, I believe that more is involved in Nussbaum's account of ecological capability than an instantiation of the value of connectedness. In her recent edited collection *Animal Rights*, she argues that "the capabilities approach does treat animals as agents seeking a flourishing existence; this basic conception ... is one of its great strengths" (Nussbaum 2004: 302). Let us begin by attempting to specify more precisely what Nussbaum's ecological capability involves (here I indulge in the deliberative license that the very general statement of the principle invites). First, the human relation to other species *per se* is not the same thing as a focus on "the world of nature." There are notable problems in (i) defining species, and (ii) determining whether species, or individual sentient beings, are the proper objects of moral concern. These goals sometimes clash (as in the reintroduction of wolves into Yellowstone, and the preservation of predator populations more generally). In addition, (iii) focus on ecological systems as complex adaptive systems with emergent properties (Levin 1999) will yield different evaluative results than focus on either species preservation, or saving sentient beings from pain, or on the flourishing of individual animals.

This finer specification reveals conflicts latent in the statement of ecological capability itself. And these internal conflicts in ecological capability must be considered in addition to what I will call external conflicts of value. As I have suggested, environmental capabilities involve us in problems of conflicts with other types of goods, including other capabilities. This matters specifically within the terms of Nussbaum's theory because capabilities are supposed to be mutually supportive. Concern for the environment may sometimes conflict with what environmental ethicists would call strictly anthropocentric concerns. If, as I believe, these conflicts cannot be finessed in all cases, then to the extent that capability theories have a distinctive anthropocentric cast, emphasizing human doings and beings, the direction of the resolution of the conflict is pretty clear – perhaps a bit clearer than it should be, if the theory is to be one of value pluralism that endorses a nonmetaphysical and political approach to differences in conceptions of the good.

Despite these problems of value conflict, there is a useful heuristic in the idea that the capabilities are meant to be mutually supportive: it prompts us to look for ways that conflicts among values may turn out to be merely apparent. In some instances we may develop technological or political means to overcome the either–or structure that tends to turn prioritization problems into tragic dilemmas. Consider an example: Pacala and Socolow's theory of stabilization wedges in carbon mitigation.

The argument is often made that reversal of global warming, and the extent of carbon mitigation required to achieve it, would require a profound technological revolution or would otherwise require an unacceptable trade-off in economic growth. To Stephen Pacala and Robert Socolow, these arguments appeared disingenuous, based less on knowledge of available science than on a desire to procrastinate about climate change, arguably the most time-sensitive of all environmental issues (Pacala, personal communication, 2004). In this context, Pacala and Socolow (2004) proposed their theory of stabilization wedges, a policy proposal to "solve the climate change problem for the next 50 years with current technologies." As the authors put it,

> Humanity already possesses the fundamental scientific, technical, and industrial know-how to solve the carbon and climate problem for the next half-century. A portfolio of technologies now exists to meet the world's energy needs over the next 50 years and limit atmospheric CO_2 to a trajectory that avoids a doubling of the preindustrial concentration. Every element in this portfolio has passed beyond the laboratory bench and demonstration project; many are already implemented somewhere at full industrial scale. Although no element is a credible candidate for doing the entire job (or even half the job) by itself, the portfolio as a whole is large enough that not every element has to be used.
>
> (ibid.: 968)

The portfolio consists of three categories (efficiency and conservation, decarbonization of electricity and fuels, and natural sinks) encompassing a total of fifteen different established and usable technologies, ranging from more efficient vehicles to biomass fuel, geological storage of carbon, conservation tillage, and agricultural soils management. Instead of construing the carbon mitigation problem as a game of waiting for spectacular technological change like the development of a hydrogen fuel, or as a contest between the advocates of wind turbines and the advocates of carbon sequestration, Pacala and Socolow showed how each of a combination of different available technologies could serve to solve some quantifiable portion (literally, a "wedge" of one-seventh) of the problem and permit net emissions to eventually drop to zero. In my view, this is a classic example of a combination of technological and policy solutions to an apparently endemic value conflict: growth versus sustainability with regard to climate change.

Nussbaum argues that

> In the human case, we often face the question of conflict between one capability and another. But if the capabilities list and its thresholds are suitably designed, we ought to say that the presence of conflict

> between one capability and another is a sign that society has gone wrong somewhere. We should focus on long-term planning that will create a world in which all capabilities can be secured to all citizens.
> (2004: 317–318)

Conclusion

The need to avoid tragic conflicts of values points out the crucial role of cognitive innovation in our deliberations about capabilities. Recall that the feature of capability theory that clearly distinguished it from problems of inattentional blindness in selective perception is the revisionary role of deliberation. And now, as promised, we turn at last to the role of deliberation in overcoming the limits of our attention. Including the environment on a list of capabilities clearly matters in cases where the basic account of capability refers to human flourishing. Because human and ecological flourishing can conflict, the use of a list establishes a place for environmental value that would otherwise be tenuous and insecure. When it comes to including the environment in capability theory, however, Martha Nussbaum's recent work makes plain that there are at least two possibilities: we can build appreciation for environment into a list of human capabilities, or expand capability theory to directly address the capability and function of nonhuman individuals. And we could, with perfect consistency, add ecosystems to Nussbaum's inclusionary agenda. Either approach gives rise to conflicts of goods between human and other functionings. And the existence of these conflicts highlights the importance of our capacity for cognitive innovation in deliberation. Capability theory here comes into contact with deliberative theory. But this is not deliberative theory as standardly conceived, as a procedure of the reciprocal exchange of reasons justifying a practical decision. Rather, the account of deliberation and conceptual innovation helps us to see how impasses in reasoning can be broken, by drawing attention to the adequacy of the concepts that we use to frame the questions, and to the limitations of the contents of our lists. Lists are ambiguous instruments that both focus and limit our attention. Deliberation permits us to reconceptualize these lists in innovative and productive ways. Is this enough to overcome the cognitive limitations that lists can induce? Sometimes.

Note

I would like to thank Charles Beitz, Oona Ceder, Stephen Gardiner, Jennifer Hawkins, Breena Holland, Vittorio Hösle, Alexander Kaufman, Sonam Kachru, John Meyer, and Michael Smith for helpful comments and illuminating discussions of capabilities and the environment; Daniel Kahneman for crucial insight into studies of attention; and Steven Pacala for helpful explanation of the underlying rationale of his theory of climate change and stabilization wedges. Thanks also to panelists and audience members at the Association for Political Theory Conference 2004 session on Politics and the Environment, members of Princeton University's DeCamp Bioethics Seminar, and participants in the Princeton Workshop on Climate Change and Risk for helpful comments and discussion. Oona Ceder and Jennifer Hawkins provided a hospitable and inspiring working environment at Eliot House, Harvard.

Bibliography

Alkire, S. (2002) *Valuing Freedoms: Sen's Capability Approach and Poverty Reduction*, Oxford: Oxford University Press.

Benhabib, Seyla (1995) "Cultural Complexity, Moral Interdependence, and the Global Biological Community," in Martha Nussbaum and Jonathan Glover (eds) *Women, Culture and Development: A Study of Human Capabilities*, Oxford: Oxford University Press.

Carpenter, Siri (2001) "Sights Unseen," *Monitor on Psychology* 32 (4): 54–57.

Finnis, John (1980) *Natural Law and Natural Rights*, Oxford: Clarendon Press.

Gould, Stephen Jay (1990) "The Golden Rule: A Proper Scale for Our Environmental Crisis," in Louis P. Pojman (ed.) *Environmental Ethics: Readings in Theory and Application*,, 2nd edn., Belmont, CA: Wadsworth.

Holland, B. (2004) "Capability Theory and Environmental Value: Linking Human Capacity to Environmental Capacity," paper presented at the Association for Political Theory Conference, Colorado Springs, Colorado, 2004.

Hurka, Thomas (1999) "The Three Faces of Flourishing," in Ellen Frankel Paul, Fred D. Miller, Jr., and Jeffrey Paul (eds) *Human Flourishing*, Cambridge: Cambridge University Press.

Kahneman, Daniel (2004) Keynote Address to the Princeton Workshop on Global Warming: The Psychology of Long Term Risk.

Nussbaum, M. (2000a) "Aristotle, Politics and Human Capabilities: A Response to Antony, Arneson, Charlesworth and Mulgan," *Ethics* 111 (1): 102–140.

Nussbaum, M. (2000b) *Women and Human Development*, Cambridge: Cambridge University Press.

Nussbaum, M. (2003) "Capabilities as Fundamental Entitlements: Sen and Social Justice," *Feminist Economics* 9 (2–3): 33–59.

Nussbaum, M. (2004) "Beyond 'Compassion and Humanity': Justice for Nonhuman Animals," in Cass Sunstein and Martha Nussbaum (eds) *Animal Rights: Current Debates and New Directions*, Oxford: Oxford University Press.

Levin, Simon (1999) *Fragile Dominion: Complexity and the Commons*, Cambridge, MA: Perseus.

Mark, A. and Rock, I. (1998) *Inattentional Blindness*, Cambridge, MA: MIT Press.

Pacala, S. and Socolow, R. (2004) "Stabilization Wedges: Solving the Climate Problem for the Next 50 Years with Current Technologies," *Science* 305 (5686): 968–972.

Russow, Lily-Marlene (1981) "Why Do Species Matter?" in Louis P. Pojman (ed.) *Environmental Echies: Readings in Theory and Practice*, Balmont, CA: Wordsworth.

Sen, Amartya (1999) *Development as Freedom*, New York: Knopf.

Sen, Amartya (2002) "Environmental Evaluation and Social Choice," *Rationality and Freedom*, Cambridge, MA: The Belknap Press of Harvard University.

Simons, D. J. (2003) *Surprising Studies of Visual Awareness* [DVD], Champaign, IL: VisiCog Productions, http://www.visicog.com.

Sunstein, Cass and Nussbaum, Martha (2004) *Animal Rights: Current Debates and New Directions*, Oxford: Oxford University Press.

10 Disability, capability, and thresholds for distributive justice

David Wasserman

The capabilities approach developed by Sen and Nussbaum grounds both a metric for distributive justice and a theory of well-being. Initially, it might appear that both are uncongenial to people with disabilities. In emphasizing what people can do with what they have, rather than what they have or what they feel, the capabilities approach might seem to preclude equality and flourishing for those who are, by definition, impaired in their performance of certain functionings. Indeed, in presenting the capabilities approach as an alternative to welfare approaches, Sen invoked the euphoria of the crippled Tiny Tim to argue that subjective welfare provides an inappropriate metric for political equality and an inadequate conception of well-being.

Yet Nussbaum has modified her initial delineation of core capabilities, which denied the prospects for equality and well-being of people with major sensory, motor, and cognitive impairments, in two important ways: (i) broadening the "individuation" of the core capabilities to accommodate a significantly wider range of ways in which they can be acquired and exercised; (ii) holding that justice requires the acquisition not of equal but only of minimum levels of each capability, achievable by almost all human beings, while continuing to reject trade-offs among capabilities in assessing justice and well-being. These features allow Nussbaum to recognize the possibilities of flourishing for people with severe impairments, while maintaining that justice demands the resources and environmental modifications necessary for them to achieve minimum levels.

This chapter endorses (i) but questions (ii). It argues that achieving minimum levels of each capability is more difficult than Nussbaum assumes and that justice may require trade-offs among individuals and capabilities that leave some people below the minima for some capabilities – even if they could achieve them with sufficient resources and accommodation. This argument for the moral necessity of trade-offs converges in several respects with Arneson's critique of the priority Nussbaum accords to the acquisition of minimum levels of each capability, an approach he characterizes as "sufficientarian."

The chapter places Nussbaum's approach to capabilities equality in the context of other "threshold" accounts of political equality, which seek to simplify distributive justice and to preserve its moral urgency. It contrasts her approach with the notion of democratic equality introduced by Amy

Guttman and taken up by Elizabeth Anderson. Guttman and Anderson seek to limit the scope of distributive justice with a "thin" metric of political participation and social equality; Nussbaum seeks to enlarge it with a "thick," comprehensive account of well-being. Yet their approaches share four important features: they are motivated to a significant extent by the inadequate or inapt response to disability offered by earlier theories of justice; they view this misguided treatment of disability as symptomatic of a broader failing to understand the purpose of distributive justice; they see the first requirement of justice as the achievement of certain thresholds of capability by all or most members of the political society; and they take education, particularly the education of cognitively impaired children, as a paradigm case. I conclude that although neither proposal is successful in achieving the promised simplification or in avoiding difficult trade-offs, both contribute substantially to the current debate on distributive justice and the integration of disability scholarship into political philosophy.

Introduction

In thirty years, disabilities have gone from being seen as falling outside the scope of justice to being regarded as a central challenge for theories of justice. Moreover, that challenge has come to be framed in terms congenial to, and influenced by, disability scholars and activists. The most often-invoked person with a disability is no longer the fictional "happy cripple," Tiny Tim, resolutely euphoric in his impairment, illness, and poverty, but the very real Sesha Kittay, whose mother, philosopher Eva Kittay, has argued for a reconstruction of Rawls's framework to encompass humans with substantial cognitive limitations like her daughter's (1997).

This chapter evaluates the progress that has been made in integrating disability into distributive justice and the challenges that remain. It focuses on two accounts – Anderson's notion of "democratic equality" and Nussbaum's capabilities approach – that take the inadequate treatment of disability in earlier theories as symptomatic of a broader failing. These approaches differ in how "thin" or "thick" a conception of well-being they adopt, but both propose a more modest goal for distributive justice than many egalitarian theories: the universal achievement of critical thresholds or minima, rather than complete or strict equality. The capabilities approach, which embraces a more comprehensive conception of well-being, may offer a more promising treatment of disability. But it still faces formidable challenges in developing a realistic and plausible account of political justice that incorporates people with disabilities.

Distributive justice and disability: an unpromising start

It is only in the past forty years that disability has even been thought of as a matter of justice. As long as disabilities were viewed as biological misfortunes, they impinged on justice only to the extent that individuals were seen as having a right to insure against them – against the loss of income they would typically bring, and for the medical and rehabilitative treatment they would typically require – or to the extent they were owed compensation by virtue of being injured on the job or in defense of their countries. Those not so prudent, injured elsewhere, or born with disabilities had to rely on the kindness, capacity, and charity of societies for whom they were a marginal concern. When, in the 1960s, Jacobus ten Broek, an influential legal scholar who was also blind, argued that people with disabilities were, in myriad ways, denied their basic "right to live in the world" (ten Broek 1966), he was breaking new ground, claiming that much disability was the result of injustice rather than biological misfortune.

At the time ten Broek was proclaiming this right, academic political philosophy had little more interest in justice than society had in disability. Scholarly interest in justice surged with the 1971 publication of John Rawls's *A Theory of Justice*, which helped restore questions about the character of a just society to the forefront of the philosophical agenda. Shortly thereafter, the reconceptualization of disability implicit in ten Broek's writing started making its way into US federal legislation. The 1973 Federal Rehabilitation Act, which applied to federal agencies and recipients of federal funding, treated the denial of employment or services to otherwise qualified individuals on the basis of disability as unlawful discrimination, and it held that the failure to provide the "reasonable accommodation" such individuals needed to qualify was itself a form of discrimination. That law was extended to all public accommodations and facilities, and all workplaces with 25 or more employees, by the now more familiar Americans with Disabilities Act of 1990 (ADA). The ADA used much the same language, and adopted the same conceptual apparatus, as the 1974 Rehabilitation Act. The notion that people with disabilities had a right to work and move about in the world was now the law of the land.

The ADA was informed by what is often called the interactive model of disability: the understanding of a disability not as a medical condition or a natural deficit, but as the interaction between an atypical physical or mental function and an unaccommodating environment. On this understanding, the disadvantages associated with disability are attributable to that environment, and the discriminatory attitudes and practices that shape it, as well as to the atypical function.

Unfortunately, the revival of political philosophy missed out on the disability rights revolution. Rawls himself stipulated that the members of his Original Position, ignorant of many of the circumstances that might bias them in their task of establishing a just basic structure for society, knew that they were physically and mentally normal. People with disabilities were not invited to the hypothetical exercise by which the basic terms of a fair cooperative scheme were established, and their special needs were to be addressed only later, at the legislative stage.

In the two decades following Rawls's landmark work, theories of distributive justice by and large alternated between a benign neglect, tabling provisions for the impaired until a just "basic structure" for society had been established, and an oppressive solicitude, treating people with impairments as having claims for the achievement or restoration of normal functioning that have greater priority than the claims of "normal" members of society to material resources. As Martha Nussbaum has pointed out in an important critique (2002, 2003a, b), the neglect of justice for people with impairments by Rawls, the leading political philosopher of the past century, arises from three factors of continuing relevance for justice and disability. One is the character of his theory of justice: following in the tradition of John Locke, it is "contractarian," deriving justice from the agreement that would be reached by self-interested bargainers ignorant of their actual position in society and conception of the good. Although this stipulated ignorance gives a moral dimension to the contract, the bargainers are still self-interested, and people with impairments tend to be excluded as less attractive bargaining partners, on the assumption that they are less productive, especially if the costs of accommodating a small minority are taken into account. The second factor is the theory's need for a simple metric of comparative advantage; deficits in physical or mental function, as well as deficiencies in access and accommodation, do not fit easily into the same metric of advantage or well-being as wealth and income. Third, and particularly relevant to cognitive impairment, the bargainers are assumed to be rational. People who cannot engage in practical reasoning, let alone elaborate calculations of expected utility, do not have an obvious place at the bargaining table.

The exclusion of people with disabilities as participants in a hypothetical bargaining process is avoided by theories of distributive justice that are "directly" egalitarian or prioritarian; that begin rather than end with the claim that justice consists in equality on some metric of well-being, or some degree of priority for the worse off in (re)distributing resources and other goods and (re)constructing society. But such theories still face the challenge of selecting a metric of well-being for political justice under which people with a wide variety of atypical anatomy or function are not consigned to the ranks of the worst off merely by virtue of their impairments.

Unfortunately, "direct" distributive theories have typically taken as simplistic a view of impairment as their contractarian rivals. They rarely display any recognition of the extent that social arrangements create disability, and assume that functions like seeing and walking are critical to many or most life plans, or to a fair range of opportunity in choosing among life plans. They have proposed a variety of special measures to compensate for the lack of, or deficits in, those functions, from a cash allowance approximating the insurance people with impairments would have purchased against the risk of their deficits (Dworkin 1981), to unlimited provisions for achieving normal functioning (Daniels 1987, 1990). Both the profound misery of the blind and crippled and their unaccountable euphoria have been invoked to criticize competing metrics as demanding too much or too little for the disabled, or of the able-bodied (Sen 1980; Cohen 1989; Dworkin 1981).

Critique and response: can distributive justice accommodate disability?

Not surprisingly, leaders of the disability rights movement and the nascent field of disability studies tended to view political philosophy, especially the distributive justice approach pioneered by Rawls, with suspicion, seeing it as perpetuating the belief that disability was either a natural misfortune outside the scope of justice, or a deficiency so profound as to demand special priority in a fair cooperative scheme. The distorted portrait of impairments that informs much mainstream political philosophy, and the special provisions for disability it offered, have led some philosophers and disability scholars to conclude that merely framing the issue of justice for people with impairments in distributive terms is to present them as defective and helpless (e.g. Silvers 1994; Silvers *et al.* 1998). They argue that in seeking to compensate people for their "natural" disadvantages, distributive justice inevitably denigrates those seen as disadvantaged. These complaints about distributive theories overlap with, and reinforce, more general objections to those theories: that their obsessive concern with the comparative welfare or resource endowment of individuals is demeaning and intrusive, requiring a detailed inventory of involuntary personal deficts as a basis for intervention; and distorting, in overlooking the source of "natural" disadvantage in discriminatory social arrangements.

In the past decade, however, political philosophy has begun, to adapt a phrase from one of its well-known practitioners, "taking disability seriously." Some philosophers have come to recognize the implications of the interactive model of disability and its distributive implications. The removal of external barriers, material or attitudinal, may be more useful and appropriate than medical correction or normalization. Once political philosophers began to see the design of the physical and social environment as a matter of justice, they were better able to respond to the concerns raised, and claims pressed, by people with disabilities.

Some proponents of distributive approaches argue that disparities in any plausible outcome metric need not be attributed to the defective native endowments of those who fare poorly, nor reduced by handouts of extra resources or material goods (e.g. Bickenbach 1993). They maintain that it is possible to recognize the social causes and interactive character of disability within a theory of distributive justice, and to prescribe their alleviation by social and environmental reconstruction as well as, or instead of, by corrective surgery or Social Security Disability Insurance (SSDI) payments.

Take the case of "the ugly and socially-awkward," offered by Elizabeth Anderson (1999) to ridicule efforts to achieve comprehensive egalitarian distribution. Anderson assumes that the disadvantages of being ugly or socially awkward would have to be compensated for with cash, if not eliminated by surgery or mitigated by drugs. But only a very naive egalitarian who failed to see the extent to which those characteristics were defined by malleable, changing sensibilities would treat ugliness and awkwardness simply as deficits in "internal resources," to be rectified by cosmetic surgery or compensated for with cash. (Even if it turned out that humans were "hard-wired" to be attracted to certain facial configurations and repelled by others, the "defective natural endowment" would arguably be in the eye of the beholder.) And only an unusually unimaginative egalitarian could fail to see that there are a variety of means to mitigate the impact of such bad luck. An egalitarian worried about the impact of physical appearance and social grace on income, status, opportunity, friendship, or self-esteem would have no reason to favor handouts of cash, Prozac, or cosmetic surgery over reforms that limited the impact of good looks or panache – reforms ranging from restrictions on advertising that promote narrow ideals of beauty to the modification of hiring practices that place a harsh premium on first impressions. Clearly, a limited government should undertake only some of these reforms itself, and its bureaucratic instincts might favor cash handouts over social reconstruction. But that reflects institutional limitations and biases, not the prescriptions of egalitarian justice.

Admittedly, accounts like Dworkin's (1981) that require equality of resources tend to take the social environment for granted when they propose a hypothetical division of resources into individual bundles, either within the present scheme of social and economic cooperation or in a state of nature assumed to evolve into a scheme like the present one through transactions among equally endowed participants. Giving people with impairments equal economic shares in a society constructed like our own, with a physical environment and social practices designed for people with standard endowments, might improve their material conditions but it would likely leave them at the margins of society. And paying them the proceeds of the insurance they would hypothetically purchase against their disabilities would increase their stigmatization as well as their bank accounts. In requiring supplemental income rather than environmental reconstruction, a scheme of resource equality would reinforce the inferior status of people with disabilities, as individuals disadvantaged by deficits in natural endowment, not by the design of the physical and social environment.

Resources equality has been subject to a broader critique, which may help clear the way for the philosophical accommodation of disability. A number of political philosophers have argued that the "currency" of political justice must lie between resources, whose accumulation eventually becomes fetishistic, and subjective welfare, which makes the requirements of justice uncomfortably dependent on malleable feelings, unrealistic expectations, and fallible judgments (e.g. Sen 1980). Such "midfare" approaches seek to assess what individuals can do with what they have; they treat both material resources and subjective welfare as affecting and constraining well-being without determining it. The most influential of these is the capabilities approach, developed in different ways by Amartya Sen and Martha Nussbaum.

The capabilities approach grounds both a metric for distributive justice and a theory of well-being. Initially, it might appear that both are uncongenial to people with disabilities. In emphasizing what people can do with what they have, rather than what they have or what they feel, the capabilities approach might seem to rule out the possibility of equality and flourishing for individuals not capable of certain functionings. Indeed, in presenting the capabilities approach as an alternative to equality of welfare, Sen invokes Tiny Tim's euphoria in arguing that subjective welfare provides an inappropriate metric for equality and an inadequate conception of well-being, thereby treating the contentment of a crippled child as presumptively suspect.

Yet the capabilities approach has the potential for a more informed treatment of impairment. It is able to recognize the social contribution to "natural deficits," because most capabilities bear only a contingent, environmentally mediated relationship to people's "natural endowment." Thus, it can abstract from physical differences between people with impaired and normal limb function to find a common claim to the means of moving about from place to place. Such means will often but not always be the same for both; they may be architectural, vehicular, mechanical, or prosthetic; they may require making places more accessible or making individuals more mobile. In some circumstances it may be harder or costlier for people with limb impairments to achieve or maintain such a capability, but the difference will not be a categorical one.

Moreover, Nussbaum, who has presented by far the most detailed account of capabilities, has framed them increasingly broadly, attenuating their connection to normal or species-typical functioning. She has modified her initial delineation of the core capabilities, which precluded equality and well-being for people with major sensory, motor, and cognitive impairments, in two important ways: (i) broadening the "individuation" of the core capabilities to accommodate a significantly wider range of ways in which they can be acquired and exercised; and (ii) holding that justice requires the acquisition not of equal, but only of minimum levels of each capability, achievable by almost all human beings, but rejecting trade-offs among capabilities in assessing justice and well-being. These features allow Nussbaum to recognize the possibilities for flourishing available to people with severe impairments, while maintaining that justice demands the material resources and environmental modifications that will enable them to achieve minimum levels.

In the section "Thick distributive justice" (p. 228), I will defend the first of these features but question the second. I will argue that achieving minimum levels of each capability is more difficult than Nussbaum assumes and that justice may require trade-offs among individuals and capabilities that will leave some people below the mimima for some capabilities – even if they could reach them with greater resources and accommodation. This argument for the inescapability of trade-offs converges with Richard Arneson's critique of the priority Nussbaum gives to the acquisition of minimum levels of each capability, and, more broadly, with his skepticism about the approaches to justice he characterizes as "sufficientarian."

I will place Nussbaum's approach to capabilities equality in the context of other recent "threshold" accounts of political equality that seek to simplify distributive justice and preserve its moral urgency. I will contrast her approach with the notion of democratic equality introduced by Amy Guttman and taken up by Elizabeth Anderson. Guttman and Anderson seek to limit the scope of distributive justice with a "thin" metric of political participation and social equality; Nussbaum seeks to enlarge it with a "thick," comprehensive account of well-being. Yet their approaches share four important features: they are motivated to a significant extent by the inadequate or inapt response to disability offered by earlier theories of justice; they view this misguided treatment of disability as reflecting a broader failing to understand the purpose of distributive justice; they see the principal requirement of justice as the achievement of certain thresholds of capability by all or most members of the political society; and they take education, especially of cognitively impaired children, as a critical challenge for their views. I will conclude that although neither proposal is successful in achieving its promised simplification or avoiding difficult trade-offs, both contribute substantially to the current debate on distributive justice and the integration of disability scholarship into political philosophy.

Thin distributive justice: social or democratic equality as setting distributive thresholds

For some political philosophers, the focus on impairments as natural deficits exposes a deeper flaw in distributive justice. Distributive theories are claimed to be at risk of neglecting the urgency of redressing *in*justice, by focusing not on the elimination of great social evils such as slavery, torture, caste, and child labor, but on the achievement of elusive goals with debatable criteria. Much of the appeal of "relational" accounts of justice such as Iris Young's (1990) is that they direct attention to such specific evils, and appear to capture the moral importance of justice better than abstract assessments of outcome disparities. Disparities in outcomes between social groups may be important evidence of discrimination, oppression, and exploitation, but they lack independent significance. The targets of a theory of justice, it is argued, should be those unjust social relationships.

In the case of disability, the relational critique maintains that distributive theories place too much emphasis on impairment as functional limitation, and too little on impairment as stigma. Impairments are relevant to justice not, or not only, because of any effect they have on the functioning of impaired individuals, but because they are, like skin color and ancestry, the markers of stigmatized, oppressed social groups. Justice for people with impairments requires the removal of stigma, oppression, and subordination, and any change in the share of resources given to people in an oppressed group would be a by-product of that more fundamental change.

The strengths and limitations of such a relational account of justice for disability policy, based on the elimination of oppressive attitudes, practices, and structures, are suggested by the antidiscrimination approach of the ADA. While that approach does not offer a complete theory of justice for people with impairments, it treats the locus of injustice as underlying attitudes of contempt and aversion and their pervasive structural and institutional manifestations. It relies on, and extends, the broad notion of discrimination that has evolved in US civil rights law over the past generation, treating impairments as the markers of an oppressed social group. The antidiscrimination approach identifies a core evil in the treatment of people with impairments and provides effective means of responding to it. But as a social policy for disability, a ban on discrimination is radically incomplete.

The argument that an antidiscrimination approach alone cannot secure justice for people with disabilities has been made frequently (e.g. Wasserman 1998, 2000; Arneson 2000), and I will not repeat it here. Rather, I will look at several accounts of distributive justice that have responded to the relational critique without adopting its vague prescriptions. In placing significant aspects of the well-being of the individuals in a society outside the scope of justice, these accounts reject the more ambitious goals of a comprehensive distributive justice in favor of what they see as the more modest goals of achieving rough social or political equality.

Thus, several recent political theorists, notably David Miller and Richard Norman, have acknowledged significant constraints on outcome distributions while rejecting the comprehensive equality demanded by prevailing theories of distributive justice. Miller (1997) argues that equal distribution is a requirement of justice only in certain very narrow contexts, often as a default – for example, where there is uncertainty about the comparative strength of individual claims – and that more comprehensive equalization is not a demand of justice or an entitlement of individuals, but merely an implication of the social equality characteristic of modern societies.

Such accounts take the concerns of relational justice as a guide to the kinds of inequality that matter. While justice imposes significant constraints on distribution, and on disparities in certain forms of advantage, it does not require equality of resources or welfare, let alone equality on a more comprehensive metric of well-being (Miller 1997, 1999; Anderson 1999). This general point, reminiscent of Scanlon's suggestion that different conceptions of well-being are appropriate in different contexts, is forcefully made by Norman (1997: 246):

> Egalitarian distribution cannot plausibly be comprehensive, and the idea that it should be … has standardly incurred the derision of anti-egalitarians. Some people are incurably shy and find it difficult to form deep emotional relationships with others. Some people are emotionally volatile, forming relationships only to destroy them and move on. Some people strike a balance between these extremes. The third group are likely to have more satisfying lives than those in the first or second group. Is this inequality a bad thing?. … [T]he commonsense answer is 'That's life.' The idea that we ought to redistribute emotional sensitivity (by genetic engineering?) so that everyone has an equally fulfilling emotional life would be a caricature of egalitarianism.

A more modest and appropriate egalitarianism would treat disparities in well-being as relevant to justice only to the extent that they undermined equality in basic social or political roles, in status and participation. Proponents of this narrow notion of political equality see its principal virtue as identifying the core injustice in various social and economic disparities – the denial of equal citizenship – and as avoiding the intrusiveness of more comprehensive egalitarian theories. It also avoids the relentless demands of such theories: justicc does not require maximizing equality or minimizing (weighted) inequality, but a kind of satisficing: bringing the members of a society up to some threshold of social equality or political participation.

The notion of a democratic threshold was first proposed by Amy Gutmann (1987) as a principle for the distribution of educational resources. Rejecting as unfair to more able children the demand that "the state devote all educational resources to educationally less able children until they reach the same level of educational attainment as the more able or the highest level that they are capable of achieving," Gutmann argued that "the democratic truth in equalization is that all children should learn enough … to participate effectively in the democratic processes by which individually choices are socially structured" (ibid.: 132–133). On this basis she argued for a principle requiring "that democratic institutions allocate sufficient resources to education to provide all children with an ability adequate to participate in the democratic process" (ibid.: 136). This principle integrates relational and distributive concerns: the objective of justice in education is to prevent the unjust relationships that arise when some citizens are effectively excluded from the political processes that affect all; justice in education is concerned not with all aspects of well-being, but more narrowly with the skills needed for political participation or competence; what such justice requires is not equality in such skills, but only the minimum necessary for political participation.

Gutmann recognized that her principle gave governments broad discretion above the democratic threshold: millions are required to reach it, but not a cent to exceed it, even if the result is staggering disparities in intellectual development. She also noted two problems that are readily apparent in her formulation of the principle: first, that not all children can acquire the ability to participate, even if unrestricted resources are available; and second, that some children could be brought up to that level only by a commitment of resources that might, cumulatively, leave more able children with little education. Gutmann rejected the suggestion that brain-damaged children must be "educated to the limits of our capacity" (1987: 155–156), concluding instead that the mix of educational and noneducational services provided for such children was best left to democratic discretion, constrained only by due-process safeguards. In contrast, she insisted that democratic principles left citizens with no discretion in deciding whether, as opposed to how, to improve the education of socially disadvantaged children currently falling below the democratic threshold. Because society has the option of meeting that threshold by expanding rather than redistributing the educational budget, the satisfaction of the principles did not require the "leveling down" of education for the more advantaged and successful students.

Gutmann's contrasting prescriptions for brain-damaged and socially disadvantaged children depends on the capacity to clearly distinguish children who can and cannot be brought up to the threshold. If, however, as Gutmann suggests, we do not know the limits of our capacity to educate brain-damaged children, we also may not know whether many or most of those children can be brought up to the threshold with enough effort and expense (an uncertainty that, I will argue, confronts more ambitious accounts like Nussbaum's as well). With the possible exception of anencephalic children, the educational potential of brain-damaged children is known only to be uncertain and elastic; we often cannot know whether the failure to reach the threshold indicates that it was beyond our technological capacity or merely beyond our willingness to pay. The uncertainty is all the greater in light of the threshold's elasticity. As Gutmann recognizes, "the threshold of an ability to participate effectively in democratic politics is likely to demand more and better education for all citizens as the average level and quality of education in our society increases." And, she might have added, the proportion of citizens who cannot be brought up to that threshold is likely to increase. But it is also the case that we can raise or lower the threshold by a myriad of decisions that affect the difficulty of "effective participation," from the design of ballots to the delegation of technical issues to agencies with limited democratic accountability.

A second concern is that the flexibility of the threshold account depends on its restriction to a specific domain. We can freely prescribe more spending for education if we do not have to worry about distributional requirements in other domains. If those other domains have equally stringent or more stringent requirements, however, we may have less discretion in satisfying the educational threshold than Gutmann suggests. A democratic threshold will impose a much more demanding constraint if it applies not only to education, but to the vast array of activities and competencies involved in participating in the social and political life of a modern society.

Such a more general threshold is proposed by Elizabeth Anderson (1999) in her account of "democratic equality." Anderson suggests that the equality required by justice can be secured for people of varying physical and mental endowments without quixotic and demeaning attempts at a more comprehensive equality. Like other philosophers who reject comprehensive equality as a social or political imperative (Miller 1997, 1999; Norman 1997, 1999; Young 1990), she regards injustice as distinct from, and more egregious than, unjustified disparities in well-being. She identifies as the core of social and political injustice what others have identified as the core evil of discrimination: the treatment of some people or groups of people as moral inferiors:

> Inegalitarianism asserted the justice or necessity of basing social order on a hierarchy of human beings, ranked according to intrinsic worth. Inequality referred not so much to distributions of goods as relations between superior and inferior persons. ... Such unequal social relations generate, and were thought to justify, inequalities in the distributions of freedom, resources, and welfare.
>
> (1999: 312)

Anderson recognizes, however, that the elimination of such hierarchy requires a certain kind of equality among the members of society, and she sketches a positive account of that equality. She draws on the capabilities approach, endorsing its focus on activity and participation. But she regards only a small set of capabilities as critical for the equality a just society should pursue:

> Negatively, people are entitled to whatever capabilities are necessary to enable them to avoid or escape entanglement in oppressive social relationships. Positively, they are entitled to the capabilities necessary for functioning as equal citizens in a democratic society.
>
> (1999: 317)

The set of capabilities Anderson finds necessary for these purposes is fairly extensive, however:

> [T]o be capable of functioning as an equal citizen involves not just the ability to effectively exercise specifically political rights, but to participate in the various activities of civil society more broadly. … To be capable of functioning as a human being requires effective access to the means of sustaining one's biological existence – food, clothing, medical care – and access to the basic conditions of human agency – knowledge of one's circumstances and options, the ability to deliberate about means and ends.
>
> (ibid.: 317–318)

While this might appear to be a tall order, Anderson emphasizes that it does not require equality in many things that people value, such as sensual pleasure, romantic fulfillment, or intellectual stimulation. By limiting the scope of justice, she avoids the demeaning prescriptions for people with disabilities offered by more comprehensive theories. They are not to be compensated for their alleged unhappiness or inefficiency, but simply assured their status as full citizens. If they are left with some residual inconvenience, it is a small price to pay for preserving their dignity.

Anderson claims that the thresholds for democratic equality are achievable in a modern society, and that any more precise, exacting, or comprehensive equality is not necessary. Both these claims are questionable. Anderson's conception of equal citizenship appears to require the indefinite expenditure of resources to achieve partial and slight reductions in inequality, while her placement of certain capabilities outside the purview of democratic equality may give such equality a disturbingly instrumental character, attenuating its relationship to moral equality.

The suggestion that democratic equality imposes thresholds that can be met by all or almost all citizens is belied by Anderson's list of relevant capabilities. Thus, for example, "effective access … to medical care" would require indefinite expenditures for citizens with chronic and degenerative health conditions, unless "effective" is understood to mean only formal or logistical access to perfunctory care. But such a spare understanding would hardly serve the purposes of democratic equality, since it would not secure (to the limited extent that current or emergent medical technology permitted) the freedom from debility and pain necessary to take part in civic life. Such freedom cannot be guaranteed; it can only be achieved to a greater or lesser extent, by a greater or lesser number of people, through the use of scarce resources.

A similar point could be made about competence in deliberation, which Anderson regards as an element of "access to the basic conditions of human agency." As I maintained in discussing Guttman's proposal, we could spend an indefinite amount on education, job training, and support services for people with cognitive impairments without enabling them to gain such competence (Veatch 1986). Protracted litigation over the meaning of the "free and appropriate education" mandated by the Individuals with Disabilities Education Act (IDEA) has made it painfully clear that very difficult trade-offs are involved even to marginally enhance deliberative competence (Howe 1996). Such trade-offs arise regardless of the extent to which cognitive disability is understood as a problem of internal function or environmental accommodation. Although cognitive disability clearly is socially constructed, in the sense that society determines the complexity of many tasks and sets minimum standards for proficiency in those tasks (Wikler 1979; Buchanan 1996), reducing the complexity of those tasks or their proficiency standards may have substantial social costs. There is no universally achievable threshold for the capability of "functioning as a human being," only a distant goal that competes with the enhancement of other capabilities.

If Anderson underestimates the difficulty of achieving "sufficient" – as opposed to equal – levels of functioning, she also fails to appreciate the harshness of excluding a wide range of capabilities from the scope of democratic equality. She offers examples of fairly trivial pursuits, such as playing cards expertly, enjoying luxury vacations, and competing in beauty pageants, as capabilities that democratic equality can safely ignore. But, to extend G. A. Cohen's criticism of Sen's capabilities approach (Cohen 1989: 918–921), an impaired individual might be able to function well "as a human being, as a participant in a system of cooperative production, and as a citizen of a democratic state" while being in constant low-grade pain, bereft of friends, lovers, and family, and lacking aesthetic or intellectual stimulation.

The proponent of a threshold approach might insist that such misery and privation were relevant to justice, because virtually any deficit in any aspect of well-being reduced the capacity for social, civic, or political participation. If such a response were successful, however, it would jeopardize the advertised economy of the democratic threshold approach. Moreover, it would display an uncomfortably instrumental attitude to treat a person's pain or misery as matters of collective concern only to the extent that they affect his or her capacities to work or vote (or to be concerned, per Gutmann, with ignorance or illiteracy only to the extent that they affected those capacities). A society that acknowledged no obligation, not even a prima facie one, to alleviate protracted pain or profound depression unless it impinged on political or civic participation would arguably treat its citizens with deficient concern and respect.

It may be, as Arneson (2000) suggests, that the more limited focus of democratic equality is useful in supplying a rough proxy for well-being, which is difficult and intrusive to measure. But the proxy supplied by a democratic threshold account may simply be too rough. We may have to accept more comprehensive measures of well-being, and the considerable intrusion into our private lives their application requires, as the price of the "equal concern and respect" (Dworkin 1981) that a state arguably must display toward its citizens.

Thick distributive justice: thresholds of capability

Nussbaum regards comprehensiveness as a strength, not a weakness: she argues that a just society must enable for all its citizens the conditions to attain all the capabilities she enumerates, "up to an appropriate threshold." She acknowledges that the appropriate thresholds are relative to the society. India, for example, given its low literacy and high poverty, may reasonably set more of a modest educational threshold for its citizens than the United States, but it must be one that demands vastly more resources than India now spends on the education of many of its citizens. On the other hand, she rejects the adoption of a different capabilities list, or different thresholds, for people with disabilities *within* a society: to have a separate list for quadraplegic or cognitively impaired individuals would further their stigmatization, and display what might be called "the ablism of low expectations." One characteristic way of stigmatizing people with disabilities is to regard their impairments as far more severe, and far less tractable, than they actually are.

Nussbaum is also ready to accept some paternalism and considerable government intrusion in the lives of citizens unable to form their own life plans and make meaningful life choices. She recognizes that for such cit izens, actual functioning in certain domains may be a more appropriate goal than capability (1999). And she recognizes that some individuals with some impairments cannot achieve the minimum level of one or more functions (2002, 2003a, b).

Nussbaum's delineation of the capabilities required for humanity and human flourishing has evolved significantly in response to disability scholarship. Her earlier formulations of the capabilities roster treated impairments as insurmountable barriers to well-being, in precluding inherently valuable functionings such as seeing, hearing, and walking (Crocker 1995). Because each capability is distinct and noncompensable, lives with impaired vision, hearing, or mobility are necessarily deficient. But Nussbaum's approach permits the modification of the capabilities roster to accommodate long-neglected or newly developed understandings of human flourishing. That flexibility has allowed her to reformulate the roster in ways that attenuate the connection between impairment and well-being. This is evident in the revised catalog of capabilities found in Nussbaum's recent work (2002, 2003b).

Nussbaum has altered her "individuation" of capabilities to take account of the high levels of flourishing achieved by many people with disabilities. Her capabilities have become more general, in part because the more broadly they are framed, the less they are precluded by specific impairments. Thus, Nussbaum has gone from making "the exercise of the five senses" a requirement of humanity – which would deny blind and deaf people the status of human beings – to making it a condition of human flourishing – which would deny that blind or deaf people can flourish – to broadening the capability to "being able to use the senses, to imagine, to think, to reason" (2003b: 256), which she sees as encompassing experience from various combinations of sensory modalities. This broader formulation acknowledges that human flourishing is possible for people who are blind or deaf and imposes an obligation on society to enable them to attain it. Yet every society will include individuals whose impairments make it a practical impossibility to reach the minimum level of at least one central capability, however broadly framed. Nussbaum recognizes that individuals with the most severe cognitive impairments simply cannot fashion their own conception of the good life, no matter how intensive the support they receive from their society. She does not regard a society as unjust in failing to enable such individuals to reach a threshold level of every capability; rather, she sees that failure as "tragic," beyond the scope of justice (2002, 2003a, b).

I have great sympathy for Nussbaum's unflinching commitment to a thick conception of well-being and her unapologetic comprehensiveness about the scope of justice. I also believe that the elasticity of her capabilities list is more of a strength than a weakness. While changes in her description of various capabilities may give their current formulation an *ad hoc* appearance, they also give her list a less dogmatic, more pluralistic character, as its accommodation of physical and mental impairments nicely illustrates. But I am afraid that to a large extent her current position on capability and justice displaces rather than resolves the problem of trade-offs.

Nussbaum insists that she has not presented a complete theory of justice (1999), and might well permit trade-offs among different capabilities once her thresholds were reached. But she cannot avoid trade-offs merely by limiting the ambitions of her account in this way. First, as Arneson points out in this volume, it is not clear how her thresholds or minima are to be set. Nussbaum defends intersocietal differences in setting thresholds, in recognition of the enormous disparities that now exist in resources and achievement. But threshold setting within a society may involve the tacit weighting of different capabilities. A society committed to aggressive intervention to preserve the social bases of self-respect, or to protect bodily integrity from internal and external threats, may give its citizens less control over their political and social environments than the minimum that would be acceptable in a society with similar resources but different priorities.

Second, a distinct sort of trade-off, also raised by Arneson, is presented by the prospect of having to choose between enabling some individuals to reach a given threshold and enabling others below that threshold to make substantial gains. Arneson finds deficient priority for the worse off in Nussbaum's emphasis on bringing as many people as possible up to her minima.

Nussbaum might deny such trade-offs by insisting, dogmatically, that individuals who could not be raised to the minima also could not make substantial progress below them. But even if this were correct – and it seems very doubtful – it would not preclude a distinct kind of trade-off, one that Nussbaum could not plausibly deny and on which I want to focus: between the uncertain prospect of raising a very few individuals to the minima and the more certain prospect of raising many individuals just above it substantially higher.

In assessing the failure of some citizens to reach some minima, the line between injustice and tragedy will often be unclear or disputed. Both the placement of those thresholds and the decision to treat the failure to meet any one of them as tragic rather than unjust reflect tacit trade-offs, the more troublesome for being unacknowledged and unguided by principle.

Again, the case of cognitive impairment illustrates this difficulty. As I argued earlier, we simply do not know how much of a yield available interventions will have, or whether research in areas from education and neuroscience will yield significantly more effective interventions. From some future vantage point, our views about the possibility of educating people with various cognitive impairments may seem as naively pessimistic as our views about protecting people from infectious disease three centuries ago. On the other hand, certain impairments may prove recalcitrant. In the face of such uncertainty, we require a great deal of resources even to make an educated guess. If our educational innovations and neurobiological research held no promise, we could deem existing limitations tragic with a clear conscience. But however bleak the prospects may now appear, dramatic progress can often be made with individual children, and far-reaching scientific breakthroughs may be just around the corner.

Would Nussbaum give lexical priority to reaching thresholds of capability over exceeding those thresholds, however great the possible increase and however large the numbers benefited, or would she reluctantly countenance trade-offs? Both alternatives are problematic. The first bears an ironic resemblance to Norman Daniels's proposal, in the Rawlsian framework that Nussbaum so forcefully challenges, to give the restoration of species-typical function lexical priority over all other distributive goals. Such absolute priority would be no more justifiable for individuals who fell below some capability threshold. It would seem unjust to deny any assistance to individuals barely above those thresholds so long as *any* perceptible progress could be made with individuals slightly below one or more of them.

The second alternative seems more appealing, at least to me, but it requires Nussbaum to consider two kinds of trade-offs she appears to deny: between different capabilities, and between the capabilities of different individuals. If justice requires that we eventually halt the asymptotic progress we can make with some severely impaired children so as to enable thousands of other children to enjoy vast increases in education, or to preserve vast tracts of endangered wilderness, or to slow disfiguring and alienating sprawl, we will have to make both kinds of trade-offs.

Nussbaum glosses over the need for trade-offs in her celebration of the IDEA and inclusive education (2003a). She fails to mention that under the leading *Rowley* case, the "free and appropriate education" mandated for all children requires merely "some educational benefit" for children with cognitive and learning disabilities. This is a modest standard indeed, especially compared to the "maximum educational benefit" advocated by the losing side. And yet there are frequent complaints that school systems are being bankrupted by even this modest standard, and that average children have paid a steep price in lost academic opportunity for very costly special education support programs yielding slight benefits for small numbers. These complaints may be grossly exaggerated, and the more important problem may be the general underfunding of public education. But difficult trade-offs would arise even in a society that valued education more appropriately, and that respected its cognitively impaired citizens.

Nussbaum concedes that the IDEA and its implementation are "imperfect," but she does not even suggest the standards by which we might seek more perfect legislation. Would she, for example, endorse William Galston's (1994) standard of "commensurate benefit", less demanding than the "maximum benefit" standard but far more demanding than the present requirement of "some benefit"? Or would she contend that that academic benefit to children of widely-varying skills was incommensurable, either because of the lack of an acceptable metric or because of the elasticity and uncertainty of human potential? Writ large, the conflicts raised by the IDEA's mandate will confront any society striving to ensure that all its citizens reach minimum levels of every capability. I see no reasonable way to isolate the achievement of those minima from the vexing trade-offs required by distributive justice; to require that every citizen either meet those thresholds or be exempted by his or her "tragic" limitations.

Moreover, the resistance to trade-offs among central human capabilities places tremendous importance on the individuation of those capabilities. If the minimum level of a capability can be reached in a variety of ways, it seems plausible that there can be trade-offs *within* that capability. For example, someone with impaired senses might reach the threshold for "Senses, Imagination, and Thought" because his sensory limitations were compensated for by a vivid imagination and a keen intellect. In contrast, compensation could not be obtained from a safe neighborhood or close friends, since those would fall under different capabilities. If so much depends on how the boundaries of the capabilities are drawn, Nussbaum must do far more than she has done to justify the way she had drawn them. For example, her latest roster places both "being able to live with others … and engage in various forms of social interaction" and "having the social bases of self-respect" under the same capability: affiliation. But those capacities appear as different from each other as either appears from "emotions" or "practical reason." Their placement under a single capability may be justifiable, but some justification is needed. More generally, without a principled basis for individuating capabilities, the possibilities for gerrymandering are endless.

Nussbaum may have a plausible way of resolving the problems of individuation, and of between- and within-capability trade-offs. But any plausible solution will add to the complexity of her account of distributive justice and, very likely, to the difficulty of satisfying its requirements. In the end, Nussbaum's attempt at simplification seems no more successful than Anderson's.

Conclusion

Some of my sympathy for comprehensive distributive justice comes from my conviction that it is difficult or impossible to separate out the aspects of well-being that should be matters of collective concern from those that should not. Some may come from a complacency shared with many native-born Americans from the latter half of the twentieth century about the alleged dangers of comprehensive distributive justice: the threat of intrusion and oppression by liberal governments bent on redistribution. It may be increasingly hard to maintain a lively appreciation of these threats as our own government becomes ever more modest in its redistributive goals, and as "liberal" becomes a political pejorative.

There is, however, a new impetus for comprehensive distributive justice in the advent, however prematurely announced, of human genetic engineering. I believe (and I am hardly the first to suggest) that among "the dizzying consequences" (Williams 1973) of the capacity to alter genetic endowment in ways that affect important traits without altering identity will be an acute dilemma for distributive justice. If the freedom to genetically enhance one's children is not to be severely restricted, justice must either become more comprehensive, treating once inviolate "internal resources" as subject to direct or indirect distribution, or tolerate increasing disparities in most aspects of well-being (Buchanan 1995). The capacity to enhance human traits is likely to place intense pressure on any threshold erected to limit the scope distributive justice, and it may trivialize or erode the distinction between medical impairment and mere imperfection. I would welcome both developments, especially the latter, though with a great deal of anxiety.

Bibiliography

Anderson, Elizabeth (1999) "What Is the Point of Equality?" *Ethics* 109: 287–337.

Arneson, Richard (2000) "Luck Egalitarianism and Prioritarianism," *Ethics* 110: 339–349.

Bickenbach, Jerome (1993) *Physical Disability and Social Policy*, Toronto: University of Toronto Press.

Buchanan, Alan (1995) "Equal Opportunity and Genetic Intervention," *Social Philosophy and Policy* 12: 159–185.

Buchanan, Alan (1996) "Choosing Who Will Be Disabled," *Social Philosophy and Policy* 13: 18–46.

Cohen, G. A. (1989) "On the Currency of Egalitarian Justice," *Ethics* 99: 906–44.

Crocker, David (1995) "Functioning and Capability: The Foundations of Sen's and Nussbaum's Development Ethic, Part 2," in Martha Nussbaum and Jonathan Glover (eds) *Women, Culture and Development*, New York: Oxford University Press/Clarendon Press.

Daniels, Norman (1987) "Justice and Health Care," in Donald Van DeVeer and Tom Regan (eds) *Health Care Ethics: An Introduction*, Philadelphia: Temple University Press.

Daniels, Norman (1990) "Equality of What: Welfare, Resources, or Capabilities?" *Philosophy and Phenomenological Research* 50, Supplement, Fall.

Dworkin, Ronald (1981) "What Is Equality? Part 2: Equality of Resources," *Philosophy and Public Affairs* 10 (4): 283–345.

Galston, William (1994) *Liberal Purposes: Goods, Virtues, and Diversity in the Liberal State*, New York: Cambridge University Press.

Gutmann, Amy (1987) *Democratic Education*, Princeton, NJ: Princeton University Press.

Howe, Kenneth R. (1996) "Educational Ethics, Social Justice and Children with Disabilities," in Carol Christensen and Fazal Rizvi (eds) *Disability and the Dilemmas of Education and Justice*, Buckingham, UK: Open University Press.

Kittay, Eva (1997) "Human Dependency and Rawlsian Equality," in Diana Meyers, ed. *Feminists Rethink the Self*, (Boulder, CO: Westview Press.

Miller, David (1997) "Equality and Justice," *Ratio* (new series) 10: 222–237.

Miller, David (1999) *Principles of Social Justice*, Cambridge, MA: Harvard University Press.

Norman, Richard (1997) "The Social Basis of Equality," *Ratio* (new series) 10: 238–252.

Norman, Richard (1999) "Equality, Priority, and Social Justice," *Ratio* (new series) 12: 178–194.

Nussbaum, Martha (1999) "Aristotle, Politics, and Human Capabilities: A Response to Antony, Arneson, Charlesworth and Mulgan," *Ethics* 111: 102–140.

Nussbaum, Martha (2002) "Capabilities and Disabilities: Justice for Mentally Disabled Citizens," *Philosophical Topics* 30 (2): 133–165.

Nussbaum, Martha (2003a) "Rawls and Feminism," in *The Cambridge Companion to Rawls*, ed. Samuel Freeman, New York: Cambridge University Press.

Nussbaum, Martha (2003b) "Capabilities and Disabilities: Justice for Mentally Disabled Citizens," Lecture I of *Beyond the Social Contract: Toward Global Justice* (*The Tanner Lectures on Human Values*, pp. 418–457, available at http://www.tannerlectures.utah.edu.nopq.thml).

Rawls, John (1971) *A Theory of Justice*, Cambridge, MA: Harvard University Press.

Sen, Amartya (1980) "Equality of What?" in S. McMurrin (ed.) *Tanner Lectures on Human Values I*, Salt Lake City: University of Utah Press.

Silvers, Anita (1994) " 'Defective' Agents: Equality, Difference and the Tyranny of the Normal," *Journal of Social Philosophy*, 25th Anniversary Special Issue: 154–175.

Silvers, Anita and Wasserman, David (1998) "Competence and Convention: Disability Rights in Sports and Education," *Report from the Institute for Philosophy and Public Policy* 18 (4) (Fall).

Silvers, Anita, Wasserman, David and Mahowald, Mary (1998) *Disability, Difference, Discrimination: Perspective on Justice in Bioethics and Public Policy* Lanham, MD: Rowman & Littlefield.

ten Broek, Jacobus (1966) "The Right to Live in the World: The Disabled and the Law of Torts," *Californa Law Review* 54: 841–919.

Veatch, Robert (1986) *The Foundation of Justice: Why the Retarded and the Rest of Us Have Claims to Equality*, Oxford: Oxford University Press.

Wasserman, David (1998) "Distributive Justice," in Anita Silvers, David Wasserman, and Mary Mahowald, *Disability, Difference, Discrimination*, Lanham, MD: Rowman & Littlefield.

Wasserman, David (2000) "Philosophical Issues in the Definition and Social Response to Disability," *Handbook of Disability Studies*, Thousand Oaks, CA: Sage.

Wikler, Daniel (1979) "Paternalism and the Mildly Retarded," *Philosophy and Public Affairs* 8 (4): 63–87.

Williams, Bernard (1973) "The Idea of Equality," in *Problems of the Self*, Cambridge: Cambridge University Press.

Young, Iris Marion (1990) *Justice and the Politics of Difference*, Princeton, NJ: Princeton University Press.

Index